New Casebooks

MUCH ADO ABOUT NOTHING
and
THE TAMING OF THE SHREW

EDITED BY MARION WYNNE-DAVIES

palgrave

First published 2001 by
PALGRAVE
Houndmills, Basingstoke, Hampshire RG21 6XS
and
175 Fifth Avenue, New York, N.Y. 10010
Companies and representatives throughout the world

PALGRAVE was formerly Macmillan Press Ltd and St. Martin's
Press Scholarly and Reference Division.

ISBN 0–333–65790–X hardback
ISBN 0–333–65791–8 paperback

This book is printed on paper suitable for recycling and
made from fully managed and sustained forest sources.

A catalogue record for this book is available
from the British Library.

Library of Congress Cataloging-in-Publication Data
Much ado about nothing and The taming of the shrew/edited
by Marion Wynne-Davies.
    p. cm. – (New casebooks)
Includes bibliographical references and index.
ISBN 0–333–65790–X
1. Shakespeare, William, 1564–1616. Much ado about
nothing. 2. Shakespeare, William, 1564–1616. Taming
of the shrew. 3. Comedy. I. Wynne-Davies, Marion. II.
Series.

PR2828 .M83 2000
822.3'3–dc21   00–062703

10 9 8 7 6 5 4 3 2 1
10 09 08 07 06 05 04 03 02 01

Printed in China

Contents

v

Acknowledgements

The editor and the publishers wish to thank the following for the permission to use copyright material:

Harry Berger Jr, for 'Against the Sink-a-Pace: Sexual and Family Politics in *Much Ado About Nothing*', *Shakespeare Quarterly*, 33 (1982), 302–13, by permission of *Shakespeare Quarterly*; Lynda E. Boose, for 'Scolding Brides and Bridling Scolds: Taming the Woman's Unruly Member', *Shakespeare Quarterly*, 42 (1991), 194–213, by permission of *Shakespeare Quarterly*; S. P. Cerasano, for 'Half a Dozen Dangerous Words' in *Gloriana's Face: Women, Public and Private, in the English Renaissance*, ed. S. P. Cerasano and Marion Wynne-Davies, Harvester (1992), pp. 167–83, by permission of S. P. Cerasano and Marion Wynne-Davies; Barbara Everett, for '*Much Ado About Nothing*: the Unsociable Comedy' in *English Comedy*, ed. Michael Cordner, Peter Holland and John Kerrigan (1994), pp. 68–84, by permission of Cambridge University Press; Joel Fineman, for 'The Turn of the Shrew' in *Shakespeare and the Question of Theory*, ed. Patricia Parker and Geoffrey Hartman (1985), pp. 138–59, by permission of Routledge; Penny Gay, for '*Much Ado About Nothing*: a Kind of Merry War' in *As She Likes It: Shakespeare's Unruly Women* by Penny Gay (1994), pp. 143–277, by permission of Routledge; Diana E. Henderson, for 'A Shrew for the Times' in *Shakespeare the Movie. Popularizing the Plays on Film, TV and Video*, ed. Lynda E. Boose and Richard Burt (1997), pp. 148–67, by permission of Routledge; Jean E. Howard, for material from 'Antitheatricality Staged: The Workings of Ideology in Shakespeare's *Much Ado About Nothing*' in *The Stage and Social Struggle in Early Modern England* by Jean E. Howard (1994) pp. 47–9, 57–72, by permission of Routledge; Natasha Korda, for 'Household Kates: Domesticating Commodities in *The*

Taming of the Shrew', *Shakespeare Quarterly*, 47 (1996), 109–31, by permission of *Shakespeare Quarterly*; Karen Newman, 'Renaissance Family Politics and Shakespeare's *The Taming of the Shrew*', *English Literary Renaissance*, 16 (1986), 131–45, by permission of *English Literary Renaissance*.

General Editors' Preface

The purpose of this series of New Casebooks is to reveal some of the ways in which contemporary criticism has changed our understanding of commonly studied texts and writers and, indeed, of the nature of criticism itself. Central to the series is a concern with modern critical theory and its effect on current approaches to the study of literature. Each New Casebook editor has been asked to select a sequence of essays which will introduce the reader to the new critical approaches to the text or texts being discussed in the volume and also illuminate the rich interchange between critical theory and critical practice that characterises so much current writing about literature.

In this focus on modern critical thinking and practice New Casebooks aim not only to inform but also to stimulate, with volumes seeking to reflect both the controversy and the excitement of current criticism. Because much of this criticism is difficult and often employs an unfamiliar critical language, editors have been asked to give the reader as much help as they feel is appropriate, but without simplifying the essays or the issues they raise. Again, editors have been asked to supply a list of further reading which will enable readers to follow up issues raised by the essays in the volume.

The project of New Casebooks, then, is to bring together in an illuminating way those critics who best illustrate the ways in which contemporary criticism has established new methods of analysing texts and who have reinvigorated the important debate about how we 'read' literature. The hope is, of course, that New Casebooks will not only open up this debate to a wider audience, but will also encourage students to extend their own ideas, and think afresh about their responses to the texts they are studying.

John Peck and Martin Coyle
University of Wales, Cardiff

Introduction

MARION WYNNE-DAVIES

I

Over the past twenty years both *Much Ado About Nothing* and *The Taming of the Shrew* have undergone a sea-change in critical terms, transforming the former's 'incarnation of light-hearted mirth' into a dark and problematic comedy, while at the same time turning *Shrew* from a play which 'almost prompts one to regret the triumph of the suffragette movement' into the 'prompt' for a wide variety of feminist interpretations, both on stage and page.[1] The present collection traces this transformation by including essays which move from a focus on character to ones that adopt a psychoanalytic approach, from those which identify historical referents in the text to those that see the plays as actively participating in social change, and from those which concentrate upon the plays' language to those that see material context as equally important. Moreover, what becomes apparent in the process of examining these works is that critical positions are as multiple and shifting as the meaning of the plays themselves, and that to appreciate the self-conscious complexities of these pieces – just as for the dramas themselves – we need to bring our own self-awareness to the processes of reading. By approaching both the dramatic and critical works in this way the immediacy of the dramatic moment, the fascination and power of the text – whether romantic, comic or horrific – will not be subsumed by scholarly researches, any more than the enterprise of criticism will be lost amidst a flurry of personalised impressions.

Today we are aware that our sense of values frequently changes, so that when we read a text or see a play we need to come prepared with a sharp awareness of our own concerns. We now recognise that time and place, as well as race, age, gender, sexuality and class, all affect our perceptions of art, or even of what we presume to be art. Similarly, the essays in this collection all attempt, in one way or another, to present their own concerns clearly; in many respects these overlap, but at the same time their backgrounds are often different from one another. Moreover, this Casebook also follows contemporary fashion, in the ordering of the two plays discussed. For, although *The Taming of the Shrew* is the earlier work (usually dated c. 1592), *Much Ado About Nothing* (dated 1598–9) is far more popular, being produced and taught more often than the early comedies as a whole. In this sense we may remain aware of the chronology of composition, while at the same time acknowledging the changing fashions of the theatre – and look first at *Much Ado* and second at *Shrew*.

II

Marriage and the complicated dance undertaken by women and men to reach that blissful state is the central narrative of both comedies. In his essay, 'Against the Sink-a-Pace: Sexual and Family Politics in *Much Ado About Nothing*' (essay 1), Harry Berger Jr uses the trope of the cinquepace (an Elizabethan dance) to uncover the way in which the concept of marriage is more complex than *Much Ado*'s happy resolution might at first suggest. In an astute analysis of the way in which the men of the play construct their subjectivity, that is develop a sense of their own identity, Berger comments that,

> The Men's Club of Messina can trace its pedigree back to the days of Egypt, Babylon, and Hercules; it adopts and rehabilitates those outworn fashions because it shares the premises of power,

cost-avoidance, and fear of love and women that have integrated the male community since summer first was leavy.[2]

Don Pedro, his adherents and his hosts, all subscribe to this Men's Club, being positioned – and positioning themselves – within the dominant male hierarchy that, as Berger points out, sustained itself through replicating a biblical, historical and classical past. Moreover, with his self-conscious play on words, particularly fitting for this drama of wit, Berger implies that our own society, with its own Men's Clubs in the form of male-dominated groups and professions, might similarly 'repeat history'. 'Against the Sink-a-Pace' thus stands at a point of transition in the history of Shakespeare criticism, allowing a close textual reading of *Much Ado*, while at the same time foregrounding the ways in which language, image and custom are subject to the fluctuations of time and taste.[3]

Another Men's Club that might appear to have been persistently repeated through history must surely be the English courts of law, and indeed, much feminist criticism in the popular press heralds judicial pronouncements with attacks against the antiquated values of the presiding judge. Yet, without defending the English legal system, we can see that such blanket assumptions are inadequate when set alongside a detailed historical analysis of contemporary laws and court records. In her scholarly essay 'Half a Dozen Dangerous Words' (essay 2), S. P. Cerasano investigates slander as a legal concept in Renaissance England:

> Considering the propensity of Elizabethans to take charges of slander to court, this background would have been familiar to the audience of *Much Ado About Nothing*, even though it is almost entirely unfamiliar to most twentieth-century audiences. Likewise, it is important for us to understand that the subordinate position of women during the Renaissance made them especially vulnerable to verbal abuse ... [and] virtually all slander suits involving women called into question their sexual morality.[4]

Cerasano sets examples of contemporary slander suits – the usual insults being 'drunkard', 'lewd liver', or 'notorious thief' – alongside Hero's 'honest slanders, / To stain my cousin with', demonstrating that 'Hero's "honest slander" is a fantasy that resists the social and legal realities of the time'.[5] Moreover, through a careful tracing of linguistic as well as legal 'precedent',

Cerasano is able to conclude that the play's seemingly harmonious conclusion 'is not really a vindication of the truth ... but an unmasking of men's "truth"'.[6] In this manner her essay couples a respect for historical sources with an acknowledgement of the impact of feminist criticism, emphasising the female roles in the play while at the same time being aware of the period's dominant discourses.

An awareness of the historical context of *Much Ado* as well as *The Shrew* has, in its various guises, permeated Renaissance criticism in the 1980s and 1990s, an impact that has already become clear from reading the first two essays of this collection. However, it is still possible to balance this approach with a focus upon character, an understanding of the psychological complexities of the play and an overall awareness of the fictional nature of the text. Barbara Everett's essay, '*Much Ado About Nothing*: The Unsociable Comedy' (essay 3), is an excellent example of such equilibrium. Everett provides us with a perceptive insight into the play's central concerns:

> *Much Ado About Nothing* reminds us, both as title and play, that though life is indeed serious, most human beings pass much of their time in little things, unseriousness; that the ordinary, social fabric of life can be very thin, made up of trivia, and we can often feel a kind of real nothingness underneath.[7]

Yet that 'nothingness' is set against the dark realities of Elizabethan life, from those 'who died in childbirth, like so many Elizabethan women', to the entangled political relations between Protestant England and Catholic Spain – 'Don John's title can hardly fail to remind an Elizabethan audience of that Don John of Austria who was similarly a Spaniard, a natural son of Philip II'.[8] It is this sense of balance that Everett sums up in her conclusion, showing that while the play is 'entertainingly "About Nothing"' it is simultaneously 'serious in its concerns'.[9]

III

To a certain extent the first three essays in this Casebook present a development of earlier theoretical positions. In the 1980s, however, Renaissance criticism was radically reworked through the advent of New Historicism. This form of approach challenged earlier versions of historical analysis as well as downplaying the exclusive focus on class and economic status that characterises Marxist criticism. Jean E. Howard in her essay, 'Antitheatricality Staged. The Workings of Ideology in Shakespeare's *Much Ado About Nothing*' (essay 5), explains one of the reasons why historical criticism needed to change:

> [It] denied literature an initiatory role in cultural transformations or social struggles, and it seemed to foreclose the possibility that literature could have an effect on other aspects of the social formation, as well as being altered by them ... [and it denied literature's] plurality and contradictions in favour of an unequivocal reading of its relation to a particular contextual ground.[10]

One of the key differences, therefore, is the way in which, for New Historicists, texts are seen not simply to reflect back their society like a passive mirror-face, but to alter actively the way people think. In order to achieve this the texts must produce plural and contradictory meanings. *Much Ado About Nothing*, Howard argues, on one level 'produce[s] and reproduce[s] class and gender differences within a social order dependent on these differences to justify inequalities of power and privilege', in effect sustaining a status quo in which the patriarchal nobility dominates.[11] But Howard then goes on to show how this naturalising of differences and inequalities is undermined by the play's frequent recourse to theatrical devices that uncover the very apparatus of power, rather than supporting it.

While looking at shifting interpretations has now become established practice in critical circles, this process has always existed in the theatre. Indeed, the need to produce new and sometimes shocking versions of Shakespeare's plays has been the very essence of dramatic production, each age searching for an appropriate vision for its own audience. Penny Gay's essay, '*Much Ado About Nothing*: A Kind of Merry War' (essay 4), traces these fluctuations in the productions of *Much Ado* from the post-Second World War era to the end of the twentieth century. From this narrative it immediately becomes apparent that the directors of the play have generally attempted to respond to the changing social climate, so that, for example,

> [John] Gielgud, an experienced entrepreneur since before the war, knew what the British public wanted at this point in twentieth-century history – elegance, and a sense of material and spiritual

bounty, a sense that the world was indeed a good place and that the social *status quo ante* offered the best possible image of order.[12]

This overwhelming need for 'style' was, however, gradually transplanted by the recognition of social upheaval, exemplified particularly in Trevor Nunn's 1968 production which responded to the 'growing assertiveness of the young',[13] and in the new feminist interpretations by the actresses. Yet while the theatre itself seemed to respond to these challenges, Gay alerts us to the conservative intransigence of the critics:

> One wonders in what olde-worlde establishment these critics pursue their 'ideals' – certainly not in the modern world, where at least in the arts, the feminist revolution has established images of women which accurately reflect their passion, their anger, their energy ... [14]

Thus, a new generation's sense of its own changing subjectivity had inevitably permeated the theatrical productions of Shakespeare's plays, just as it had influenced the critical essays already discussed. And what if these radical interpretations did cause an uproar in the conservative establishments of drama and textual critic alike? If so, all the better. For, by demanding, even projecting, such a regenerated and at times revolutionary response *Much Ado* may be seen to have successfully participated in the construction of our own social identity, as well as in that of Shakespeare's own time.

IV

In turning from *Much Ado About Nothing* to *The Taming of the Shrew*, two aspects for consideration immediately present themselves: first, that the play seems to have invited a good deal of radical interpretation, especially from feminist critics, and second, that productions, whether on stage or film, have always been problematic, the last scene of the play in particular. These two issues are united in Diana E. Henderson's essay, 'A Shrew For the Times' (essay 10), in which she immediately identifies the play's recalcitrance,

> [o]f all Shakespeare's comedies, *The Taming of the Shrew* most overtly reinforces the social hierarchies of its day [with] ... an anachronistic plot premised on the sale of women.[15]

Despite its seeming anachronism the play has been frequently filmed, mainly at times, Henderson suggests, 'of "backlash" when advances in women's political participation outside the home have prompted a response from those who perceive a threat'.[16] Thus, if the stage participates in on-going social dialogue from a challenging perspective, it appears that the Hollywood studio system took quite the reverse approach, negotiating for, rather than against, the *status quo*. For example, we can contrast Nunn's 1968 production of *Much Ado* with its 'vitality and nonconformity'[17] with Zeffirelli's 1967 version of *Shrew* which, at one level, worked 'to naturalise a traditional sex-gender system all the more doggedly'.[18] Indeed, Henderson is left wondering if 'a new millennium [will] ... produce a more experimental filmic rendering of this resistant tale'.[19]

If the celluloid *Shrew* has lacked radicalism, however, in critical terms this early Shakespearean comedy has produced an overwhelming number of inspired and inspiring pieces, and not only from feminists. The earliest essay included in this collection is the late Joel Fineman's 'The Turn of the Shrew' (essay 6) in which he begins with a series of simple propositions and questions, asking at the end of his first paragraph:

> Is it possible to voice a language, whether of man or of woman, that does not speak, sooner or later, self-consciously or unconsciously, for the order and authority of man?[20]

In the essay, which is now recognised as a classic, Fineman demonstrates a remarkable ability to present his arguments with a fine sense of lucid rationality that allows the reader a clear insight into even the most complex forms of psychoanalytic theory and Derridean deconstruction. Both these theoretical schools and their key theorists – Freud, Lacan and Derrida – are invoked by Fineman as he undertakes a close reading of *Shrew*, sets the play within its cultural context, and finally analyses the current critical debate between the very theories he employs. Thus, concluding his supremely self-aware account of the gender/theory 'war', Fineman comments ironically that readers should not have to 'in their theory or their practice act out what they read', suggesting, in other words, that we can read about the battles between theorists and spouses without having to take sides.[21]

The focus on language and its inevitable ambiguity found in 'Turn of the Shrew' is equally present in Natasha Korda's essay, 'Household Kates: Domesticating Commodities in *The Taming of the Shrew'* (essay 9), in which she locates a conjunction between the name 'Kate' and the noun 'cates' – meaning 'goods that are purchased'.[22] Korda's work is clearly informed by the feminist debate on *Shrew*, but it sidelines this regularly reworked field for a Marxist approach. As Korda notes herself:

> What differentiates *The Taming of the Shrew* from its precursors is not so much a concern with domestic economy – which has always been a central preoccupation of shrew-taming literature – but rather a shift in *modes of production* and thus in the very terms through which domestic economy is conceived.[23]

She traces this economic evolution of the Elizabethan housewife from 'skilled producer to savvy consumer',[24] showing how the conspicuous consumption of goods denotes class identity, in particular that of the aspiring bourgeois. Thus, when Kate destroys her cap at the end of the play, Korda argues that she has learned – from Petruchio – how to consume 'nothings' in order to display an external vision of wealth that in itself serves to draw actual capital. In this way, rather than interpret the problematic final scene in feminist terms, Korda concludes with an adaptation of Marx:

> The movement of subjects within the play takes the form of a movement made by things, and these things far from being under their control, in fact control them.[25]

If, however, Korda redirects the conclusion of *Shrew* away from the gendered debate, the other essays collected here engage fully with various feminist issues. Certainly, Henderson and Fineman make clear referents to the ongoing argument that has increasingly formed itself under the framework of a historicised feminism. In addition, Karen Newman approaches *Shrew* from this latter perspective in her essay, 'Renaissance Family Politics and Shakespeare's *The Taming of the Shrew*' (essay 7), although she moves away from the question of 'woman's' identity to the category of 'femininity'.[26] Newman begins with the true tale of the drunken Nicholas Rosyer and his 'shrewish' wife and suggests that

> [t]he entire incident figures the social anxiety about gender and power which characterises Elizabeth culture.[27]

Having located Shakespeare's play within the firm context of its social and chronological field of production, she then demonstrates that

> The theatrically constructed frame in which Sly exercises patriarchal power and the dream in which Kate is tamed undermine the seemingly eternal nature of those structures by calling attention to the constructed character of the representation rather than veiling it through mimesis.[28]

The emphasis upon the cultural construction of gender hierarchies and the way in which the text's own self-referential allusions undercut the sense of a mirror-like representation of reality, thereby allowing the play an active role in constructing femininity, echoes Jean E. Howard's assertions about *Much Ado About Nothing*. Korda, like Howard, moreover, aligns herself not only with feminism but also with New Historicism.

The substance of historicism, its artifacts and objects, forms the basis of Lynda E. Boose's essay, 'Scolding Brides and Bridling Scolds: Taming the Woman's Unruly Member' (essay 8). At the beginning of her piece, Boose notes the discomfort which *Shrew* has often induced in the members of its audiences (male and female alike) from the first performances of the play, and the way in which 'directors, players, audiences, and literary critics' have tried to see the final scene as one of reconciliation and mutuality between Kate and Petruchio.[29] For this reason, Boose argues, it is essential to historicise the play and to take note of the 'real village Kates who underwrite Shakespeare's character',[30] those women who, being deemed 'shrews' by their communities, were subjected to the horrific tortures of the cucking stool and the scold's bridle. The subsequent descriptions of the forms and uses of the scold's bridle might seem, as one commentator put it 'far from close reading [of the text]', but as Boose notes:

> The sheer fact that the excluded brutalities lie suppressed in the margins of the shrew material also means that they travel, as unseen partners, inside the more benevolent taming discourse that Shakespeare's play helped to mould.[31]

Indeed, these 'unseen partners' may only be uncovered by a self-aware and investigative reading of the text, or viewing of the drama/film. While Boose's essay might therefore initially appear – with its detailed socio-historical enquiry – to be far distant from the other pieces collected here, it echoes their processes of questioning the assumptions about the play, which have previously been held as 'natural'.

V

This Introduction began with an explanation of how *Much Ado About Nothing* and *The Taming of the Shrew* have changed in our perceptions over the centuries. In the following sections the essays included in this New Casebook were described and were shown to engage with the most recent alterations in our appreciation of the plays. Moreover, the changing fashions are reflected in the productions of the plays on stage and screen as well as in the most conventional literary criticisms. As such, this New Casebook offers an insight into the texts themselves and into the processes of critical appreciation by which *Much Ado About Nothing* and *The Taming of the Shrew* may be understood.

NOTES

1. These quotations are taken from a description of the 1882 performance of *Much Ado About Nothing* with Ellen Terry as Beatrice (*Saturday Review*, quoted in the Arden Shakespeare's *Much Ado About Nothing*, ed. A. R. Humphreys [London, 1981], pp. 37–8), and from the 1960 *Observer* review of *The Taming of the Shrew* quoted in Penny Gay's *As She Likes It* (London, 1994), p. 97.

2. See p. 25 below; Berger describes the men in the play as 'The Men's Club of Messina', from which Benedick becomes separated.

3. Harry Berger's essay is reprinted in his latest book, *Making Trifles of Terrors. Redistributing Complicities in Shakespeare* (Stanford, CA, 1997), pp. 10–24.

4. See p. 35 below.

5. See pp. 31, 34 and 48 below.

6. See p. 48 below. This essay was included in a collection, co-edited by S. P. Cerasano and myself, which looked specifically at the role of women in the English Renaissance: *Gloriana's Face: Women, Public and Private, in the English Renaissance* (London, 1992).

7. See p. 59 below.

8. See p. 61 below.

9. See p. 67 below.

10. See p. 103 below. This essay by Jean Howard is taken from a chapter in her book *The Stage and Social Struggle in Early Modern England* (London, 1994) in which she uses New Historicism as a starting point for the investigation of a range of Early Modern plays.

11. See p. 105 below.

12. See p. 71 below. Penny Gay's consideration of *Much Ado About Nothing* is taken from her book, *As She Likes It: Shakespeare's Unruly Women*.

13. See p. 80 below.

14. See p. 99 below.

15. See p. 226 below.

16. See pp. 227–8 below.

17. See p. 81 below; this quotation is taken from Penny Gay's essay.

18. See p. 237 below

19. See p. 248 below. Henderson's essay was originally published as one of a collection of essays in *Shakespeare, the Movie*, ed. Lynda E. Boose and Richard Burt (London, 1997), in which several plays are traced through a much more optimistic and inventive series of productions. Lynda Boose is represented separately in this Casebook by her essay, 'Scolding Brides and Bridling Scolds: Taming the Woman's Unruly Member' (see pp. 166–91 below).

20. See p. 124 below.

21. See p. 144 below.

22. See p. 193 below.

23. See p. 193 below.

24. See p. 194 below.

25. See p. 216 below.

26. Although I have taken Newman's essay from the journal *English Literary Renaissance*, 16 (1986), the piece is republished in her book, *Fashioning Femininity and English Renaissance Drama* (Chicago and London, 1991).

27. See p. 149 below.

28. See p. 154 below.

29. Unfortunately, because of the constraints of space and finance, I have been unable to include the whole of Lynda E. Boose's excellent essay in this collection. The quotation above and the description of the first part of that piece will, I hope, both serve to elucidate the subsequent excerpt for the reader, as well as to do justice to the complex historicised argument Boose makes. Lynda E. Boose, 'Scolding Brides and Bridling Scolds: Taming the Woman's Unruly Member,' *Shakespeare Quarterly*, 42 (1991), 179–213, 181.

30. See Boose (1991), 181.

31. See p. 170 below.

1

Against the Sink-a-Pace: Sexual and Family Politics in *Much Ado About Nothing*

HARRY BERGER, JR

> For, hear me, Hero: wooing, wedding, and repenting is as a Scotch jig, a measure, and a cinquepace: the first suit is hot and hasty like a Scotch jig (and full as fantastical); the wedding, mannerly modest, as a measure, full of state and ancientry; and then comes Repentance and with his bad legs falls into the cinquepace faster and faster till he sink into his grave.
>
> (*Much Ado About Nothing*, II.i.63ff)[1]

'Sink-a-pace' is the way Sir Toby Belch pronounces the name of the five-step dance, and I borrow his pronunciation here because it signifies a slowing-down that beats against the galliard tempo of the dance. In Beatrice's formula, marriage, the afterlife of the wedding, is renamed repentance, and its tempo is divided into the two mutually intensifying rhythms suggested by placing Toby's pronunciation in tandem with Beatrice's description: on the one hand, the decelerating sink-a-pace of the yoke of boredom, the long dull anticlimax to the fantastical jig and stately measure; on the other hand, the frenetic re-action in which the penitent tries ever more desperately and vainly to escape back into jigtime, tries to make himself giddy with acceleration and spin himself into forgetfulness. The state and ancientry of the wedding indicate the influence of the older generation, the father's interest in and control of the alliance that seals his daughter's future. Since Repentance is male, the bad-legged dancer may suggest either the husband himself or else the dominant tone which he – the dominant partner – gives to the monogamous relationship he finds himself unnaturally confined in by what Gloucester, in *King Lear*, called 'the order of law'.

Beatrice begins her little lecture with 'hear me, Hero', and it is difficult, on hearing the ear pun, not to add it to the senses of her name.[2] Most of the 'noting' about which there is much ado consists of hearing or overhearing. Hero, who says almost nothing in the first two acts, hears a great deal, probably more than what is good for her. If she notes what we note, she hears enough to make her feel that her fate in life is to be her father's passport to self-perpetuation, a commodity in the alliance market, the spoils of the love wars – inevitably a conquered Hero, 'overmastered with a piece of valiant dust' who guarantees her anonymity by giving her his name and making her the prisoner and trophy that validates the name. Hero's name threatens to be her fate: Mrs Hero. Yet even this most male-dominated of heroines betrays more than once her sense of her complicity in the sexual politics of Messina.

The first clue to this sense appears in the brief dance scene beginning at Act II, scene i, line 75. When Hero responds to the masked Don Pedro's request for a promenade, the conditions she imposes sound like a self-description: 'So you walk softly and look sweetly and say nothing, I am yours for the walk' (II.i.76–7). It is as if she is quite conscious of the principle of behaviour to which she conforms, and in offering her role to the Prince she may, by a mere shift of the shifters, indicate the value and objective of that behaviour: 'So long as I walk softly and look sweetly and say nothing, I am yours for the walk', and for the sink-a-pace as well. During all but one (line 32) of the first 141 lines of the play she had looked on sweetly and silently, saying nothing while her cousin Beatrice crossed swords with Benedick and the other men, and saying nothing while her father entertained a vapid joke or two about her legitimacy and his own easy assurance that he is no cuckold. 'Is this your daughter?' Pedro asks:

> Leontes   Her mother hath many times told me so.
> Benedick   Were you in doubt, sir, that you asked her?
> Leontes   Signior Benedick, no: for then you were a child.
>   (I.i.94–6)

And Pedro, after a gibe at Benedick, graciously responds that 'the lady fathers herself. Be happy, lady, for you are like an honourable father' (I.i.98–9). Benedick will not leave this alone: 'If Signior Leonato be her father, she would not have his head on her shoulders for all Messina, as like him as she is' (I.i.100–2). Bizarre as that image is – Hero wearing her father's bearded and greying head as a mask or visored helmet – it may have some truth as an emblem.

After Act I, scene i, line 32, Hero is silent until Act II, scene i, line 5, where all she can summon up is one softly and sweetly limping line in support of Beatrice's comment that Don John's sour looks give her heartburn: 'He is of a very melancholy disposition' (II.i.5). It is therefore a pleasant surprise to hear an unexpected surge of spirit in her dialogue with the Prince at the masked ball. Remember the situation: the Prince had offered to woo her for Claudio but had been wrongly overheard by her Uncle Antonio's man, who thought Pedro wanted her for himself. As a result, Leonato decided to break the good news to her so 'that she may be the better prepared for an answer'. Thus when the visored Prince says, 'Lady, will you walk about with your friend', she seems to know who her friend is, and has her answer ready:

> **Hero** So you walk softly and look sweetly and say nothing, I am yours for the walk; and especially when I walk away.
> **Pedro** With me in your company?
> **Hero** I may say so when I please.
> **Pedro** And when please you to say so?
> **Hero** When I like your favour, for God defend the lute should be like the case!
>
> (II.i.76–83)

Hero peels off her mask of soft, sweet silence and becomes frisky. She tries to flirt, then to banter like Beatrice, and we suddenly see why the Prince's bastard brother had called her 'a very forward March-chick' (I.iii.49). Her carrying-on keeps the Prince from getting to the point – telling her he is Claudio – before they move out of earshot. He has to coach her in the art: 'speak low if you speak love' (II.i.87) – 'not so loud, not so fast, let's go off by ourselves and be serious'. Since he does not know that she expects his proposal (so that if he pretends to be Claudio she will think it really is the Prince pretending to be Claudio), and since these are the last words we hear, even the audience is not entirely sure of what happens until over a hundred lines later. When Hero next comes on stage, at Act II, scene i, line 190, it is in time to hear herself compared to a stolen bird's nest being returned to its owner, and to be traded to Claudio by her father as part of a package deal that includes Leonato's fortunes. She seems easily to reconcile herself both to the match and to the role of commodity, but I think we are allowed at least a momentary doubt as to whether she and Leonato would not have preferred the Prince to Claudio, especially when she hears the Prince casually offer himself to Beatrice after giving Claudio back his bird's nest.

Even if we do not seriously entertain this doubt, we cannot help noticing something else about these scenes, namely that Hero's silence is the correlative of Beatrice's witty noise. Beatrice hogs the stage, and does not let Hero and Claudio savour their betrothal by basking in the limelight; she manages the scene, gives them their cues, gets the affair quickly settled, and then, pushing it aside with 'Good Lord, for alliance' (II.i.285), redirects attention to herself and her brief flirtation with the Prince. It is not only that the absence of parents seems to give her a freedom Hero might well envy: since no honourable father's head burdens her shoulders, she can father herself and fight men with their own weapons. It is also that in Hero's presence she continually puts down the norms Hero is trained to respect and the institutional functions Hero is destined to fulfil.

What I find most interesting about all this is that Hero seems both to admire and envy Beatrice and to disapprove of her. This is suggested in her responses to the masked Prince. Her pert 'I may say so when I please' (II.i.80) reflects a struggle between two contrary pieces of advice she had just heard: on the one hand, Leonato warning Beatrice that 'thou wilt never get thee a husband if thou be so shrewd of tongue' (II.i.16–17) and Antonio counselling Hero to be ruled by her father (II.i.43–4); on the other hand, Beatrice countering Antonio's advice with 'Yes, faith. It is my cousin's duty to make curtsy and say, "Father, as it please you", But yet for all that, cousin, let him be a handsome fellow, or else make another curtsy, and say, "Father, as it please me"' (II.i.45–6). Hero follows with an attempt to masquerade briefly as Beatrice while respecting her filial obligation. If we agree with the Pelican editor that she is flaunting 'her permission to say "yes"', then her 'when I please' takes on a cutting edge, since it means 'when my father lets me'.[3] Her effort to say 'as it please me' and emulate Beatrice fails in the utterance and turns instead into an implicit rejection of Beatrice's rebellious attitude.

If Hero's behaviour during the rest of the play lends support to these narrowly based interpretive remarks, then she is a much more interesting character than she has been made out to be, for she not only reflects the limitations of her culture but also betrays a dim awareness of them. This comes out more clearly in her behaviour during the gulling of Beatrice. She tells Ursula that when Beatrice hides to overhear them

> Our talk must only be of Benedick.
> When I do name him, let it be thy part
> To praise him more than ever man did merit.
> My talk to thee must be how Benedick
> Is sick in love with Beatrice. Of this matter
> Is little Cupid's crafty arrow made,
> That only wounds by hearsay.
>
> (III.i.17–23)

Their parts had obviously been assigned by Don Pedro, the Cupid who devised these crafty practices, and to whom Hero had promised – with a fine concern for both her own image and the smooth functioning of society – that she would 'do any modest office ... to help my cousin to a good husband' (II.i.334).

Though she goes into the scene with an altruistic motive, helping soon turns into hunting. With Ursula she eagerly takes up Cupid's arrow, birdbolt, and fishhook, and marches into ambush, impatient to see the golden Beatrice-fish 'greedily devour the treacherous bait' (III.i.28), the 'false sweet bait that we lay for it' (III.i.33). But the bait turns out to be neither false nor sweet, and Hero makes sure the hook of love is sharp, so that when the wounded Beatrice swallows the bait she will also swallow her pride. Hero's reciting her part in the Prince's script – she is to speak of Benedick's love-sickness – only prepares us to see how far she strays from it. For she is herself a weapon of the Prince, and of her father, and of the Men's Club of Messina, and what she wants to harp on is Beatrice's disdain. The vigour with which she berates her cousin suggests that she is doing more than pretending for Beatrice's benefit. She only pretends to pretend; the game of make-believe is a self-justifying blind, an altruistic mask, from behind which she can stalk Beatrice with 'honest slanders' (III.i.84), letting her know what she really thinks of

her, what she really feels, without (for once) being interrupted or
put down:

> Disdain and scorn ride sparkling in her eyes,
> Misprizing what they look on: and her wit
> Values itself so highly that to her
> All matter else seems weak. She cannot love,
> Nor take no shape nor project of affection,
> She is so self-endeared.
>
> (III.i.51–6)

The implied contrast is of course to her own quiet, reliable, unap-
preciated girl-scout self. Unlike herself, Beatrice 'never gives
to truth and virtue that / Which simpleness and merit purchaseth'
(III.i.69–70).

> No, not to be so odd, and from all fashions,
> As Beatrice is, cannot be commendable.
> But who dare tell her so? If I should speak,
> She would mock me into air; O, she would laugh me
> Out of myself, press me to death with wit.
>
> (III.i.72–6)

Hero thinks it wrong to rebel against fathers and husbands.
The world must be peopled, and it is disconcerting to be told that
marriage is virtue's repentance rather than its reward. Yet something more than her own wounded pride comes through in the
language she uses to humble her cousin. There is a touch not only
of envy but of grudging admiration in such images as the fish
with golden oars cutting the silver stream, and the haggards of
the rock whose spirits are 'coy and wild' (III.i.35). And consider
the following passage, in which Shakespeare oddly allows the
usually quiet Hero to break into epic simile: she tells Ursula to
bid Beatrice

> steal into the pleachèd bower,
> Where honeysuckles, ripened by the sun,
> Forbid the sun to enter – like favourites,
> Made proud by princes, that advance their pride
> Against that power that bred it.
>
> (III.i.7–11)

This is a displaced analysis of the whole situation, as well as a
figurative embodiment of Hero's complex attitude. Beatrice is the

rebellious favourite advancing her virgin pride against the masculine forces that ripen it – the solar energy of parents, princes, and admirers. But comparisons are odorous, and the simile does not quite work the way Hero wants it to: the courtly figure strains against the positive quality of its floral subject.

It seems natural, lovely, and even fulfilling for honeysuckle to transform the sun's pride and power into its own, to ripen a fragrant shade, make an enclosed garden where women might protect themselves from princely or paternal penetration. What the imagery implies about Hero is that although she criticises Beatrice's rebellious pride and independence, she finds them attractive and could even, perhaps, wish for the spirit to photosynthesise her own disdain. With the scorn sparkling in her eyes, Beatrice models an enviable alternative that calls into question Hero's pliant submission to the sun. According to the logic of her image, the alternative chosen by Hero is not pollination but pruning: to be married is to have womanhood's natural ripening into freedom interrupted by the wrench that will reduce her to a sprig worn by some conquering hero. Thus by putting down Beatrice and helping her to a husband, Hero will either eliminate the shadow cast over her own self-effacing commitment, or else she will triumph over Beatrice by reducing her to her own level – that is, by condemning her into everlasting redemption.

Beatrice's view of marriage as a sink-a-pace of repentance is by no means exceptional in *Much Ado About Nothing*. Benedick seems to share it:

> Is't come to this? In faith, hath not the world one man but he will wear his cap with suspicion? Shall I never see a bachelor of three-score again? ... An thou wilt needs thrust thy neck into a yoke, wear the print of it and sigh away Sundays.
>
> (I.i.175–9)

Don John agrees: 'What is he for a fool that betroths himself to unquietness?' (I.iii.41). It is conventional male wisdom that women are not to be trusted: 'O, my Lord, wisdom and blood combating in so tender a body, we have ten proofs to one that blood hath the victory' (II.iii.154–6). Leonato says this for the benefit of the listening Benedick, but as his response to his daughter's defamation later shows, that is no indication that he does not accredit its truth. The ease, indeed the alacrity, with which Leonato, Claudio, and the Prince seize on Hero's guilt confirms what they already suspect, and what they seem happy to suspect. It validates the conventional wisdom, and it affords them the added pleasure of having their sense of merit injured.

It is difficult, however, to reconcile the opinion that men are more sinned against than sinning with another which seems to have equal weight:

> Sigh no more, ladies, sigh no more!
>   Men were deceivers ever,
> One foot in sea, and one on shore:
>   To one thing constant never.
>   Then sigh not so,
>   But let them go,
> And be you blithe and bonny,
> Converting all your sounds of woe
>   Into Hey nonny nonny.
>   (II.iii.59–67)

The Prince acclaims this as 'a good song' (II.iii.73), and I think his behaviour throughout the play shows that although in this instance he may be referring to the music, in general he agrees with the sentiment. However playfully, he treats courtship as a military campaign, or a hunt, or a set of behind-the-back manoeuvres – *practices*, as he calls them. He promises Claudio to take Hero's 'hearing prisoner with the force / And strong encounter of my amorous tale' (I.iii.292–3); like a good engineer and physician, he will bridge the flood of Claudio's passion, and fit his disease with a remedy (I.i.284–93). Since, as Benedick concludes, 'man is a giddy thing' (V.iv.106), men as well as women can be tricked into giving up their avowed and natural resistance to love and marriage. And in fact, not only *can* they be so deceived; they *must* be, for they would never march off willingly to what both know is a prison that constrains all their natural urges.

The difference between men and women in this respect – so goes the regnant ideology of the play – is that women are responsible for their sins but men are not. Male deception and inconstancy are gifts that God gives, and their proper name is Manhood. But woman has an awesome responsibility. Since she bears her father's fame and fortune into the future as if – to borrow Benedick's image – she wore his head on her shoulders, and since by marrying she assumes the management not only of her husband's household but also of his reputation and honour, she is expected to conquer blood with wisdom even though the odds are ten to one against it. It may be that men dislike the virtue they both praise and lay siege to: they seem to demand the perfections of Diana only in order to prove that Diana, like Astraea, fled the earth long ago, in the time of good neighbours, leaving it to the corruptions of Venus. Claudio's bitter but obvious satisfaction in being victimised owes partly to the fact that it reaffirms his moral superiority: '... as a brother to a sister', he whines, I 'showed / Bashful sincerity and comely love' (IV.i. 51–2), while,

> You seem to me as Dian in her orb,
> As chaste as is the bud ere it be blown;
> But you are more intemperate in your blood
> Than Venus, or those pamp'red animals
> That rage in savage sensuality.
> (IV.i.55–9)

A virgin who under false pretences seeks associate membership in the Men's Club of Messina deserves whatever sentence she receives.

On the other hand, the song tells the members of the club that 'the fraud of men was ever so, / Since summer first was leavy' (II.iii.70–1). Men are born deceivers whose nature is to be inconstant, untrustworthy, lustful, contentious, and obsessed with honour, status, and fortune. This enables them to think better of themselves, and worse of women. Not only can't they be blamed for what they cannot help, but their inability to control themselves proves their passionate and virile manliness; it is only their inability to control sinful women that threatens to unman them. Having persuaded themselves of this, they are both more ready to suspect, and more willing to excuse, each other. It is to be expected, for example, that the Prince will swerve from his announced plan, and end up wooing Hero for himself. But the fault is more Hero's than his, according to Claudio: 'for beauty is a witch / Against whose charms faith melteth into blood' (II.i.161–2). And though Hero's subsequent betrayal is a heinous crime against the whole Men's Club, Claudio and the Prince find themselves guilty only of a pardonable error in judgement, a position they coolly maintain in the face of Hero's announced death.

The members of the Men's Club are securely joined together by the handcuffs of fashion. 'Come,' says Dogberry, 'let them be opinioned' (IV.ii.61), and he conspires with his colleagues and

Borachio to bring forth their opinionator, the deformed thief, Fashion, who 'goes up and down like a gentleman' (III.iii.117–18):

> **Borachio**   Seest thou not ... what a deformed thief this fashion is? how giddily 'a turns about all the hot-bloods between fourteen and five-and-thirty? sometimes fashioning them like Pharaoh's soldiers in the reechy painting, sometime like god Bel's priests in the old church window, sometime like the shaven Hercules in the smirched worm-eaten tapestry, where his codpiece seems as massy as his club?
>
> (III.iii.121–8)

> **Dogberry**   ... And also the watch heard them talk of one Deformed. They say he wears a key in his ear, and a lock hanging by it.
>
> (V.i.294–6)

In his stimulating essay on Dogberry, John Allen spells out the relevance of 'Borachio's thumbnail sketch of fashion's way with gallants': 'Freely interpreted, fashion first creates the model soldier, gorgeously arrayed but overconfident and bent on vengeance as a means of gaining honour; then it supplies him with the outward attributes of one who cherishes a sacred trust, although he secretly abuses it; and finally it ushers in his destined role as a uxorious lover, tricked by appetite into an unmanly servitude which passes for devotion to his female captor.'[4]

> Fashion, as Borachio sees it, signifies the conception of one's self which one presents, or wishes to present, to the public eye ... Like a 'deformed thief' ... fashion steals from men their knowledge of themselves, reducing them to posturing automatons who nourish the illusion of their individuality while actually possessing none, because they do not even choose the fashions they will wear but, whether they will or not, are fashioned to them ... The spoils of fashion are most frequently the qualities ... which nurture and solidify essential interpersonal bonds.[5]

Allen perhaps overstresses the extent to which the play presents men as the slaves of fashion. A clue to their own complicity in fashioning the fashion that robs them is given in Dogberry's charge to the watch. He tells them that 'the most peaceable way' to keep order is not to interfere with those who disturb the peace. Item:

> **Dogberry**   If you meet a thief, you may suspect him, by virtue of your office, to be no true man; and for such kind of men, the less you meddle or make with them, why, the more is for your honesty.

Second watchman If we know him to be a thief, shall we not lay hands on him?

Dogberry Truly, by your office you may; but I think they that touch pitch will be defiled. The most peaceable way for you, if you do take a thief, is to let him show himself what he is, and steal out of your company.

(III.iii.47–56)

The Prince had observed in his first speech that 'the fashion of the world is to avoid cost' (I.ii.86), and the constable whose office is 'to present the Prince's own person' (III.iii.69) agrees: 'indeed the watch ought to offend no man' (III.iii.74–5).

Dogberry's instructions for maintaining respectability are worthy of Erasmus' Folly. The comic paradox giving them their point is that by refusing to associate with thieves (i.e. refusing to apprehend them) the watchman becomes their associate. He confirms his illusion of honesty and joins the community of thieves in one and the same act. And he is indeed superior to the known thief in his ability to hide his thievery from himself, to rob himself of self-knowledge, by redistributing complicities. Avoiding the cost and preserving the peace of the self-deception Folly called *philautia*, he becomes, like the thief, 'no true man', and he thrives on the ethical confusions of his situation, confusions which are beautifully expressed in the watch's language:

Dogberry Are you good men and true?

Verges Yea, or else it were pity but they should suffer salvation, body and soul.

Dogberry Nay, that were a punishment too good for them if they should have any allegiance in them, being chosen for the Prince's watch.

(III.iii.1–6)

It is by meaning and trying to be good men that they both enable thievery and legitimise their complicity. This does not make them less good and true; it only suggests that 'being good' as Shakespeare presents it is a more difficult, a more complex and maculate, process than the purer whole-cloth conception of goodness – and of their own goodness – entertained by the characters. It seems unavoidable, then, that Shakespeare's 'good' characters should merit salvation and damnation simultaneously. To suffer salvation, to be condemned to redemption, is to suffer the self-deception of *philautia*. Yet this very illusion of self-esteem is inseparable in most human beings from their good intentions no less than from the more questionable consequences of their actions. That the watch should be punished for their allegiance to the Prince extends this reasoning to the principal characters. The use of the term *Prince* itself implies this. Since Leonato is listed in the *dramatis personae* as the *Governor* of Messina, and Pedro as the *Prince* of Arragon, 'Prince' in this scene comprehends both of these ethically 'vagrom' figures, one the leading elder of the group and the other its self-confessed love-god. Thus the watch 'presents' in its collective person the principles that underlie and unify the play's two wars – that is, between generations and between genders. And this extension from subplot to main plot is manifested in other ways.

According to Dogberry, the ideal watchman is 'desartless', literate, and 'senseless', one who can 'comprehend all vagrom men' but can talk himself into releasing them on the grounds that 'they are not the men you took them for' (III.iii.8–45). This standard makes 'desartless' an accurate term, fusing 'unworthy' with 'disingenuous', and it makes 'senseless' mean 'self-blinding'. Combined with the requirement of literacy, the formula produces an exact description of the members of the Men's Club of Messina. They create and empower the deformed thief that robs them of the qualities which, in Allen's words, 'nurture and solidify essential interpersonal bonds'. Self-robbing thieves who preserve self-esteem by appropriating Fashion's image, they enable the deformed thief to present their person and go 'up and down like a gentleman', an *arbiter elegantiae*. 'Fashion' is roughly synonymous with Erasmian folly and *philautia*. It is in part the ability to avoid cost to oneself by inflicting and blaming it on others. But it is more than that, as Borachio's words reveal.

Passing from Pharaoh's soldiers through the priests of Bel to the shaven Hercules, his speech charts a move from war through specious veneration of an idol to virility unmanned by love. The connection of Bel to the themes of the play is less apparent, but Shakespeare may have chosen *Bel* because as the root of both *bellum* and *bella* it provides an etymological transition while referring to an instance of false devotion directed presumptively toward concern for the idol but actually toward oneself. The devotion of Cupid's proud subjects is not unlike that of the priests of Bel. The point of the sequence is borne out by the general sense that in Messina war and love are interchangeable, because war is the paradigm of love. Love *of* contention gives way to love *as* contention, and the honeyed rhetoric in which Claudio describes his transformation does not conceal the interchangeability suggested both by his syntax and by his subsequent behaviour: now that 'war-thoughts / Have left their places vacant, in their rooms / Come thronging soft and delicate desires' (I.i.269–71). The fashion that turns the hot-bloods about reflects their apprehensive reliance on power, their secret worship of self-gratification, and their excessive attachment to *machismo*. But as attempts to avoid cost, these styles of behaviour only bring it on; Borachio's examples are all losers, defeated by the true God and woman. And since men were deceivers and self-deceivers ever – since 'the fraud of men was ever so' – today's hot-blood adopts styles as fusty and worn as the art that communicates them. The Men's Club of Messina can trace its pedigree back to the days of Egypt, Babylon, and Hercules; it adopts and rehabilitates those outworn fashions because it shares the premises of power, cost-avoidance, and fear of love and women that have integrated the male community since summer first was leavy. If the gallants of Messina are doomed to repeat history, it may be because they enjoy their pain. Their chosen fashions betray their misprision of power, their allegiance to the fine art of self-defeat and its long history. Perhaps they avoid cost at one level only to encounter it at another. Like Leonato they come to meet their trouble and embrace their charge too willingly (I.i.85–93). Their club insignia may be the badge of which the messenger spoke: 'joy could not show itself modest enough without a badge of bitterness' (I.i.19–21).

If I may digress for a moment to cite a northern analogy, the same by-laws are in effect in the Gloucester Chapter of the Gentleman's Club of Old Britain. Gloucester, an old hand at cost-avoidance, tells Kent that Edmund's mother was fair, 'there was good sport at his making, and the whoreson must be acknowledged' (*King Lear*, I.i.19–23). If that sport smells of any fault, it belongs to the mother for her intemperance and carelessness, and to her son for his saucy disobedience in not remaining nothing. The father's language identifies the mother as a whore, and Edmund not as *his* bastard but as *her* son, and it suggests that mother and son conspired against father in producing the knave before he was sent for. It is thus to father's credit that he overlooks the inconvenience they have caused him, and assumes the consequences of their fault as his own burden: 'His breeding, Sir, hath been at my charge' (*King Lear*, I.i.8). This piece of bravery is partly a brag, alluding to his notorious accomplishment in lusty stealth, and partly a disclaimer of full responsibility. He seems eager to impress on Kent his paired accomplishments, in good sport and in sportsmanlike conduct, and this, incidentally, may throw some light on the convenient presence in Messina of Don John the Bastard. 'Never came trouble to my house in the likeness of your grace' (I.i.88–9), Leonato tells the Prince, and this is because trouble comes in the likeness of Don John, who seems eager to claim even more culpability than he deserves. The Prince drags him around on a leash, like a pet Caliban, so that Don John may receive blame for the trouble which, although it arises from the very foundation of Messina's 'dissembly', is orchestrated by Don Pedro's practices. Both brothers, in fact, are practitioners, and the chief difference between them is that the Prince is much better at it.

Don John is a comic villain who can hardly twirl his moustache without scratching his eye.[6] The ease with which his practice (put into play by Borachio and Conrade) succeeds, therefore, tells us more about the susceptibility of Messina than about the Bastard's motiveless malignancy. For the villain to succeed, everyone has to collaborate in helping him on with his bumbling villainies. But this is not something it would be useful for him to find out, for he struts his autonomy and – like Edmund in *King Lear* – takes a certain swashbuckling pride in virile and honourable professions of plain-speaking wickedness, though the pleasure of feeling himself to be a *man*, more sinning than sinned against, is occasionally justified by an appeal to his status as a pariah, more sinned against than sinning. It is sometimes hard to distinguish his own wing of the Men's Club from his brother's. Conrade matches Claudio and Borachio Benedick in the collegiate locker-room of wit-crackers, while the latter two show better stuff before the play ends. The play's two scapegoats are a bastard named Trouble and a woman named Hero, and his bastardy tells us where the blame lies: like Edmund, no doubt, he is a testimony both to his father's prowess and to his mother's sin – a by-product of the frailty named Woman.

If this is how men choose to distribute praise and blame, we can understand why they expect women to fail to live up to their responsibilities. If men are deceivers ever, their first deception will be to trick women into loving them. And since women have to be won by the practices of men who flaunt their God-given powers of deception and inconstancy as the jewels of manhood, there is no reason to expect the ladies to honour their commitments. On the other hand, there is no reason not to demand it of them and chastise them when (as is likely) they betray their menfolk into shame. For women are, after all, in a double bond: they are to be wives as well as lovers. That is, they are not only prizes of war, but also commodities in the marriage market. Daughters are ducats. Marriage is a woman's vocation: it is her formal induction into the Men's Club; it is therefore her salvation; to be condemned into everlasting redemption is the fate she was born for. Man, however, was not born for wedlock. It is an accidental inconvenience of the system that after a man has amused himself in hunting his lawful prey, and succeeded in trapping her, he is then expected to deny his nature and spend his life by her side.

Men have, then, a bad conscience about their use and abuse of women in both love and marriage. They know that they do not deserve the loyalty and respect they command women to give them; *they* suspect their place, and they also suspect that *women* do. But this raises a question: If they are apprehensive about their own ability to be good husbands, is it *because* they choose to believe themselves born deceivers, or does it work the other way round? That is, could it be *because* marriage strikes them as a difficult, confining, and dull sink-a-pace that they choose to accept their fate as deceivers who are by nature unfit for it? Like the swan-brides in Spenser's *Prothalamion*, they resist the sink-a-pace because in various ways domesticity presages helplessness and death. For one thing, it means committing their reputation to wives in whom the power of cuckoldry is legally invested. For another, it spells the death of their most precious experience: their companionship with other men. The solidarity of the locker room; the shared vicissitudes of love and war; the easy trust and distrust engendered in friends who are second selves to each other; their common allegiance to self-deception – these are doomed to dissolve after the wedding. Wooing bonds men together in a competitive or cooperative association that marriage threatens; therefore when marriage beckons, men no less than women have to be forcibly separated from the arms of their loved ones. Thus Claudio clings to the Prince before his wedding, begging to escort him to Arragon as soon as the marriage is consummated. At the end of the play, Benedick dallies among his fellow bachelors, and finally, as the turncoats fall away, the Prince sadly stands alone, like the Farmer in the Dell's proverbial cheese.

Male solidarity is never more in evidence than at its twilight. Everyone in the last scene does a Scotch jig to avoid the imminent dispersal through marriage. Benedick and Beatrice resume their earlier roles and seem for a moment ready to shy away from conjugation. The college of wit-crackers shoot off their last salvo of bad marriage jokes, and reaffirm their commitment to inconstancy. After the events of the fourth act, during which everyone was divided against everyone else, all have succeeded in escaping from that dream of unhappiness-come-true, and now, deceivers ever, they wake themselves with laughing (II.i.308–9) and take their hearing prisoner with the lock of fashion. One after the other, the men rejoin the ranks and redirect their suspicions away from themselves toward the fugitive Don John. At last the Men's Club is back together; but only for a moment. The Club is about to be dismembered. The work – that is, the play – of Leonato, Claudio, and Benedick is over, even the Prince is urged to marry, and all will soon scatter to their newly full or empty households. *Much Ado About Nothing* is an *endless moniment* for short time, and what it celebrates, as the machinery of the sink-a-pace turns over, is the ending of happiness.

This ending begins 'aspiciously' enough when Claudio addresses his second wedding as one of the reckonings to be settled, a debt he owes and is owed, or a score he must repay. The first reckoning is with Benedick, who has just genially insulted him:

> **Claudio** For this I owe you. Here comes other reck'nings.
>   Which is the lady I must seize upon?
> **Antonio** This same is she, and I do give you her.
> **Claudio** Why, then, she's mine. Sweet, let me see your face.
> **Leonato** No, that you shalt not till you take her hand
>   Before this friar and swear to marry her.
> **Claudio** Give me your hand before this holy friar.
>   I am your husband if you like of me.
> **Hero** And when I lived I was your other wife;
>   And when you loved you were my other husband.
> **Claudio** Another Hero!
> **Hero** Nothing certainer.
>   One Hero died defiled: but I do live,
>   And surely as I live, I am a maid.
>
> (V.iv.52–64)

The language emphasises the forms of *apprehension*. Claudio's is aggressive ('the lady I must seize upon'), Leonato's defensive.

Having prayed at her 'tomb', the wolves continue to prey (V.iii. 251). But this time Hero is more than a match for Claudio. The parallels between lines 60 and 61 bring out the biting contrast produced by the difference between 'when I *lived*' and 'when you *loved*': his 'love' is no more real than her 'death', and we do not forget that the first marriage failed to take place. Nothing is 'certainer' to Hero than that, although she was defiled by slander, her virtue has triumphed over all efforts – and especially over Claudio's – to kill it. Her emphatic assertion of virginity pronounces Claudio guilty. She has the advantage and knows how to call in 'other reck'nings'. To borrow Portia's words, she capitalises on 'my vantage to exclaim on you' (*Merchant of Venice*, III.ii.174).

Hero makes it clear that the new Hero is simply the old with a vengeance, and though Claudio tries to shuffle off the implication with '*another* Hero', the Prince accepts it: 'The former Hero! Hero that is dead!' (V.iv.65). Her words reflect mordantly on the friar's self-delighting penchant for staging spiritual scenarios.[7] They remind us that this community harbours no twice-born souls. The friar's practice is a travesty on religious psychology, conversion, and ethical self-transformation. It conspicuously excludes what it parodies, and substitutes a mere plot mechanism equal in ethical quality or causality to the bed trick. His terms of death and rebirth, being metaphorical and counterfactual, work by contraries to affirm that Hero and Claudio remain the same. No one is new-created by verbal or theatrical magic. The dialogue quoted above glances toward the conventional reconciliation. But the parties to it would have to be reborn in a new heaven and earth, a new Messina, before they could enter into a relationship free of the assumptions of their community. Their words, and the friar's game, evoke this possibility only to dispel it. They do not cut through the bond; they only nick it, and the play happily concludes, for *Much Ado* is a Shakespearean comedy – that is, an experience which ends in the nick of time.

From *Shakespeare Quarterly*, 33 (1982), 302–13.

NOTES

[Harry Berger's essay is reprinted in his latest book, *Making Trifles of Terrors, Redistributing Complicities in Shakespeare* (Stanford, CA, 1997), pp. 10–24. This collection testifies to the enduring impact of Harry Berger Jr's work, and places the essay on *Much Ado* in the context of his Shakespearean criticism in general. Berger has always utilised contemporary theory in a way which facilitates a close reading to the text and as such stands at a point of transition in the history of Shakespeare criticism, between a concentration upon language, image and custom, and an application of theoretical formulae. Ed.]

1. All quotations are from *William Shakespeare: The Complete Works*, ed. A. Harbage (Baltimore, MD, 1969).

2. The significance of Beatrice's speech, and its usefulness as a kind of leitmotif for the themes with which this essay is concerned, were first pointed out to me by D. S. Manning.

3. J. W. Bennett, Introduction to *Much Ado About Nothing*, ed. Harbage, p. 275.

4. J. A. Allen, 'Dogberry', *Shakespeare Quarterly*, 24 (1973), 42–3.

5. Allen calls him 'a bumbling minor-league Iago' ('Dogberry', p. 36).

6. Cf. Allen's excellent comment on Borachio in 'Dogberry', p. 39.

7. On this point I part company with Allen's reading in 'Dogberry'. He idealises the friar by way of dismissing or minimising the problematic elements so perceptively discussed in the earlier pages of his essay, and steers the play back into the comic mode and happy ending. On this disagreement in general, see Richard Levin's interesting 'Refuting Shakespeare's Endings', Parts I and II, *Modern Philology*, 72 (1975), 337–49, and 75 (1977), 132–58. I am committed to the ironic reading of Shakespeare that Levin criticises, and while I am not directly concerned to refute his refutation of the refuters, the present essay is an implicit critique of a strategy employed by both Levin and Allen: overstressing the magic power of the ending – and of the comic genre and conventions – to resolve or dissolve settled ambivalences of attitude inherent not merely in particular actions or characters, but in the community of the play.

2

Half a Dozen Dangerous Words

S. P. CERASANO

In Act III, scene i of *Much Ado About Nothing*, Hero tries to encourage Beatrice's love for Benedick by staging a conversation with Ursula which she expects Beatrice to 'overhear'. During their discussion Hero dismisses the possibility of confronting Beatrice openly with Benedick's passion because Beatrice cannot be trusted to respond positively. She 'turns every man the wrong side out', Hero decides; therefore, since the match between the would-be lovers cannot end happily, Hero teasingly suggests that Benedick should be encouraged to fight against his love and ultimately to reject Beatrice. In aid of this course of action Hero contrives a plot:

> And truly I'll devise some honest slanders,
> To stain my cousin with, one doth not know
> How much an ill word may empoison liking.
> (III.i.84–6)[1]

Hero's playful proposal to employ 'honest slander' brings ironic repercussions for her later in the play, for it is the 'dishonest slander' that poisons Claudio's affections, disrupts Hero's marriage, prompts Leonato's rejection of his daughter, and requires finally that Hero 'die', only to return to marry the man who earlier mistakenly condemned her to death by destroying her reputation. In this way, the possibilities presented by Hero's love game initiate the makings of a more serious matter. In the course of the play Shakespeare reveals that maintaining one's reputation is more complex than simply managing to avoid slander. The private language of 'honest slander' raised by women like Hero in order to unite lovers becomes, in the mouths of men like Don John, a publicised 'dishonest slander' by which relationships and particularly the women involved in them, can be destroyed. Moreover, *Much Ado* implicitly dramatises the plight of women and slander within the actual legal structure. Although several critics comment that the play seems to lack a final trial scene in which to absolve Hero and set things right (as, for example, occurs in *Measure for Measure*)[2] the causes and circumstances of slander – namely, the use and abuse of language – are put on trial publicly in the church scene and tested implicitly throughout the play. Finally, the language of slander is shown to be a fabrication of the social and sexual values which are mirrored and married (literally and figuratively) in the cultured discourse of the play.

The adjudication of slander suits in the Renaissance has been described by some critics (Lisa Jardine and Valerie Wayne, for instance) as following a well-established procedure and offering the possibility for the offended party to find justice under the law. Although they do not imply, for a moment, that a slander suit was a pro forma matter, their examples, being drawn from records of the consistory courts (which were ecclesiastical courts), do not reflect the enormous changes in the way slander was conceptualised and adjudicated during the sixteenth century. Throughout the Middle Ages, slander was construed by the Church courts as the telling of lies. It was treated as a spiritual offence and the guilty party was sentenced to do penance, which could take a variety of forms including 'humiliating [public] apology'. This conception of slander was consistent with the type of court which was addressing the offence, and the penalty was consistent with the sort of compensation that the Church courts could legally extract. Although slander was treated as a sin (capable of being ameliorated through holy acts), at some unspecified time before 1500 the courts began to allow a fee to be substituted for penance. Consequently, a blurring of the distinction between the spiritual and the civil spheres of redress occurred, and this confusion overshadowed the litigation surrounding slander suits throughout the sixteenth century.[3]

A further move from spiritual to civil in slander cases occurred with the decline of the local and ecclesiastical courts in the first half of the sixteenth century. Slander thus became actionable in the common law courts. However, the common law courts had inherited the ecclesiastical precedent that slander was a 'spiritual offence', which fell slightly outside the judicial domain that the civil law was best able to adjudicate. There was no debate among the courts at Westminster, all of which acknowledged that the telling of lies was morally wrong; but the courts were bound to specific modes of redress. Slander could not be treated as an action of trespass in the common law courts unless 'damages' could be assessed. Restricted to this criterion, the courts did not consider slander as assault, and they were reluctant to award damages for 'evanescent or indirect harm', although that was the type of damage slander most often caused.[4]

But the complications do not stop here. As a result of Henry VIII's break with the Church the ecclesiastical courts gradually began to vanish, and as they did slander suits lost their natural legal venue. In addition, there was a growing awareness that slander constituted not only a moral offence but a breach of the peace, sometimes instigating violence. In recognition of these realities the common law courts eventually found themselves in the unhappy business of trying to deal with slander in a purely civil context. By 1550 slander had become part of the everyday business of common law, in particular of the Court of King's Bench.[5] Before long – and owing in part to the allegations of conspiracy frequently accompanying slander charges – the equity courts also became involved. The Court of Star Chamber, in which assault was integral to the pleadings, became steeped in slander suits.[6] And because of its lower costs and its tradition of expediency, the Court of Requests started to deal with slander on a regular basis. By Shakespeare's day at least three major courts were forced to decide large numbers of cases, although the legal mechanisms through which they operated were ill-suited to deal with the charges at issue.

The judicial precedent established by the common law courts meant that the legal atmosphere was, in some ways, inhospitable to any claimant, and doubly inhospitable to claims by women. Perhaps the latter fact is not surprising, given the well-documented tendencies towards cultural misogyny, as well as women's general disadvantages under the law at the time. Women could not, for instance, plead for themselves without a male guardian. Yet the serious difficulty in adjudicating slander suits resided in the ephemeral nature of verbal assault. Proving that a statement was slanderous was contingent upon issues involving personal identity, and determining tangible damages caused further problems. Both factors were difficult to address and complicated to adjudicate. Then, as now, the textbook definition was clear enough. Slander was:

> a malicious defamation ... tending either to blacken the memory of one who is dead, or the reputation of one who is alive, and thereby expose him to public hatred, contempt and ridicule.[7]

Commonly, name-calling was the precipitating activity in slander suits, such as that exemplified in the case in which Thomas Lancaster told 'diverse persons' that John Hampton was a 'cosening knave'.[8] Given the necessity of showing that Hampton had somehow suffered damages, the outcome of the lawsuit depended upon evidence demonstrating that Lancaster had wilfully spread false information about Hampton with the intention of destroying his reputation; and further, that damage to Hampton's professional or personal status (his marriage, for example) had ensued as a result of Lancaster's rumour.[9] The usual insults for which people brought suit – 'drunkard', 'quarreller', 'lewd liver', 'notorious thief', 'beggar' or 'runnegate' – might be distasteful; but legal retribution was impossible without demonstrable evidence that harm had been done.[10] And the legal process of proving that the verbal assault had taken place, such as Lancaster really calling Hampton 'a cosening knave', was often circuitous. Unless the defendant had made some egregious comments in public or performed activities such as singing songs or reciting rhymes before a large audience of reliable citizens, showing that the slanderous situation had indeed transpired was difficult. Reliable evidence had to include a number of witnesses, frequently living at a distance, who could 'document' a rumour as it spread.

Therefore, even a cursory reading of cases in a common law court, such as the Court of Requests, shows that it was easy to be violated by verbal abuse but difficult to succeed in pressing charges. Plaintiffs did sometimes manage to extract public apologies and monetary redress for their 'damages'. However, the law was fundamentally incapable of remedying losses to one's reputation. As a result, the courts do not seem to have been consulted because litigants could expect their public images to be restored through legal action. In part, the courts acted as verbal boxing rings, mediating the hostility between litigants and providing a stage whereon actors such as Thomas Lancaster and John Hampton could each audition for the role of victim, more sinned against than sinning. If, in the end, Lancaster was found guilty of slandering Hampton, then Hampton 'succeeded' in court but also had to cope with any residual damage to his reputation. If, on the other hand, Lancaster was found innocent, then he had essentially been slandered by Hampton who, by bringing charges, had implied that Lancaster was a slanderer and a criminal.

Considering the propensity of Elizabethans to take charges of slander to court, this background would have been familiar to the audience of *Much Ado About Nothing*, even though it is almost entirely unfamiliar to most twentieth-century audiences. Likewise, it is important for us to understand that the subordinate position of women during the Renaissance made them especially vulnerable to verbal abuse. Women were expected to be 'chaste, silent, and obedient', and the high social value placed upon women's chastity left them deeply susceptible to claims of whoredom.[11] In fact, virtually all slander suits involving women called into question their sexual morality. A typical case occurred in rural Shropshire in the early seventeenth century; C. J. Sisson later identified it as a provincial version of *The Old Joiner of Aldgate*.[12] In this situation two young men, Humphrey Elliot and Edward Hinkes, were charged with performing 'scandalous and infamous libelous verses, rhymes, plays, and interludes' about Elizabeth Ridge, a young woman of the same village. According to Elizabeth's account the young men hoped to characterise her as 'vile, odious, and contemptible' and, through social pressure, to force her to marry one of them. Moreover, Elizabeth laid the charge that the men conspired against her 'out of a most covetous & greedy desire to gain' her father's sizeable estate, to which she was the sole heiress. Elizabeth Ridge's reasons for taking legal action centred upon the damage done to her reputation, as did Hampton's in the former example. However, the concept of reputation was complicated by gender issues. Like other women Elizabeth was concerned that once she was labelled a 'fallen woman', no man would want to marry her. As a young woman in a small rural village she might well have perceived the opportunities for a suitable match to have been few and far between. Also, the close-knit nature of village life would have ensured that the slanderous rumours spread to most of the inhabitants of the village by the time the case came to trial. On top of these events – by which a young woman like Elizabeth Ridge would have felt violated anyway – there were the further harrowing experiences of undergoing the process of law and of demonstrating that harm had arisen. As a single woman she could not show loss of or damage to her marriage; as a young woman of her class, not engaged in meaningful work or a trade, she could not claim 'damage' to her professional life; as a woman, denied full status as a citizen, she could not easily assert that her public presence had been 'damaged'. If a woman was called a 'whore', she had little compensation to look forward to. Not surprisingly, given the personal costs involved, no woman felt that she could afford to ignore a public allegation such as slander. Even the young Elizabeth I, about whom rumours circulated to the effect that she was pregnant by Thomas Seymour in 1548–9, felt obligated to set the record straight. On 23 January 1549 she wrote to the Lord Protector:

> My lord, these are shameful slanders ... I shall most heartily desire your lordship that I may come to the court after your just determination that I may show myself there as I am.[13]

At the same time women had to face the fact that the law was particularly inept to assist them in reclaiming such an intangible commodity as reputation, and that the potential consequences of slander for them were vastly different from those for men. The potency of language as it related to sexual status was clearly in the control of men like Elliot and Hinkes, and the process of the law favoured men, whether they were plaintiffs charging other men or defendants against complaints brought by women.

For Renaissance women, reputation, that which was synonymous with a 'good name' or a 'bad name', defined identity in an ideological, as well as in a legal, sense. A 'fair name' was essential in order for a woman to maintain her 'worthiness'; and as a woman was treated as the property of her father, husband or guardian, her name was treated as property which could be stolen, usurped or defiled. In *As You Like It*, for instance, Duke Frederick warns Celia that Rosalind 'robs thee of thy name' (I.iii.76).[14] Related to the theme of property was an economic discourse that determined the value of a woman's name, and it was always the 'fair name' that was stolen, for the 'black name' could only be 'bought' (suggesting prostitution): 'she hath bought the name of whore, thus dearly' (*Cymbeline*, II.iv.128).[15] Moreover, reputation could be 'disvalued' (see, for instance, *Measure for Measure*, V.i.220).[16] Nor was a woman's name her own property to 'sell' as she thought fit. A woman's reputation belonged to her male superior, who 'owned' her and to whom she could bring honour or disgrace. In so far as a woman was 'renamed' when she was slandered and her identity thus altered, her husband lost his good name and was rechristened with abuse – slandered by association. If the characterisation of a woman as 'loose' was true, that was all to the worse. In articulating the dual sense of *name*, signifying both 'reputation' and 'a malicious term', and in describing his wife's effect on his reputation, Frank Ford rails to the audience of *The Merry Wives of Windsor*:

> See the hell of having a false woman: my bed shall be abused, my coffers ransacked, my reputation gnawn at, and I shall not only receive this villainous wrong, but stand under the adoption of abominable terms, and by him that does me this wrong. Terms! Names! Amaimon sounds well; Lucifer, well; Barbason, well: yet they are devils' additions [names], the names of fiends. But cuckold? Wittol? Cuckold! The devil himself hath not such a name.
>
> (II.ii.280–9)[17]

The comic overtones of Ford's tirade are balanced, however, by the more severe associations of a bad name with prostitution. When Othello upbraids Montano, he remarks:

> The gravity and stillness of your youth
> The world hath noted, and your *name* is great
> In mouths of wisest censure [judgement]: what's the matter,
> That you *unlace your reputation* thus,
> And *spend your rich opinion* [reputation], for the name
> Of a *night-brawler*?
>
> (*Othello*, II.iii.182–7; emphasis added)[18]

M. R. Ridley glosses 'unlace' as 'not the simple "undo" ... but the stronger hunting (and carving) term'. The 'undoing' of Montano is suggestive of a literal 'gutting' of his personal value. Othello implies that his unwillingness to 'unlace' himself and 'spend' his rich opinion is a sign not only of Montano's weakness but of his sexual vulgarity. Montano loses his reputation to a 'night-brawler', the disclosure of which costs him dearly in excess of what he has already 'spent' for sexual favours. For the Elizabethans the rhetoric was pungent. Privileging 'dishonour in thy name' makes 'fair reputation but a bawd', and slander creates 'the wound that nothing healeth' (*The Rape of Lucrece*, ll. 621–3, 731).[19] The language of a sullied reputation – whether or not that reputation belonged to a man or a woman – was constantly associated with female sexuality gone amiss, as if no Montano would ever go astray were it not for the presence of a bawd to tempt him and rob him of his wealth.

The church scene in *Much Ado About Nothing* is replete with just these sorts of legal and ideological associations. At its opening Claudio first breaks the terms of the pre-marital agreement that Don Pedro had arranged for him. He then explicitly rejects Hero and openly refuses to accept her as his property: 'There, Leonato, take her back again' (IV.i.30). After Claudio's dispossession of Hero he calls her 'rotten orange' (IV.i.31) and 'an approved wanton' (IV.i.44), but he waits until he has dissociated himself from her completely so that her reputation and moral state cannot sully his own. In a particularly brutal and unambiguous manner he states that he does not wish: 'to knit my soul. / To an approved wanton' (IV.i.43–4). Claudio's choice of language identifies Hero with prostitution, a suggestion that acts as a powerful verbal cue inciting the other men in the scene to join in his abuse of her. Don Pedro casts her as 'a common stale [whore]' (IV.i.65). Leonato declares that she is 'fallen' (IV.i.139), her very flesh is 'foul-tainted' (IV.i.143), that her sin 'appears in proper nakedness' (IV.i.175). To destroy Hero's identity further, Claudio attempts to reduce her image, her very being to 'nothingness':

> Would you not swear,
> All you that see her, that she were a maid,
> By these exterior shows? But she is *none*:
> (IV.i.37–40; emphasis added)

In Claudio's eyes Hero has dissolved from a facade of 'seeming' to 'none' ('no one' – that is, nothingness). The tactics that reduce Hero's status and deny her humanity creep in throughout Claudio's speech in this scene. His language becomes increasingly insidious as he first appeals to the others (primarily the men) to believe that Hero bears a false front, and then turns directly against Hero herself. Intriguingly, he tries to make her name potent and worthless at the same time:

> **Hero**   O God defend me, how am I beset!
>   What kind of catechizing call you this?
> **Claudio**   To make you answer truly to your name.
> **Hero**   Is it not Hero? Who can blot that name
>   With any just reproach?
> **Claudio**   Marry, that can Hero;
>   Hero itself can blot out Hero's virtue.
>
> (IV.i.77–82)

While Hero seeks an explanation as to 'who' ('what person') can blot her name with just cause, Claudio replies that 'Hero itself' can stain her honour. On his rhetorical terms, she cannot possibly win. But whether he means that her tainted name 'itself' can dishonour Hero, or whether she is being symbolically reduced to a genderless object ('Hero *itself*) Claudio's response is tempered with the sexual values of his society. He would not call a man 'wanton' because it is so explicitly a male term of opprobrium for a woman.

When Claudio slanders Hero in such an extreme manner his rhetoric has the effect of uniting part of the male community behind him, with the exception of Benedick (who, with Beatrice, stands outside the rhetorical and social codes to which Claudio and the others subscribe) and the Friar (who immediately takes steps to attempt to turn slander to 'remorse' [IV.i.211]). Nevertheless, Leonato, Don Pedro and Don John all take an active verbal role in Hero's persecution, knowing that Claudio's slander could well lead to grievous injury. Leonato, in fact, demands Hero's extinction, even her death, as a justifiable retribution for her presumed digression and for jeopardising his name. When Hero swoons, Leonato responds:

> O Fate, take not away thy heavy hand!
> Death is the fairest cover for her shame
> That may be wished for ...
>
> Do not live, Hero, do not ope thine eyes;
> For did I think thou wouldst not quickly die,
> Thought I thy spirits were stronger than thy shames,
> Myself would on the rearward of approaches
> Strike at thy life.
>
> (IV.i.115–17; 123–7)

Slander and death are familiar bedfellows throughout Shakespeare's plays. The slandered victim, spoken of in terms that relate to discredit, sexual defilement and disease, was finally described as an outcast. Slander, popularly thought of as 'the transient murderer', if not actually the cause of literal death, was thought to lead to public alienation and metaphorical death. As Antony succinctly points out concerning his political opponents:

> These many men shall die; their names are prick'd.
>
> He shall not live. Look, with a spot I damn him.
>   (*Julius Caesar*, IV.i.1,6)[20]

The urgency of the Friar's proposal to turn slander into remorse recognises the price Hero will have to pay for Claudio's slander. Her alternatives are to be reborn ('a greater birth' [IV.i.213]) and to begin anew with a pure reputation (possibly to be slandered again at some future time) or to be hidden away 'in some reclusive and religious life' (IV.i.242). But finally, the Friar urges that death and resurrection is the best course – 'Come, lady, die to live' (IV.i.253) – regardless of the fact that Hero initially 'died upon his [Claudio's] words' (IV.i.223) and that Claudio makes no attempt to repair her shattered emotions at the end of the scene, simply going off and leaving her for dead.

In describing the violation of Hero as the conspiracy of 'eyes, tongues, minds, and injuries' (IV.i.243), Friar Francis reminds us of the other ways in which those in Messina are slandered and violated, and of the covert strategies that stand in the way of the characters' ability to negotiate meaningful interactions. Chief among these undercurrents is that presented by the atmosphere of Messina itself, an environment which revolves around tale-telling, eavesdropping and spying, all purportedly performed in the name of some legitimate purpose. From the opening of the play, where Beatrice asks for 'news' of Benedick, the characters seem caught up in a web of gossip and surface appearances. Marriages are arranged by proxy, while men and women woo and wed behind masks – literal face-coverings and social expectations alike. This tendency towards doubling encourages naïve young men like Claudio to cling to the traditional male sphere of war in public, and to accept the less-than-gratifying pose of Petrarchan lover in his private life.

As long as conversations are witty and frivolous, Messina's social code is attractive; but as soon as serious issues are at stake, the community opens itself up to misrepresentation and slander.[21] As much as Hero is slandered by Claudio's words she is also slandered by his eyes, by his predisposition to distrustfulness, and by his need to spy on her in order to test her virtue. And because the men in Messina are so willing to accept what they (mis)perceive and (mis)hear, they easily become impulsive and abusive. Leonato and Claudio will trust each other through a process of male bonding, but they will equally trust impersonal and unsubstantiated 'report'. As a result, they condemn Hero on the basis of slight evidence without allowing her to defend herself. The natural tendency of the residents of Messina is towards gullibility, inconstancy, unpredictability and slander; and also towards giving short shrift to personal identity, individual circumstances or motivations, patience and constancy.

The ways in which characters identify each other in public give another indication of their reduced status as individuals. This is especially true of women and others, such as foreigners, who are disadvantaged by their social role, and all of whom are categorised by the term 'none'. The gentlemen killed in the war before the play opens are described as 'none of name' (I.i.6); and although Beatrice asks about the well-being of 'Signor Montanto', the messenger knows 'none of that name' (I.i.30). It is only when Hero interposes, identifying Beatrice's enquiry as that concerning 'Signor Benedick of Padua' (therefore an alien [I.i.33]), that the messenger recognises the man to whom Beatrice refers. Likewise, after Claudio's first meeting with Hero he initially identifies her by everything other than her name, thereby renaming her. She is 'the daughter of Signor Leonato' (I.i.150–1), 'a modest young lady' (I.i.153), 'a jewel' (I.i.168) and 'the sweetest lady' (I.i.174). It is at the moment when he wishes to acquire Hero that he finally names her: 'if Hero would be my wife' (I.i.182). And like the name-calling in the church scene, other men are quick to pick this up. Subsequently, Don Pedro privileges Hero's name and her identity at a point that involves acquisition: 'Claudio, I have wooed in thy name, and fair Hero is won' (II.i.280–1). Interestingly, when Hero is defamed her name is used repeatedly and made an object of mockery (as is her identity):

> **Don John** The lady is disloyal.
> **Claudio** Who, Hero?
> **Don John** Even she, Leonato's Hero, your Hero, every man's Hero.
> (III.ii.93–6)

Sadly but predictably, Hero herself ends up condoning this practice – that which encourages women to exchange or surrender their identity willingly – when she interprets her restoration in Act V, scene iv:

> One Hero dies defiled, but I do live
> And surely as I live, I am a maid.
> (V.iv.63–4)

Indeed, Hero's act of giving up her name to restore her relationship with Claudio metaphorically prefigures the time when she will actually relinquish it – when they marry and she takes his name.

In contrast with Hero, the male characters of the main plot have firmly fixed names and identities, and they spend a fair amount of time using their names and reassuring themselves of their identities. When their names are exchanged for titles ('Don Pedro' for 'the prince', for instance) it is to enhance their status. There are two intriguing exceptions to this generalisation, however, and both relate to men bearing dishonourable names. One is the character of Don John, a social outcast who cannot hide his bastard status or his melancholy temperament behind the mask of an honourable name: 'I cannot hide what I am: I must be sad when I have cause, and smile at no man's jests' (I.iii.12–14). (The name 'john' was coterminous with 'waiter', 'footman', or other subservient at the time.) The other exception occurs in Act IV, scene ii, when Dogberry tries to get Conrade and Borachio to answer for their offences by taking on the name and identity of 'false knaves' (false names, although surely a pun is intended here). Every time Dogberry challenges them with this label, one or the other counters: 'we are none' (IV.ii.23, 28). But both instances occur in the subplot; the main male characters in the play appear to have more control, both over their own names and over the names they apply to others. Moreover, the speed with which they confer and change nomenclature to suit whatever they hope to accomplish allows them to take a cavalier approach to identity – and a cavalier approach, as well, to the harm that an individual suffers when misidentified and slandered. While the women are defending the names of the men (**Hero**: 'Indeed he [Benedick] hath an excellent good name [III.i.98]) the men jest about slandering inanimate things (**Balthasar**: 'Oh, good my lord, tax not so bad a voice, / To slander music any more than once' [II.iii.44–5]). Their power resides in the choice they maintain – and take for granted – to determine their own identities. Even in the game-playing-teasing between Antonio and Ursula at the dance, Antonio guards his name as the ultimate signifier of his reputation. Ursula identifies Antonio by the wagging of his head, but his recourse is verbal. He refuses to accept her label: 'At my word, I am not [Antonio]' (II.i.110).

Janice Hays concludes that when Hero faints in the church scene she is exhibiting a distinctly feminine sort of power. The 'going down in order to come up' imitates 'the Demeter–Persephone pattern of responding to experience'. In psychological terms Hays explains Hero's faint as suggestive of the power of giving birth, but also as replicating the coping mechanism that women have developed in order to be caretakers. In other words, it is another testimony to the way in which women are socially expected, and conditioned to put themselves in a position of weakness in order to maintain their femininity.[22] Were this not enough of a sacrifice, Hero's response is complicated by what can be demonstrated through lawsuits to have been the severity of the legal-cum-social code of the times. The danger of slanderous language, as it affected women, expands upon David L. Stevenson's sense that *Much Ado* is marked by 'mimetic realism' – what he aptly describes as 'the natural, this-worldly atmosphere', especially as regards the 'potency of language' used in the play.[23] Not only does the play imitate the quality of everyday language used during Shakespeare's day. More than this, it reflects the real threat of the language of conflict, with all its sexual and erotic overtones. Therefore Hero faints not only from shock and because the violence of Claudio's rhetoric is akin to a physical assault, but also because she realises that neither the legal process, her father's position in Messina, the force of her own argument, nor the testimony of her friends can ultimately exonerate her.

The violence of war in foreign parts, alluded to at the beginning of the play, becomes the violence of rhetoric at home. Aggression becomes domesticated. Perhaps because the nature of war forbids it, the men in the main plot seem unaccustomed to verbal communication, so that too often they respond in silence, in excess, or in ways inappropriate for times of peace. For example, when Leonato grants his permission for Hero to marry Claudio and asks for everyone's 'amen', Claudio is strangely silent and has to be prodded by Beatrice: 'Speak, Count, 'tis your cue' (II.i.286). Claudio doesn't really know what to say, so unaccustomed is he to the intercourse of peace, so he ends up clumsily offering what he thinks is a compliment, but is finally an oddly self-reflexive transaction:

> Silence is the perfectest herald of joy; I were but little happy, if I
> could say how much. Lady as you are mine, I am yours; I give away
> myself for you and dote upon the exchange.
>
> (II.i.288–91)

What he is doting on is obviously himself. Not fully understanding
language, Leonato is dismissive of words, convinced that words are
air, that they are totally without substance: 'Charm ache with air,
and agony with words' (V.i.26). It is partly this insensitive disregard
for language that motivates the men's careless use of language
throughout the play, despite the fact that they are effusive, and that
Much Ado About Nothing is largely a play about men talking to
one another. Antonio would like to pin the responsibility for
slander on the young men:

> God knows I lov'd my niece,
> And she is dead, slander'd to death by villains,
> That dare as well answer a man indeed
> As I dare take a serpent by the tongue.
> Boys, apes, braggarts, Jacks, milksops!
>
> What, man! I know them, yea,
> And what they weigh, even to the utmost scruple,
> Scrambling, outfacing, fashion-monging boys,
> That lie, and cog, and flout, deprave, and slander,
> Go anticly, and show outward hideousness,
> And speak off half a dozen dangerous words,
> How they might hurt their enemies, if they durst,
> And this to all.
>
> (V.i.87–91, 92–9)

Yet it is not a fault limited to young men. After Hero faints,
Leonato continues to rail for almost forty lines before he loses
steam. In a play in which words are so very cheap, language is
superfluous. Echoing the play's title, Leonato's abundant rhetoric is
essentially 'much ado' and worth 'nothing'.

Beatrice cries: 'Sweet Hero, she is wronged, she is slandered, she
is undone' (V.i.299). The language of the church scene places the
audience as witnesses of the misogynist ends to which language
could be – and was, at times – put. It also shows the way in which
men use language to set up the law for their own advantage, and
how they continually use language to diminish women to nothingness. Claudio, knowing 'nothing' of Hero as an individual and only
inaccurate gossip about her behaviour (itself 'nothing'), metaphori-

cally condemns her to death and symbolically to 'nothingness'. By the last scene he seems to have changed but little. Although the epitaph on Hero's monument is blatant ('Done to death by slanderous tongues, / Was the Hero that here lies' [V.iii.3–4]), he asks for pardon from the goddess of the night, herself a symbol of darkness, absence, 'nothingness'.

Claudio cannot, of course, create something from nothing; but the 'honest slander' of the subplot involving Beatrice and Benedick does. This is the point at which I believe that those critics who argue that Hero's 'honest slander' does not raise the same issues as Claudio's slander are in error. To begin with, the Beatrice–Benedick subplot displaces the Claudio–Hero plot through the sharp juxtaposition of reality and fiction, for Beatrice and Benedick show a healthy distrust for the conventions of idealised love. In this way they know how to 'name' themselves, how to deal with the pitfalls of language, and how to stand back from romantic conventions:

> **Benedick** The savage bull may [bear the yoke]; but if ever the sensible Benedick bear it, pluck off the bull's horns and set them in my forehead, and let me be vilely painted, and in such great letters as they write, 'Here is food horse to hire', let them signify under my sign,
> 'Here you may see Benedick, the married man.'
>
> (I.i.243–8)

> **Beatrice** And, Benedick, love on, I will requite thee,
> Taming my wild heart to thy loving hand.
> If thou dost love, my kindness shall incite thee
> To bind our loves up in a holy band;
> For others say thou dost deserve, and I
> Believe it better than reportingly.
>
> (III.i.111–16)

In one sense 'honest slander' complements the other forms of reconciliation in the play, helping to explain why the Beatrice–Benedick subplot is rhetorically richer than the main plot. Claudio's 'malicious slander' is balanced out by the 'honest slander' that helps to bring Beatrice and Benedick together, as Claudio's fantasised love is balanced out by the more genuine, mature love of Beatrice and Benedick. Similarly, Claudio's 'nothingness' is countered by the avowal of the love shared by Beatrice and Benedick, which is brought on by Claudio's denunciation of Hero in the church scene:

> **Benedick**   I do love nothing in the world so well as you – is that not strange?
>
> **Beatrice**   As strange as the thing I know not. It were as possible for me to say I loved nothing so well as you, but believe me not; and yet I lie not, I confess nothing, nor I deny nothing. I am sorry for my cousin.
>
> (IV.i.266–72)

However, Beatrice's verbal potency is limited. Later in the same scene, when she bids Benedick to kill Claudio and the former refuses, she realises that as a woman she has only language – not action – within her power, and that is not always effective:

> But manhood is melted into curtsies, valour into compliment, and men are only turned into tongue, and trim ones too: he is now as valiant as Hercules that only tells a lie and swears it. I cannot be a man with wishing, therefore I will die a woman with grieving.
>
> (IV.ii.316–23)

The fact that 'honest slander' is a concept created by one of the women in the play, and it is implemented by women, prompts questions about language and 'real' slander in the 'real' world – or rather, about slander in the world that men have constructed. In Act III, scene i, Hero and Ursula toy with the invention of 'honest slanders' because they realise how ambiguous language (and slander) can be. Language, they think, can exist on two levels: one serious, and one in which potentially serious values such as truth and falsehood may be determined in a game-like fashion; and as the women fabricate their account of Benedick's love they believe that they are playfully creating truth from a fiction.[24]

> **Hero**   Our talk must only be of Benedick.
>   When I do name him, let it be thy part
>   To praise him more than ever man did merit:
>   My talk to thee must be how Benedick
>   Is sick in love with Beatrice. Of this matter
>   Is little Cupid's crafty arrow made,
>   That only wounds by hearsay.
>
> (III.i.17–23)

The women, however, understand well the profound distinction between 'honest' and 'dishonest' slander, and they realise that it is more a matter of language creating reality than creating illusion. Some critics find the solution of *Much Ado* an unsatisfactory one: in the words of Roger Sale, 'the apparent triumph of this dishonest illusion'. But the play's conclusion is not so simply paraphrased as 'Tricking into marriage is honest, whereas tricking out of marriage is dishonest'.[25] Don John – the bastard without legitimate name – reveals, by his fictional account of Hero's transgressions, that to name things is to make them real. Yet concurrently, while language can slander it can also be chaste:

> Fie, fie, they are not to be nam'd, my lord,
> Not to be spoken of!
> There is not chastity enough in language
> Without offence to utter them.
>
> (IV.i.95–8)

Much Ado's resolution might be temporary and fictional, but the fictions that language creates are consequential. The power of language to bring about order or chaos is treated throughout the play; and whether we observe Margaret, called 'Hero' by Borachio at the chamber window, or Hero, called 'wanton' by Claudio, it is the preservation of 'chastity in language' by women and Hero's vision of 'honest slander' that bring about the resolution of the play. For if there was 'dishonest slander' alone, the play could not end as it does. Carol Neely observes: 'patriarchal marriage customs conveniently coalesce with romantic rhetoric, enabling him [Claudio] to maintain Hero as object of social exchange and possession.' Claudio's slander, then, is an expression of masculine anxieties about marriage and about male sexuality.[26] But Hero – by presenting the possibility of 'honest slander' – offers the vision of a different rhetoric. Claudio essentially becomes trapped in his own language; by his slander he loses Hero. And through the 'honest slander' used by women we learn that honest interaction can exist in Messina. In creating an alternative rhetoric, Hero suggests that the female characters can empower themselves through language within the patriarchal system that confines them. Hence, her final 'naming' is a naming of doubles, of alternatives that subvert the notion and the process of 'dishonest slander'. In this she is also seeing possibilities that promise to free both women and men from the rhetoric that contains them and simultaneously distances them from each other. Here her gesture and her language come together strongly as she 'unmasks' (literally and symbolically) by offering alternatives:

> **Hero** (*unmasking*) And when I liv'd, I was your other wife;
> And when you lov'd, you were my other husband.
>
> (V.iv.60–1)

If Claudio is thought to have become at all enlightened in the final moments of the play, the conclusion of *Much Ado* suggests that the deceived can be led to a new understanding. But what of the central deception of the play itself – that 'honest slander' can exist? Following Hero's path, if men choose to slander women on the basis of 'nothing', then they deserve to be manipulated with the language of their own fictions. And women must accept that they will be controlled by men until they create their own rhetoric (fictions). Conversely, as the members of the audience are eavesdroppers on the play, they end up falling in with Claudio as he spies on Hero, however much they might think that they emphathise with Hero. Shakespeare himself knew the workings of the law,[27] and to raise the ghost of slander at all before his audience was to present a situation that, in reality, disallowed a comic ending. Hero's 'honest slander' is a fantasy that resists the social and legal realities of the time. Thus, when the official (legal and social) discourses on the issue of slandering women break down, they can be taken up only by dramatic discourse, as the theatre allows for greater latitude in ideology. The members of the audience might be cheered by the play's altruism, but they also have to accept Hero's language in order for the play to end on so unlikely a note; and language, as *Much Ado* shows us, is fickle. 'Honest slander' is created at a price. Hero's 'renaming' is not really vindication of the truth or the affirmation of her former self but an unmasking of men's 'truth' through the creation of a second reality. As she states:

> One Hero died defil'd, but I do live,
> And surely as I live, I am a maid.
>   (V.iv.63–4)

Finally, Hero invents the personal language she needs to survive the fiction of Claudio's idealism, its dangerous consequences, and the failure of a public legal system to redress violations on women. Hero puts Claudio's language on trial. In so doing she demonstrates that 'dishonest' slander is every bit as fictional as the play itself. And also, in so doing, she bankrupts the patriarchal power of language to hold sway over women.

From *Gloriana's Face: Women, Public and Private, in the English Renaissance*, ed. S. P. Cerasano and Marion Wynne-Davies (Hemel Hempstead, 1992), pp. 167–83.

NOTES

[This essay was included in a collection, co-edited by S. P. Cerasano and myself, which looked specifically at the role of women in the English Renaissance: *Gloriana's Face: Women, Public and Private, in the English Renaissance* (London, 1992). It demonstrates a respect for historical sources combined with an acknowledgement of the impact of feminist criticism, thereby allowing contemporary literary theory to inform a thorough and scholarly use of historical evidence. Cerasano's work is one of the finest examples of feminist historicism. Ed.]

1. All quotations are from *Much Ado About Nothing*, ed. A. R. Humphreys (London and New York, 1981).

2. See, for instance, K. Newman, *Shakespeare's Rhetoric of Comic Character* (New York and London, 1985), pp. 111ff. It is in the context of deciding whether the play is a comedy, a dark comedy, or a romance that most discussion about its conclusion arises. C. Neely also touches on the issue of the absence of a trial scene in *Broken Nuptials in Shakespeare's Plays* (New Haven, CT and London, 1985), p. 39.

3. L. Jardine and V. Wayne restrict themselves to evidence drawn from the consistory courts, for example, in V. Wayne (ed.), *The Matter of Difference* (Hemel Hempstead, 1991), p. 161. Here, Wayne is drawing on Jardine's forthcoming essay about *Othello* in particular. It should be noted that the commentary on slander in Renaissance literature is fast-growing, and not all of it can be cited here. However, readers should see J. H. Sexton, 'The theme of slander in *Much Ado about Nothing* and Garter's *Susanna*', *Philological Quarterly*, 54 (1975), 419–33. For information on slander and the law, see J. H. Baker, *An Introduction to Legal History* (London, 1979); W. S. Holdsworth, *History of English Law* (London, 1922–6), vol. VIII, pp. 333–78; D. M. Walker, *The Oxford Companion to Law* (Oxford, 1980); J. A. Sharpe, *Defamation and Sexual Slander in Early Modern England: The Church Courts at York* (York, 1980); P. Hair (ed.), *Before the Bawdy Court: Selections from Church Courts and other records relating to the correction of moral offenses in England, Scotland and New England, 1300–1800* (New York, 1972).

4. Baker, *An Introduction to Legal History*, pp. 364–5.

5. Ibid., p. 368.

6. C. J. Sisson, *Lost Plays of Shakespeare's Age* (London, 1970), p. 10.

7. Sir Thomas Edlyne Tomlins, *The Law Dictionary* (London, 1820). The term 'spoken libel' was coterminous with slander, as cases such as PRO, STAC8/71/15 show.

8. PRO, REQ2/220/8. I have modernised spelling and punctuation throughout my quotations from lawsuits.

9. A. K. R. Kiralfy, *Potter's Historical Introduction to English Law and Its Institutions* (London, 1958), pp. 430–5.

10. Some cases in which common insults are recorded are (all REQ2): 53/16, 156/3, 220/8, 402/25.

11. Standard sources discussing the social place of women during the Renaissance include the now outdated C. Camden, *The Elizabethan Woman* (London, 1952) and W. Notestein, 'The English woman, 1580 to 1650', in J. H. Plumb (ed.), *Studies in Social History* (London, 1955).

12. PRO, STAC8/250/31. See also Sisson, *Lost Plays*, pp. 140 ff.

13. As quoted in M. Perry, *The Word of a Prince* (Woodbridge, Suffolk, 1990), pp. 61–2.

14. *As You Like It*, ed. A. Latham (London, 1975).

15. *Cymbeline*, ed. J. M. Nosworthy (London, 1965).

16. *Measure for Measure*, ed. J. W. Lever (London, 1965).

17. *The Merry Wives of Windsor*, ed. H. J. Oliver (London, 1971).

18. *Othello*, ed. M. R. Ridley (London, 1959).

19. *The Rape of Lucrece*, in F. T. Prince (ed.), *Shakespeare's Poems* (London, 1960).

20. *Julius Caesar*, ed. T. S. Dorsch (London, 1958).

21. See also Barbara Everett, '"Something of great constancy"' in J. R. Brown (ed.), *'Much Ado About Nothing' and 'As You Like It'* (London, 1979), pp. 102–3; and P. and M. Mueschke, 'Illusion and metamorphosis', pp. 130–48 in the same volume. [See also Barbara Everett's essay on *Much Ado* in this Casebook; below, pp. 51–68. Ed.]

22. 'Those "soft and delicate desires": *Much Ado* and the distrust of women', in C. Lenz, G. Green and C. Neely (eds), *The Woman's Part* (Urbana, IL, 1980), pp. 79–99; this material is from pp. 88–9.

23. D. L. Stevenson (ed.), The Signet Edition of *Much Ado About Nothing* (New York, 1964), p. xxiii.

24. R. Nevo, *Comic Transformations in Shakespeare* (London and New York, 1980), p. 171.

25. R. Sale, *'Much Ado About Nothing'* (London, 1990), pp. 98–9.

26. Neely, *Broken Nuptials*, p. 44.

27. S. Schoenbaum, *William Shakespeare: A Compact Documentary Life* (New York, 1977), p. 289, cites the lawsuit of Susanna Shakespeare Hall against John Lane Jr for slander in 1613. This case, of course, postdates *Much Ado* by quite a few years. I offer it only by way of historical example.

3

Much Ado About Nothing: The Unsociable Comedy

BARBARA EVERETT

Social workers sometimes speak of people 'falling through the net'. That's what it can seem that *Much Ado About Nothing* has done, critically speaking. Audiences and readers rarely like it quite as much as the two comedies by Shakespeare which follow it, *As You Like It* and *Twelfth Night*: they feel that by comparison it lacks some sort of magic. Professional critics can take this vague disappointment much further, almost echoing the nineteenth-century charge that the heroine Beatrice is an 'odious woman'. In case it appears that we have changed all that, it may be worth mentioning that what is probably still the only full-length handbook on the play describes Beatrice (at least in her earlier unreformed phase) as 'self-centred', 'the embodiment of pride', a person who '*cannot love*', 'a crippled personality, the very antithesis of the outgoing, self-giving character [Shakespeare] values most highly'. Nor is this study by J. R. Mulryne exceptional.[1] A leading paperback edition cites it approvingly and itself describes both Benedick and Beatrice as 'posing', 'showing themselves off as a preparation for mating'; and it regrets that this pair of lovers fails to 'arouse in an audience the warmth of feeling' evoked by a Portia or a Rosalind. The writer of this Introduction, R. A. Foakes, can only conclude that 'The contrast between [Claudio and Hero] and Beatrice and Benedick was surely designed in part to expose the limitations of both couples.'[2]

'This lookes not like a nuptiall', Benedick murmurs helpfully as the catastrophic Wedding Scene of *Much Ado* gets under way: and the reader of the play's criticism can often feel the same.[3] Particularly given that we are considering a love-comedy by Shakespeare, the remarks I have quoted all seem to me to be startling judgements. For opinions to differ so much can provoke useful thought. Perhaps Shakespeare's mature comedies, once recommended literary fodder for school-children on the grounds of their charming pure-minded simplicity, are – whatever their other characteristics – not so simple after all. When Shakespeare first staged *Much Ado*, fairly certainly in 1598 or '99, he was coming to the end of a decade of extraordinary achievement and invention. The first Tragedies, the earlier Histories and Comedies lay behind him, *The Merchant of Venice* immediately preceded *Much Ado*, and Shakespeare had probably written most of both parts of *Henry IV*. The dramatist of *The Merchant of Venice* and *Henry IV* was in no way unsophisticated or unambitious. If he gave the three comedies we now choose to call 'mature' his most throwaway titles, they aren't throwaway plays. Possessed as they are of a profound sense and vitality which suggest the popular audience they were written for, their lightness nonetheless recalls that 'negligent grace' (*sprezzatura*) which the aristocratic culture of the Renaissance aspired to. The very unpretension of *Much Ado About Nothing*, its affectionate straightforward transparency have been invented to deal with human experience dense enough and real enough to produce notably different reactions from given human beings.

These comedies have become so familiar that it can be hard to think of them freshly. I want therefore to begin by approaching *Much Ado* from a slightly unexpected angle – because sometimes, when we are surprised, we see things more clearly. I'm going to start by thinking about one of the comedy's textual cruces, involving a few words spoken by Leonato in the first scene of Act V. An interestingly shaped play, whose structural rhythm the dramatist was to use again in *Othello* (a fact which alone may say something about the work's seriousness), *Much Ado* has its main plot's climax, which turns out to be a pseudo- or anti-climax, in Act IV: in the big, bustling, peopled and very social Wedding Scene, which sees the gentle Hero, unjustly shamed by the machinations of the villains, publicly humiliated and jilted by her courtly fiancé Claudio

– though the fidelity to her of her witty though here grieving cousin, Beatrice, brings to Beatrice's side her own lover, the humorous Benedick.

In marked contrast, Act V opens with a quiet scene between two suddenly aged men, Hero's father Leonato and his brother Antonio. Critics have often thought it the most feeling moment in a drama they otherwise find cool. Leonato rebuffs his brother's philosophical comfort; he will be stoical, Leonato says bitterly, only if so advised by one who has suffered precisely as, and as much as, himself:

> If such a one will smile and stroke his beard ...
> Patch griefe with proverbs, make misfortune drunke
> With candle-waiters: bring him yet to me,
> And I of him will gather patience.
> (I.i.15, 17–19)

I have edited this, cutting out a line which both the early texts, the 1600 Quarto and the 1623 Folio, are agreed on, but which the great late-Victorian New Variorum edition fills two and a half of its large minutely printed pages of Notes discussing: and which all modern editors emend, in various slightly unconvincing ways. In the authentic texts, Leonato says that his despised comforter would be one to

> stroke his beard,
> And sorrow, wagge, crie hem, when he should grone,
> Patch griefe with proverbs

– and so on.

I want to talk for a few moments about what I think Leonato really said (which is not quite what modern editors make him say). It's necessary to add that, as the New Variorum records in its textual apparatus, fortunately or unfortunately an excellent American scholar named Grant White printed in his edition of 1854 the emendation I'm going to propose: but, since he dropped the emendation in his second edition, and didn't explain or gloss it in the first place, the field remains reasonably clear. He thought, and I too had thought independently, that Leonato describes his would-be comforter angrily as 'sorrow's wagge' – 'And, sorrow's wagge, crie hem, when he should grone': a compositorial mistake very easy to account for; for, in the old Secretary hand which Shakespeare had learned to write in, the terminal letter 's' to a word was written as a kind of scrawled loop very like a topped comma. Let the comma lose its top because of a shortage of ink and the text reads just as in the Quarto and Folio.[4]

It's an interesting fact that the editor of the New Variorum, the scholar Furness, urges us to find these early texts 'irredeemably corrupt' – not even to try, that is, to emend their version of the line. And he does so because the line shocks him as it stands. No editor, however authoritative (he says) 'can ever persuade me that Shakespeare put such words, at this passionate moment, into Leonato's mouth. There is a smack of comicality about "wag" which is ineffaceable.'[5]

There is indeed. But perhaps Shakespeare put it there. The seriousness, even the genius of *Much Ado* may be to bring in precisely that 'smack of comicality' where we least expect it – just as its dramatist invents peculiarly English constables for his Sicilian play, to stumble fat-headedly into arresting the villains and bringing about the play's happy ending. A 'wag' is a word and a social phenomenon that is nearly obsolete now, though I can remember my own mother using it drily, with something of Furness's rebuke. A wag is or was a person who habitually, even desperately, tries to be funny. But in Shakespeare's time the word hadn't progressed to this degraded condition – it had not, so to speak, grown up: it remained the 'little tine boy' of Feste's song. For the most familiar colloquial usage of 'wag' in the poet's own day was in the tender phrase, 'Mother's wag'. The word denoted a mischievous small prankster, amusingly naughty as little boys often are. Only a few years before *Much Ado*, Greene in his *Menaphon* has, 'Mothers wagge, prettie boy' – and Falstaff calls Hal his 'sweet Wagge' in Part I of *Henry IV*.

Leonato says that the father who, having lost a child, could still find or accept words of comfort would be 'Sorrow's wagge': he means the man would be himself a child, immature. And the phrase has an element of oxymoron that defines his shock and outrage. Like Furness after him, this decently conventional, hierarchical, even conservative old man thinks that certain conjunctions of what they would have called the grave and the gay, of grief and humour, are 'irredeemably corrupt'.

Before we agree with them both, we ought perhaps to pause and ask whether Shakespeare has not shaped this encounter of the two old men so as to prevent us doing just that. The 'passionate moment' which the Victorian editor points to is surely something odder than passionate – and is odd in a way that is relevant. For (and this is my chief topic here) *Much Ado About Nothing*'s real achievement may be to make us think very hard indeed about this quality of the 'passionate' in human beings.

In this scene, Leonato and Antonio wear something that is easy to call, at sight, the dignity of the bereaved; and they wear it consciously. But this is odd because, though Hero may be disgraced, she is certainly not dead. And both Leonato and Antonio know it. Moreover, we in the audience know that even Hero's disgrace is rapidly melting into air: for the grieving scene is linked to the Church Scene by, and is immediately preceded by, the comic bridge-scene in which the ludicrous constables – the more senior proclaiming, with something of Leonato's own self-important fury that he 'hath had losses' – have apprehended the villains and are at this moment hotfoot bringing a full disclosure to Leonato.

Later in this Fifth Act, Don Pedro and Claudio will make solemn acknowledgement at the quasi-tomb of Hero. This action has its own meaning – the moment's music allows the gesture a dimension of the symbolic: the scene mutedly articulates some sadness which all grown-up 'understanders' of this highly civilised, social comedy know to be intrinsic to most passion seeking social embodiment. In the very preceding scene, Act V, scene ii, Benedick has lightly told Beatrice that she doesn't live in 'the time of good neighbours', if it ever existed; that 'if a man doe not erect in this age his owne tombe ere he dies, hee shall live no longer in monuments, then the Bels ring, & the Widdow weepes' – i.e., not long. But symbols are one thing, and facts another, even in our greatest poetic dramatist. Hero still isn't dead. And the fact that she isn't, and that we know that she isn't, and that her family, too, know that she isn't, turns this grieving ceremony at the tomb into something like the masked dances which characterise this sophisticated comedy: an art, a game, a pretence – a deception exonerated by having been proposed in good faith and by a man, so to speak, of the cloth.

Much Ado's tomb-trick may in short be considered as not unlike those bed-tricks in the two later, much darker comedies, *Measure for Measure* and *All's Well That Ends Well*. Greater, much more intense, these two plays tell us far more about Shakespeare's interest in the tragi-comic – though neither they, nor any other play written by him is truly identifiable with the genre as the Continental aristocracy of the period knew it. But *Much Ado* shares one striking characteristic with them. It has the tragi-comic concern with love in society, a society for which some version of the political, the power-issue, is serious: a world which defers to Courtship and to social hierarchy. From this point of view, the tomb-trick is like the bed-tricks in working as a special kind of 'good deceit' or virtuous untruth, a device of worldly accommodation in a light but moral art. The clever courtiers, with Don Pedro at their head, have de-scended on Leonato's provincial family, and have done these simpler if still socially aspiring people some harm. Now the tables are pleasingly turned, the foolers are fooled, and Leonato and Antonio regain something of their lost honour merely by the silent superiority of knowing what they know.

But if this is conceded, something else must follow. The tomb-trick is peculiarly like those forms of wise comfort (and the word comfort actually means 'self-strengthening') angrily rejected in the grieving scene by the passionate Leonato. The music of the tomb-scene, shortly after, though saying nothing true, can still both calm and resolve. It thus performs the act at first denied by Leonato in the scene I started from: it can, like the wag's wisdom, 'Charme ache with ayre, and agony with words'. While the old man scorns sorrow's wags, something wise in the play embraces them.

I have used the word 'embrace' here deliberately – and not only because it is a love-comedy we are concerned with. For Elizabethans, the chief image of Love itself was as a 'wag': as the Puck-like armed baby, Cupid – naughtily dangerous, even disturb-ing to the coolly rationalistic eye of the Renaissance, yet in these comedies also the medium of great good. Puck himself is, after all, in the service of Oberon the King. Yet Puck moves in the night, 'Following darkenesse like a dreame', and the wood where the lovers wander is a distressing and frightening place. These complex-ities make Shakespeare's Love, and love's Happiness, a pair of twins, springing from the circumstances of sorrow: sorrow's wags.

I am hoping to suggest that in this casual phrase, a local crux in the text of a light comedy, we have some suggestion of the kind of rich complexity, of fruitful half-paradox, which gives *Much Ado* the vitality and depth by which it now survives. The comedy's Italian director, Franco Zeffirelli, once referred to it as a 'very dull play'. And *Much Ado* is indeed simple if we compare it, for in-stance, to its predecessor *The Merchant of Venice*. But that play's fascinating intellectual battles, its energy of contrasts embodied in Portia and Shylock, the market-place and Belmont, leave behind at the end a disquieting dissatisfaction, a sense of something unjust or unresolved. This is a subject I shall return to. For the moment I want only to suggest that *Much Ado* may have chosen to be a 'very dull play', to be simple to the eye.

But its simplicity is a solidity. Shakespeare uses the *novelle* sources from which he has taken his main plot to generate a special, almost novelistic sense of the real, of a world where people live together to a degree that is socially and psychologically convincing, and new in the poet's work. And this realistic, even novelistic comedy deepens itself by containing, indeed we may say, with Leonato in mind, by *embracing* contradictions everywhere beneath its smooth and civil surface. If there is, to Leonato's mind, a troubling indecorum, an unconventionality in the juxtapositions, momentarily glimpsed by him, of sorrow with joy and of play with love, then it has to be said that such vital oppositions pervade the play, and are its life. Let me touch on one famous passage. At one point Don Pedro finds himself proposing marriage to Beatrice. He does not love her, nor she him. He has been led into it by his belief in the kindness of his own impeccable manners: a self-defeating trap from which he is released by Beatrice, who of course has led him into it in the first place, with the neat licentious speed of some brilliant Court Fool. Panting slightly, the courtly Don Pedro tells Beatrice that she was 'born in a merry howre' (II.i.313–14). She wins again, both wittily and touchingly: 'No sure my Lord, my Mother cried, but then there was a starre daunst, and under that was I borne' (II.i.315–17). This nicely hints at some of the reasons why this (to my mind) superb heroine has been and can still be disliked by a whole host of male scholars, both past and present. She is Shakespeare's true heroine, woman as 'wag', the sharp and comical child of sorrow.

Beatrice does something far more waggish than merely walking along a razor's edge of good behaviour with a visiting grandee. Indecorum is embodied in the fact that she and her story, which a formal criticism calls 'the sub-plot', take over the play, edging aside the main-plot story of Claudio and Hero. It's well known that Charles I wrote against the title of his text of the play 'Benedik and Betrice', and the sympathy of most succeeding readers has agreed with him. But the high originality of this comic structure can leave editors behind. Much in accord with the New Penguin Introduction which I quoted earlier, the New Arden confronts as the chief critical problem the question, 'What can or should be done to balance the play?' and proposes as answer: 'Hero and Claudio can gain in prominence; Benedick and Beatrice can be less salient.'[6] But perhaps the comedy has its own balance, which can only be impaired by these adjustments: and this balance has to do with the delicate poise of energies suggested by the phrase, 'sorrow's wag'. I have lingered over this conceit because of all it can suggest about the essential principles involved in a Shakespearean comedy: principles necessitating both light and dark, both seriousness and laughter.

It can be a struggle to explain why these romantic comedies carry the value that they do – why, seeming to be 'About Nothing' (as their ironic or nonchalant titles suggest) they nonetheless evoke from those who truly like them words like 'true' or 'brilliant' or 'profound'. The 'Nothing' of the *Much Ado* title is now, of course, somewhat undercut by our understanding that Elizabethans could pronounce 'Nothing' as 'Noting'. The plot of the comedy certainly turns on what this pun implies: note-taking, spying, eavesdropping. No other play in Shakespeare introduces so much eavesdropping – each new turn of the action depends on it. The confusions of Don Pedro's wooing of Hero for his protégé Claudio, the machinations by which his bastard brother Don John deceives Claudio into believing Hero unchaste, the trick by which Beatrice and Benedick are persuaded that each loves the other, the discovery of the villains by the comic constables – all these are effected by the incessant system of eavesdropping. Yet underneath the noting there is nothing. The play's first act is filled by a flurry of redoubled misunderstanding which scholars often assume to be textual confusion or revision. This seems to me a mistake. The dramatist plainly wanted his comedy to be this way: he wanted the world he had invented to be swept through by these currents of pointless energetic bewilderment. Later, after all, he almost unwinds the villainy of the main plot before our eyes, by having the pretend-Hero address her villainous lover as 'Claudio', a naming which would have left the heroine all but guiltless. Shakespeare's change of all his sources in this main plot is important here: what they presented as evidence, he converts to mere inference. An editor once complained that the omission of the 'Window Scene' does an injustice to Claudio. Perhaps; but it was meant to. And this stress in Shakespeare's play on the insecurities of mere social inference even touches the other lovers. In the last scene, the obdurately individual Beatrice and Benedick show signs of being as near as makes no matter to a readiness to back out of each other's arms: loving each other 'no more then reason', 'in friendly recompence', taking each other 'for pittie', yielding 'upon great perswasion'.

Much Ado About Nothing reminds us, both as title and play, that, though life is indeed serious, most human beings pass much of their time in little things, unseriousness; that the ordinary, social fabric of life can be very thin, made up of trivia, and we can often feel a kind of real nothingness underneath ('hee shall live no longer in monuments, then the Bels ring, & the Widdow weepes ... an hower in clamour and a quarter in rhewme' [V.ii.72–3 and 75–7]). Benedick's light definition of human void is a striking one, peculiarly apt in the theatrical world which has produced it, where revels are always 'now ... ended'. He evokes it in a context congenital to Shakespearean comedy, that of the presence or absence of real human feeling: love in a world which is defined as recognisably *not* 'the time of good neighbours', and in which the sound of the bells is short, of weeping even shorter.

Shakespeare's comedies are a 'Nothing' concerned with serious things; and these serious things are the principles of true human feeling, in a world in which a wise man knows that so much is nothing. To be at ease in such reflections demands at once ironic detachment and feeling participation. Consonantly, if we are trying to describe the power, the real survival-value of even the poet's earliest comedies, it has to do with his ability to bring laughter together with tenderness. We think of Launce and his dog in *The Two Gentlemen of Verona*; of the tough slapstick of *The Taming of the Shrew*, resolving into Katherine's sober devotion; or the weeping of the angrily jealous Adriana in the brilliant fast farce of *The Comedy of Errors*. The coolest and most intellectual of aristocratic revues, *Love's Labour's Lost*, ends with a father dead and Berowne sent, in name of love, to 'move wilde laughter in the throate of death'; and it includes the memory of a girl, Katherine's sister, who died of love: 'He made her melancholy, sad, and heavy, and so she died: had she beene Light like you, of such a merrie nimble stirring spirit, she might a bin a Grandam ere she died.' Titania, similarly, in *A Midsummer Night's Dream*, tells of her loyalty to the friend who died in childbirth, like so many Elizabethan women:

> she being mortall, of that boy did die,
> And for her sake I doe reare up her boy,
> And for her sake I will not part with him.
>   (*MND* II.i.135–7)

I quoted Beatrice's 'No sure my Lord, my Mother cried'. Immediately after, with Beatrice sent out of the room, Leonato tells that, by Hero's report, Beatrice has 'often dreamt of unhappinesse, and wakt her selfe with laughing'. Something very similar might be said of Shakespeare's comedies in themselves: their character from the beginning has to do with finding a way of being 'sorrow's wag'. His art recognises the interdependence of the dark and the light in life, especially at those points of love and friendship where feeling is most acute, and often most complex. The mature comedies seek to perfect a style or condition in which happiness exists not just despite unhappiness but through it, because of it, yet charitably and sympathetically, like Patience smiling at grief. There must in the end be the co-existence, the smiling and the grief. In *The Merchant of Venice*, for all its brilliance, there is no final co-existence: something has been sacrificed to the desired achievement of extreme contrarieties, of the play of light and dark. As the sociable Bassanio has to use the lonely loving Antonio, so in the end the golden Portia must destroy the embittered, dark-housed Shylock, the greatest personage in the comedies.

It's in the art of co-existence that *Much Ado's* supremacy lies: this, the first of Shakespeare's mature comedies in which very different human beings believably live together. Its 'dullness' (to quote Zeffirelli) is only the prosaic quality of the novel as against the poem. Yet this temperate, equable and witty world Shakespeare has created has surprising resonances, depths and possibilities. If prose is the comedy's dominant medium, the work's very coherence and inventiveness is a poetic achievement of a high kind.

That creativity is first manifested by Shakespeare's making of 'Messina'. That the dramatist calls his play's setting Messina, and makes his elderly Leonato, father to Hero and uncle to Beatrice, Governor of it, does not have to be taken too seriously – seriously in the sense of literally. 'Messina' is any romantic place lived in by rich and relatively important people. But, off the literal level, 'Messina' has extraordinary self-consistency and convincingness. The fantasy-place also functions as the grounding of the real; and, immediately below the surface, things hold together. I will give one small example from the first lines of the play: it says something about the way the poet's imagination has worked on his fantasy-place, and may even give some hint as to why Shakespeare chose this Sicilian port as his locality. *Much Ado* begins with the descent of grand visitors, heralded by formal letter and Gentleman-

Messenger, on the excited and grateful Leonato: the visitors being the well-born and triumphant young warriors, Don Pedro and friends. The stage 'Messina' is thus flooded by a desired and aspired-to standard of Court behaviour, one evidenced in the battle just won (the chief occupation of a Court culture was warfare); and also in the good manners everywhere, the formal wit, the letters, the vivid sense of worldly hierarchies.

But directly this Court standard is initiated, we feel its ambiguity. Don Pedro brings with him the brother he has just defeated, the villainous Don John. The opening words of the drama speak of the distinguished visitor by his Spanish title – he is '*Don Peter of Arragon*'; and his brother Don John's title can hardly fail to remind an Elizabethan audience of that Don John of Austria who was similarly a Spaniard, a natural son of Philip II. Oddly enough, it was at the port of Messina that the fleets gathered before the great battle of Lepanto, where 'Don John of Austria' rode 'to the wars'. Catholic Spain was at Lepanto the defender of what Renaissance Christians held to be true civilisation against the barbarian hordes of the East. But she was also the lasting, unchanging threat to English supremacy at sea – and she represented a Church thought by many of Protestant Elizabeth's subjects to be wickedly authoritarian: a double face, as the play's courtliness will shift between light and dark.

For, though Leonato welcomes Don Pedro's visit as a high honour, Don Pedro brings with him the bastard brother, Don John, the at least nominal source of all the play's troubles, his dark, surly, lonely ill-nature an interesting shadow to Don Pedro's all-too-glittering sociality. And young Claudio, Don Pedro's friend, is as amiably disagreeable as he is conventional. It is entirely unsurprising that he should later indicate his interest in Hero by making certain that she is her father's heir; that his deception by the villains should be as rapid as his consequent repentance; and that the girl he readily accepts at Leonato's hand as second bride should be 'Another Hero'. In the triviality of their love is the necessary stability of their society.

The story of his two independent individualists, Beatrice and Benedick, Shakespeare seems to have invented for himself. But the main Hero-and-Claudio plot of his play he took from the great stock of international Renaissance romance. These facts are perhaps suggestive: they may tell us something about the kind of world Shakespeare saw himself creating in this comedy of 'Much Ado'.

'Messina' is a figure for the most courtly, most worldly aspirations of ordinary people. The society of 'Messina' is governed by decorum, convention and fashion. Its only alternative, bred within itself, is the hostile isolationist Don John, the lawless brother who has determined 'not to sing in my cage'. Everyone else does sing in the cage – the cage being Leonato's great house with its arbour-full of secrets for a garden, a world of spiky high-level chatter where formal compliments intertwine with informal insults. It's not surprising that the comic policemen get the impression that the villains are led by one Deformed, a man of some fashion. Even Shakespeare himself sings in his cage: amusedly inventing at one point the babble of *Vogue* magazine, telling us that Hero's wedding-dress will be worth ten of the Dutchesse of Millaine's 'cloth a gold and cuts, and lac'd with silver, set with pearles, downe sleeves, side sleeves, and skirts, round underborn with a blewish tinsel' (III.iv.18–20).

'Messina' is tinsel itself, and yet very real. It can't be satirised or politicised out of existence, nor even assumed to be a mere preserve of the rich. The constables who enter the play in its third act to resolve the problems of their nominal superiors are just as much given to chat and argument as anyone else in Messina, and as interested too in social status. They are rustic, obdurately English instead of Sicilian, and often very funny ('We will rather sleepe than talke, wee know what belongs to a Watch' – 'Nothing' operates here, too). 'Messina' represents a mundane if aspiring social reality which we recognise at sight: that social world which is, as Wordsworth remarked, the 'world / Of all of us', and in it, we 'find our happiness, or not at all'. When Benedick resolves to marry, he remarks briskly that 'the world must be peopled', and we all (of course) laugh. Yet he is serious too; and this is what *Much Ado* portrays in 'Messina' – the world of people that 'must be peopled'.

This wonderfully real and recognisable world Shakespeare brings alive in the very style and structure of his comedy. 'Messina' talks a fine and formal, conversational yet mannered prose, which in the genuinely intelligent becomes admirably flexible. Only those who are unusually deeply moved (Beatrice in love, Hero's family in and after the Church Scene) speak in verse, and that not often. The play is a very Elizabethan work, yet it sometimes sounds to the ear almost like Restoration Comedy, at moments even like Wilde. Its structure has the same tacit expressiveness. The action falls naturally into Messina's large crowded scenes of social encounter – the opening arrival of the soldiers, the evening dance in mask, the church wedding, the final celebration. It is because of these thronged and bustling scenes that the moment when Benedick and Beatrice speak their love to each other, left alone on the stage after the interrupted marriage, has such startling effect.

Despite the eventfulness of what we call the main plot, nothing really happens to the more social characters of the play, who are precisely defined as people to whom nothing can happen (hence, 'Another Hero'). Late in the play, after Hero has been cruelly rejected on her wedding-day and is believed to be dead by all but her family and friends, there is a decidedly subtle and embarrassing encounter between the young men, as Don Pedro and Claudio think to take up again their old verbal teasing of Benedick, and can't realise by how much he has now outgrown it. This unawareness is the continuity of the social, the process by which it survives: 'Messina' lives in a perpetual present, where salvation depends on the power to forget. It has all been, after all, 'Much Ado About Nothing'. And yet there is of course an exception to this. Beatrice and Benedick do change. And the index of this change, their falling in love, is the great subject of the comedy.

Beatrice and Benedick are most certainly inhabitants of Messina. Hero's cousin and Claudio's friend, they belong in their world, possessed by a social realism summed up in Beatrice's 'I can see a Church by daylight'. Moreover, there is a real sense in which we are glad to see the cousins and friends join hands again at the end of the play, with a sensible patient warmth foreshadowing that romantic yet worldly wisdom which keeps the families joined, if at some distance, at the end of *Pride and Prejudice*.

Yet Beatrice and Benedick do still change. Modern Shakespeareans who work assiduously to banish this change, to work the hero and heroine back into those borders of the action from which they come, seem to me to be in serious error, and to be breaking the back of a work of art. *Much Ado*'s very originality of action and structure, that power of mind which animates Shakespeare's lightest comedies, here depends on the growing importance of two people who, though their intelligence gives them authority from the beginning, are socially on the margins of the action, subordinate in interest to the possibly younger Hero and Claudio. But, where the trick played on Claudio by Don John destroys his shallow love for Hero, Don Pedro's fooling only releases real depths of feeling in Beatrice and Benedick, the two unsociable individuals who think themselves determined to resist the enforcements of matrimony.

There has been in much recent criticism a comparable resistance to the originality of *Much Ado* itself, one evidenced by the repeated insistence that Beatrice and Benedick do not change and fall in love in the course of the play: they are (the argument goes) in love when it begins. Again, I have to say that I find this near-universal assumption entirely mistaken. Despite all the sophisticated techniques of the modern psychological novel, the analysis of actual human feeling often lags far behind Shakespeare still. Beatrice and Benedick begin their play attracted to each other, but not in love. Both are children of 'Messina'; both play its games; both belong to a social world for which such attraction is an ordinary datum of experience. 'Messina' assumes that men and women are always after each other and always betraying each other: 'Men were deceivers ever'; and Benedick joins in with Leonato's social by-play of distrusting his own child's legitimacy.

But both from the first see beyond, and through, the merely social, as Benedick really prefers 'my simple true judgement' to what he is 'professed' or supposed to think. This soldierly preference for sincerity suggests that he might similarly like to be truly in love with Beatrice. But he isn't. When he finally does fall, he is honest enough – in a fashion both comic and heroic – to tell her how 'strange' he finds it to feel so much. Earlier, though, what has angered Beatrice is this sense of a mere conditionality in Benedick, which might never have become fact. With an allusive dimension of past and future which distinguishes the two senior lovers from the rest of timeless Messina, Beatrice has two curious references to time past which have puzzled critics. She tells of the moment when Benedick 'challeng'd Cupid at the Flight', and was in turn challenged by Leonato's fool. This narrative anecdote works, I believe, as a conceit of analysis, a definition for a pre-psychological age: she is saying that Benedick may think his resistance to love so clever and aristocratic, but really it is just stupid. This is Beatrice the 'odious woman', descended from Katherine the Shrew; but Shakespeare has deepened the moment and justified the rudeness. With a touch of Lear's Fool in her, Beatrice is the true human heart, struggling against the mere manners of Messina.

And this becomes plainer in her Second-Act answer to Don Pedro, who tells her she has 'lost the heart of Signior *Benedicke*':

> Indeed my Lord, hee lent it me a while, and I gave him use for it, a double heart for a single one, marry once before he wonne it of mee, with false dice, therefore your Grace may well say I have lost it.
>
> (II.i.261–4)

This is less private history than a fine open act of analysis. Beatrice describes what the courtly Don Pedro, without knowing it, means by 'heart': a world of mere lending and borrowing, a scene of mere winning and losing. The dice are false. Charmingly, wittily and sometimes politely, Beatrice is looking for something else again. Her brisk, tough and cool character belongs – and this is Shakespeare's profound insight, in the most psychologically interesting romantic comedy he has yet written – to one of the most romantic and idealistic of human beings. But she isn't intending to discuss her heart in Messina, a world which is, in her own words, 'civill as an Orange, and something of a jealous complexion'.

With these views, Beatrice may well, as she knows herself, 'sit in a corner and cry, heigh ho for a husband'. And Benedick is as true an individual as herself. Despite the friendly effervescence of his successful social being, there is another Benedick who is most himself when he 'sits in a corner'. In a curious small scene (II.iii) he complains of the change in Claudio: and his soliloquy is prefaced, in a way that editions don't explain, by his sending of his boy to fetch the book 'in my chamber window' for him to read 'in the orchard'. The vividness of this is on a par with the thorough realism elsewhere in *Much Ado*: and it throws up a sudden image of the solitude of the real Benedick, whom we see when no one else is there. The book in the hand is for Elizabethans a symbol of the solitary.

In short, here are two people who could easily have remained divided from each other, in a state of irritated or quietly melancholy resentment at themselves and at life. This Elizabethan comedy brings alive what we may think of as a datum of peculiarly modern experience, the randomness, the accidentality of existence: the fact that many things in the life of feeling remain 'a perpetual possibility / Only in a world of speculation'. Attraction starts up socially but there need be no happy endings; there is only 'Much Ado About Nothing', a waste of wishes and desires.

The two difficult lovers owe much to the courtiers for bringing them together, a debt which justifies the forgivingness of the last scene. Yet neither Beatrice nor Benedick is precisely dependent on the tricks of a trivial milieu for their feeling. Orthodox Elizabethans believed that God indeed made 'Much' out of 'Nothing', the Creation out of Void. The change of these two intelligent and principled lovers asks to be comparably explained. They come together over the quasi-dead body of Hero, at the end of the Church Scene.

They are, that is to say, drawn together by their shared sympathy for the wronged girl. It is this tertium quid outside themselves that permits Benedick to say at last, 'I do love nothing in the world so well as you, is not that strange?' and Beatrice to answer, 'As strange as the thing I know not, it were as possible for me to say, I loved nothing so well as you.'

I am hoping to suggest that there is a paradox here not far from the oddity of 'sorrow's wag'. The moment is so romantic because not romantic – or not so in the Messina sense; it is the true romanticism of the real. Benedick is at heart a kind man, which to Elizabethans meant 'kinned', 'brotherly'. He is deeply grateful to Beatrice, and besides can't bear to watch her crying. All this, on top of her usual attraction for him. She responds in precisely the same way, not merely changing the subject when she says firmly: 'I am sorry for my cousin.' It's as if she were drawing up the rule-book for the rest of their lives. Both Beatrice and Benedick are individuals who have feared love because it means so much to them; when they do lose their heart, as here, it won't be a 'double' one, in the sense of *dishonest*. What brings them together at last is neither trick nor fluke, but the conjunction of shared principle – a principle which depends on their independence, even their loneliness as human beings. As a result, their professions of love are deep with risk and danger, which is why their bond is involved with a girl in some sense dead, and why Beatrice must ask Benedick to 'Kill *Claudio*'. He doesn't, and it's as well that he doesn't obey the whim of a wildly angry woman. But he's ready to. There is therefore a kind of death in their love, for both of them. 'Sitting in the corner' is the posture of a prizefighter or duellist; when the two advance to the centre, someone may lose, and something must die. There is a delightful, comic, humorous charm and truth in the fact that, as soon as the trick is afoot and love declared, both start to feel terrible: Benedick gets toothache and Beatrice a fearful cold. Many critics assume a pretence on their part, but I think not.

When Shakespeare borrowed his immensely widely disseminated main-plot story from many sources, he did something strange to it. He used a legend that turned on strong evidence of infidelity, and he took the evidence away. There is no 'Window-Scene' in our comedy. The poet has thereby transformed a tale of jealousy into something much nearer to a definition of love, which asks the question: 'How in the world do we ever *know*?' The answer of *Much Ado* is: 'By whatever we take to be the dead body of Hero' – a character whose very name is suggestive. Leaving aside the Leander-loss, we may say that in *Much Ado About Nothing* one kind of hero and heroine is replaced by another. Comparably, one kind of social, winning-and-losing false dicing love finds itself quietly upstaged by something quite different: a feeling intensely romantic, because involving real individuals, yet grounding itself on something as sober, or we could even say 'dull', as an extreme and responsible human kindness. And the true lovers are kind, to each other and others, because they are aware that life necessitates it even from the romantic. They are both, that is to say, sorrow's wags.

Beatrice and Benedick, 'sitting in the corner' of life, each resent marriage because they are helplessly individual beings. But their very independence and individuality, their corner-view, gives them what no one else in the comedy really has – truth of feeling. Their thinking and feeling for themselves has as its high-water-mark that famous moment, already quoted, at which Beatrice, always quick off the mark, thinks almost too much for herself. As she weeps angrily in the church after Hero's rejection, Benedick makes his vital move – he lets Don Pedro's party leave without him, and stays to comfort Beatrice, asking gently if he can help her. Yes, she says, he can; he can kill Claudio. The play is a comedy precisely because Benedick, always the sounder in sizing up the mark he is being asked to get off, doesn't have to kill Claudio; and we can hardly regret the fact that 'Messina' survives. Here is a co-existence we can like as well as finding likely. But we can't regret either the two individuals who are, as Benedick says, 'Too wise to wooe peaceablie'. The comedy needs their wisdom, just as it needs the constables' folly. Intensely romantic, therefore, as well as consistently funny, *Much Ado* is serious in its concerns while always wearing the air of being entertainingly 'About Nothing'.

From *English Comedy*, ed. Michael Cordner, Peter Holland and John Kerrigan (Cambridge, 1994), pp. 68–84.

NOTES

[Barbara Everett's essay balances an understanding of historical context with a focus upon character, an understanding of the psychological complexities of the play and an overall awareness of the fictional nature of the text. As such Barbara Everett's work on *Much Ado About Nothing* demonstrates an equilibrium between a more traditional reading of the play and the impact of contemporary criticism. In addition, this essay furthers a sense of balance in that Everett contributed a piece on *Much Ado About Nothing* to the original Casebook on the play: 'Something of Great Constancy' in John Russell Brown (ed.), *Much Ado About Nothing and As You Like It* (London, 1979), pp. 94–117. Brief bibliographical references have been provided by the editor. Ed.]

1. J. R. Mulryne, 'Shakespeare: *Much Ado About Nothing*', *Studies in English Literature*, 16 (1965); reprinted as 'The Large Design' in the original Casebook series, *Much Ado About Nothing and As You Like It*, ed. John Russell Brown (London, 1979), pp. 117–29.

2. R. A. Foakes (ed.), *Much Ado About Nothing* (London, 1968), pp. 7–27.

3. *Much Ado About Nothing*, IV.i.86. All other act and scene numbers have been added parenthetically by the editor.

4. R. G. White (ed.), *Mr William Shakespeare's Comedies, Histories, Tragedies, and Poems* (Boston, 1884).

5. H. H. Furness (ed.), *Much Ado About Nothing* (Philadelphia and London, 1899).

6. A. R. Humphreys (ed.), *Much Ado About Nothing* (London, 1981).

4

Much Ado About Nothing: A Kind of Merry War

PENNY GAY

Much Ado About Nothing takes place not in a 'world elsewhere' – Illyria or Arden – but in Messina, Sicily. From its very opening lines it insists that the audience recognise on the stage a simulacrum of the 'real world', with its townsfolk, householders and their families, servants and visitors – and its gossip. In this *Much Ado* is much more akin to *Romeo and Juliet* or *Measure for Measure* than it is to the other 'romantic comedies' with which it is usually grouped. This is not a world in which a girl can disguise herself as a boy and not be recognised even by her lover; it is, rather, a society structured very like the Elizabethan one which first witnessed it, in which the niceties of interpersonal behaviour are directed by accepted rules. And although those standard tropes of farce, disguisings and tricks soon enter the narrative, they are not its principal dramatic interest; they are merely there to help along the plot which has from the first held the audience's chief attention – the courtship of Beatrice and Benedick. The bringing together of two prickly, unconventional adults in marriage – into conformity with the structures of society which they have hitherto managed to flout – holds a gleeful fascination for the audience, as it does for the 'audience' on stage – all the other members of Leonato's household. None can finally escape the powerful coercion of our social system: 'The world must be peopled!' (II.iii). Despite Benedick's apparent libertarian bravado here, what he means and what the play means is a world peopled via the ceremony of Christian marriage only. The play's triumph is to make the audience assent to its vision of a community always to be revitalised from within, by the incorporation of rebellious energy, not its expulsion. It does this by presenting, in Beatrice and Benedick's dialogues, such an 'erotic friction' (in Stephen Greenblatt's term) that our profoundest desire is to see that friction come to its bodily consummation. 'Peace, I will stop your mouth' – the talking only ceases when the lovers' bodies come together in a kiss. (In modern terms, we may read Benedick's 'domineering' action here as a playful and self-conscious taking-on of his social role as 'Benedick the married man'; but we might also remember that in Act II, scene i Beatrice quite unselfconsciously suggests that the roles can be reversed when she says to the newly engaged Hero, 'Speak cousin. Or if you cannot, stop his mouth with a kiss, and let him not speak, neither'.)

The play achieves its conservative victory also by flattering the audience's intelligence, encouraging us to despise the callow foolishness of the conventional Claudio (and to a lesser extent, of Hero) and to identify with the witty, unconventional Benedick and Beatrice. Marriage, it argues, is not just for dull people – in fact, they are lucky to be allowed a second go at finding an appropriate mate. Shakespeare seems particularly interested in the workings of gender in society in *Much Ado*. Claudio's immature behaviour is grounded in his dependence on the hierarchical brotherhood of the military and its ideology of male honour; Hero's helplessness arises from her being the protected daughter of a still-living father, bound to consult and obey him in all matters. Beatrice, by contrast, is, like Rosalind, a 'poor relation', without living parents: one who survives on her wits, intelligence, and the affection and tolerance of her oddities freely given by Leonato's family. The text also suggests that she and Benedick have had some sort of love-relationship in the past ('Marry, once before he won it [her heart] of me, with false dice' [II.i]); that is, that she is no stranger to the vagaries of sexual love and the ways of the social world. But ultimately, for a woman in a solidly-structured patriarchal society such as this one, there are no prospects other than marriage or a barely-tolerated maiden-aunt status. Beatrice's fantasy of spending eternity 'where the bachelors sit, and there live we, as merry as the day is long' (II.i.) is recognisably that – a fantasy – in the context of the clearly divided male and female spheres of the society which the play presents. By showing the gaps between ideal and reality in the Hero and Claudio story, Shakespeare deconstructed the gender-ideology of separate spheres; and offered in Beatrice and Benedick an image of the '*merry* war' that may exist between two strong-willed characters resistant to the behavioural restrictions of conventional gender roles. However, once these two acknowledge their sexual attraction, they cannot avoid society's discourse of romantic love and marriage; the best they can do is to meet it with wit, fully conscious of their own absurdity: 'Thou and I are too wise to woo peaceably' (V.ii). It is this shared consciousness of the delicious playfulness of language which can always circumvent the dead hand of convention that makes Beatrice and Benedick such an attractive pair: the audience's fantasy of the intelligent, witty, and caring heterosexual couple. The permutations of that image, and of the society which permits it (more or less) to flourish, are typically varied in performance.

1949–61

For many critics John Gielgud's Stratford production of *Much Ado About Nothing*, which premiered in April 1949 and was revived and toured intermittently until 1955, was unsurpassable. Above all, it had 'style', and critics forty years later were still nostalgic for the undemanding, profound pleasure that this production offered both in design and acting. Gielgud, an experienced entrepreneur since before the war, knew what the British public wanted at this point in twentieth-century history – elegance, and a sense of material and spiritual bounty, a sense that the world was indeed a good place and that the social *status quo ante* offered the best possible image of order. He invited the Spanish artist Mariano Andreu to design both the sets and the costumes – signalling, as it were, that the war had been won, and the preservation and continuity of European culture was once again in the right hands. Andreu responded by providing rich and highly elaborate Renaissance designs, reminiscent of Italian painting of the late fifteenth century; one reviewer wrote,

> The scenery opens, shuts, wheels and turns inside out. Gardens become banqueting halls, and by a turn of the hand gaily attired ushers transport us from the pillared exterior of a church porch to the Byzantine reaches of a far-flung nave. These transformations are in excellent taste, but all the same they are slightly distracting.
> (*Birmingham Post*, 21 April 1949)

The audience, in fact, greatly enjoyed and applauded the clever scene changes – their pleasure, that is, was not only in illusion but (as Gielgud, with his family's theatrical history stretching back a century, would know) in the amazing transformations of pantomime. This technical facility added to the air of richness and confidence of the production.

As for the costumes, heavy and elaborate though they were, they clearly delighted an audience sick of wartime austerity. The *Birmingham Post* commented, 'Mariano Andreu has celebrated the end of clothes rationing by providing a glittering array of costumes', and the critic of the *Leamington Spa Courier* (23 April 1949) noted the psychological effect of this justified extravagance:

> costumes and decors were not only a joy to those who saw them – they had a subtle but quite definite effect upon the actors, who seemed to catch light and style from their costumes and the garden where they disported themselves.

This air of euphoria characterised the acting of the quartet of lovers. The production did not question the innocence and ardour of youth: Claudio and Hero were played as 'star-crossed children', innocent victims of the wicked Don John. They had 'violent fits of uncontrollable giggles' during the overhearing scenes; Claudio 'wept openly during his accusations of Hero's infidelity. ... The impression was of impassioned, youthful impetuosity overcome with emotion'.[1] Similarly, the production's view of more adult relationships was uncomplicated: Anthony Quayle was 'engaging and manly' as Benedick, Diana Wynyard 'gay, charming and fiery' as Beatrice (W. A. Darlington, *Daily Telegraph*, 20 April 1949); 'a plain soldier and a mocking maid too much interested in each other to ape the airs of the court', said *The Times* (27 April 1949). Clearly Gielgud's production aimed to reinforce a sense that social (and sexual) relations had returned to normal after the extraordinary conditions of the war. But any description of 'normality' is embedded in the dominant ideology; in this case – still shadowed by the war – that the ideal man is a 'plain soldier' and the ideal woman a 'maid' worth both honourable defence and chivalrous attack in the 'merry war'. In fact, some adventurous critics found Wynyard and Quayle perhaps the tiniest bit dull, lacking in erotic chemistry. 'A warm glow is substituted for the sparkle', said the *Birmingham Post*, and the critic of the *Manchester Guardian Weekly* (28 April

1949) 'had the impression that they had really been married for ages'.

A sense of cosiness and stability underlying the richly elegant style: what more could a war-weary audience want? W. A. Darlington concluded his review by saying, 'I prophesy for it a great popularity', a prophecy amply fulfilled in the next five years, as it ran and ran. Gielgud revamped it for the 1950 season with a new cast, including himself and Peggy Ashcroft, and a new touch to the costumes – extravagant hats, which allowed him, in particular, to lift Benedick from the 'plain man' of Quayle to a fantastical dandy; he 'meets Benedick's changing moods in a succession of remarkable hats – blanc-mange mould, floral cartwheel, tarboosh – worn with an air of amused disbelief' (Richard Findlater, *Tribune*, 16 June 1950).

It is this version of the production, this partnership (occasionally varied by Diana Wynyard replacing Ashcroft) which has gone down in theatrical history as a yardstick by which to judge later *Much Ados*. 'This is a perfection of acting', Brian Harvey reported, 'to which a humble and grateful salute can be the critic's only gesture' (*Birmingham Gazette*, 7 June 1950). What were the characteristics of Ashcroft and Gielgud's Beatrice and Benedick which produced such a unanimous effect on their happy auditors? Peter Hall remembers their 'extraordinary display of quick-tongued wit, unbelievably fast',[2] which suggests that they had rediscovered the 'erotic friction' of the text. Philip Hope-Wallace noted, at the time, something further about its embodiment by these two performers:

> Mr Gielgud's strong suit remains the distraught, the tragic, or the whimsical rather than cocksure bantering, and Miss Ashcroft's best cards are those of a yielding and womanish pathos without the astringent manner of a natural Beatrice. This involves some playing 'against the grain' and that little obstacle in temperamental affinity which brings out the best in fine artists which would explain the energy of the rallying matches between these devoted enemies.
>
> (*Manchester Guardian*, 9 June 1950)

It appears that these two highly acclaimed actors, whose pre-war partnership (in, for instance, *Romeo and Juliet*) was legendary, in playing roles for which they were not typecast, made visible an edge of vulnerability in their characters, allowed their 'humanness' to be seen. Of Gielgud, it was generally agreed that 'his comedy is the highest of high comedy, urbane and light, essentially of the drawing-room or the arbour' (*New Statesman*, 11 June 1950) – hence, in his unsoldierly Benedick, a self-deprecating 'modesty' noted by *The Times* (7 June 1950), and hence the ironical head-gear. Gielgud later said that 'over the years', he 'kept trying to make Benedick into more of a soldier. ... I decided [the hats] had not much to do with Shakespeare's play, and I gradually discarded them and wore leather doublets and thigh boots and became less of the courtier'.[3] He retreated, under the pressure of the post-war ideology of gender, into a more conventionally masculine 'soldierly' characterisation. Observe here how conscious the actor is of the semiotics of costume: how a person is dressed is a sign of how closely he or she conforms to gender models.

Ashcroft was also strongly aware of the signals given by costume. Her portrayal of Beatrice demonstrated her intuition that the idea of gender is implicated with that of class; according to Gielgud:

> Diana Wynyard played it much more on the lines I imagine Ellen Terry did – the great lady sweeping about in beautiful clothes. When Peggy started rehearsing she rather jibbed at that and said 'I'm not going to wear those dresses, they're too grand for me.' ... She wore much simpler dresses and created a cheeky character who means well but seems to drop bricks all the while (perhaps she got it from me). Everybody thinks Beatrice will never marry because she is too free with her tongue and is rather impertinent to people without intend-ing any rudeness.[4]

Richard Findlater found her 'somewhat too anxious and vulnerable' for the 'merry' Beatrice. But he concluded, as did all the critics, that 'her Beatrice is radiant with wit and grace'. It would seem that Ashcroft provided a model by which to judge later Beatrices not because of her 'style' but because she allowed the audience to see an individual Beatrice who could be hurt, rather than a 'lady' pro-tected by her grand costume. Gielgud's early fantasticality (as opposed to his later revivals and to Quayle's 'manliness') by the same token opened the way for a much later exploration of a slightly camp Benedick, a man whose reluctance to marry sprang from an unresolved narcissism. But that was not a line to be ex-plored till thirty years later.

The Stratford production which eventually followed Gielgud's much-loved version was in many superficial respects not unlike it. It certainly had 'style'; it also shared a choreographer with the earlier production – Pauline Grant – the dances, with music by

Christopher Whelen, were much remarked on. The whole production had the air of a light opera, an association deliberately made
by the director, Douglas Seale, in a publicity note: 'the producer is
staging *Much Ado* in the 1850s, in the Italy of Verdi and Rossini, a
period in which the play has not been set before and which reflects
its romantic, witty and at times melodramatic situations'. The sets
by Tanya Moisiewitsch and costumes by Motley were 'chocolate-
box' pretty: ten different scenes, accomplished with painted back-
drops, wrought-iron garden furniture and village carts (and an
elaborate church scene which harked back to Irving's atmospheric
masterpiece of the 1890s); the women in summer muslins, parasols
and flat hats, the men resplendent in hussar-type uniforms. A few
months earlier *My Fair Lady* had opened its enormously successful
career at Drury Lane; the over-the-top elegance and sheer entertainment value of this musical must have had an influence on Seale and
his designers (Seale's previous production at Stratford had been a
sober *Henry VI*). It was as though 'Shakes vs Shav' was being
played again, this time with music, in an attempt to win the public
out for a good night's entertainment – that public which would not
subject itself to the 'modern drama' of 1958: *Endgame, A Taste of
Honey, A Resounding Tinkle*. Richard Johnson's Don John was
regularly hissed by a clearly delighted audience, who felt no real
threat to the comic-opera community presented on stage.

For *Plays & Players*, it was among the year's best productions;
other critics, while enjoying it, had some reservations, largely
arising from an uneasy sense that the play had more to offer than
this production did (the same, of course, could be said for
Pygmalion and *My Fair Lady*):

> Already it is more than half-way to being a successful musical ...
> [with] lots of Palm-Court style music and many gay dance routines
> ... a dazzling feast for the eye ... [But] there is a point at which cos-
> tumes and setting become as dangerous to an actor as a child or a
> dog in the cast and that point was reached last night. ... Miss
> Withers and Mr Redgrave [the Beatrice and Benedick] substituted
> only a charming playfulness for the anticipated courtship.
>
> (*Star*, 28 August 1958)

The critic of the *Spectator* (5 September 1958) thought the 'elaborate, spectacularly irrelevant scenery and costumes' were a sign of 'a
fear of the text'. For Googie Withers, however, whose performance
as Beatrice gave great pleasure, there was no question that elaborate

staging was an advantage: 'people came to the theatre to see the play and to be enchanted. Otherwise, they could merely listen to a lecture', she said at a forum in Stratford (*Stratford Herald*, 5 September 1958). Her Beatrice was a triumph of the old school of thought about *Much Ado*:

> [she] sails magnificently through the play with all her comedy guns firing – and reaching their mark. ... She is no shrew, but a woman of fine spirit and keen intelligence who will make marriage a splendid adventure instead of merely 'dwindling into a wife' ... a performance that glows, sparkles, and makes every man in the audience a surrendered Benedick.
>
> (*Stage*, 28 August 1958)

This critic is reading Withers's Beatrice with the help of a later dramatic model, Congreve's Millamant, as one who is essentially of her society (the cynosure of a male gaze) rather than on the margin of it. But there was no equivalent Restoration toughness or worldly cunning in Michael Redgrave's good-natured, easy-going Benedick, 'quick to renounce his bachelor's creed and go[ing] almost eagerly to marriage' (*Coventry Evening Telegraph*, 22 August 1958) – though a number of critics noted that Redgrave, a serious Method actor, seemed ill at ease in the Victorian operetta *mise-en-scène*.

The play looked ripe for the 'Peter Hall treatment' under the new regime at Stratford; a darker re-presentation in his ground-breaking series of the middle comedies. But, for reasons presumably commercial, the first *Much Ado* in the newly-honoured Royal Shakespeare Theatre (1961) was backward-looking, offering no advance on the light-operatic charm of Seale's production. Michael Langham, from Stratford, Ontario, had directed a strikingly successful *Merchant of Venice* in 1960 at the Shakespeare Memorial Theatre; for this *Much Ado* he brought with him from Canada a rising young star, Christopher Plummer, as Benedick, and teamed him with the 'lightweight' Hero of the 1958 production, Geraldine McEwan. Once again the production style was that of operetta, and the period setting was nineteenth century. The only notable differences from 1958 were in Desmond Heeley's designs: the costumes were those of Regency England or Second Empire Europe (the men especially resplendent in their military costumes, in which they remained throughout the performance, giving rise to critical jibes about 'chocolate soldiers'); and there was only a single set – a garden *capriccio* with a wrought-iron staircase and balcony attached to

nothing. The *Birmingham Mail's* critic was one of many who felt
that the permanent set was 'infuriating ... [it] spoilt the church
scene, looming like some fantastic harvest-festival decoration
scheme' (5 April 1961). For no apparent reason the decor suggested
early autumn:

> Thunderstorms darkened the blue Messina skies, the guests at Hero's
> wedding wiped their feet at the cathedral door. Sere and yellow were
> the vines on the trellis of Leonato's house, chill the ornamental
> wrought-iron staircase which Desmond Heeley can flog at any time
> to Tennessee Williams.
>
> (Felix Barker, *Evening News*, 5 April 1961)

This suggestion of a possibly darker reading of the comedy was not
carried through in Langham's production. Critics complained of its
fussiness, its hurry; 'There is far too much flurry on the stage', said
Desmond Pratt (*Yorkshire Post*, 5 April 1961). 'The actresses either
screech like agitated hens or giggle like schoolgirls. There is also
too much comic business.' However, he added, 'What this production lacks in subtlety, it gains in youth, enormous zest and energy.
It has the bounce and flavour of a musical comedy ...' All agreed,
however, that the production lacked the 'poetry' that they remembered from the Gielgud production. This was partly nostalgic senti-
mentality for a more gracious age of theatre – 'We, who have seen
our Gielguds and our Ashcrofts and our Wynyards playing in the
sempiternal sunlight of this almost Mozartian comedy, felt frustrated', sighed Caryl Brahms (*John O'London's*, 13 April 1961).
The production had a plebeian air, most notably in the relation of
Beatrice and Benedick:

> Miss Geraldine McEwan dispenses almost entirely with the airs and
> graces of the traditional Beatrice and plays her as a modern young
> woman who thoroughly enjoys the Elizabethan notion of repartee.
> There is something a little hoydenish in her enjoyment but she is in
> her prosaic way very effective.
>
> (*The Times*, 5 April 1961)

'Mr Plummer walked off slapping Miss McEwan's bottom –
so much for wit', commented the *New Statesman* (5 April 1961).
R. B. Marriott thought that Christopher Plummer was 'more of a
watered-down provincial Petruchio than a Benedick in whom we
can take real interest' (*Stage*, 6 April 1961); of Geraldine McEwan's
Beatrice, Philip Hope-Wallace said 'she can be amusing, but her

range seems all too small and her melting into love carries no sort of conviction' (*Guardian*, 6 April 1961). Demonstrating once again the importance of costume, particularly in creating a female character, McEwan later said, 'I loathed playing Beatrice in a Regency dress. I would like to play her as a Renaissance lady – the full-blooded thing. It's a wonderful complex part; it's got everything' (*Plays & Players*, March 1974). But the director's and designer's 'concept' did not allow the actress to explore the complexity she saw in the role. There was a general disappointment that this Beatrice and Benedick's 'merry war' did not seem to *matter*: 'Mr Langham misses completely the heartbreak that lies within the core of his play's boring heartiness', said Robert Muller. 'Neither Geraldine McEwan nor Christopher Plummer managed to communicate more than its shadow. We lost all the nuances of this superb, erotic fencing match which must end in sweetest reconciliation' (*Daily Mail*, 6 April 1961).

Lacking an exciting Beatrice and Benedick, audience attention may turn to the other pair of lovers, Claudio and Hero, in the hope of finding an emotional thrill. This was provided for many critics by the idealised portrayals given by Barry Warren and Jill Dixon. The sexual politics of the Claudio–Hero story were not yet a matter for concern – neither, for that matter, were Plummer's bottom-slapping exploits – and Marriott, among many, admired

> a striking Claudio, with his fresh true-ringing ardour, his moving display of anger and grief, and his simple but shining gladness when Hero is restored to him. Jill Dixon also impresses, with a charming Hero. These two, in fact, provide the most completely pleasing and satisfying aspects of the production.
>
> (*Stage*, 6 April 1961)

Most notably. Don John emerged at last from the melodramatic stereotype which had been his previous dramatic incarnation, in a striking performance by a saturnine, stammering Ian Richardson: 'a surprisingly good Don John, drawing the usually incredible villainy of this character out of a neurosis of romantic self-pity and somehow making it seem plausible' (*The Times*, 5 April 1961). Richardson, a powerful and highly intelligent actor, was obviously encouraged to explore his character in a way that the four lovers, stereotypes of the early 1960s ideology of gender, were not.

1968

If Langham's production lacked the erotic thrill and the exploration of subconscious motivation that audiences were beginning consciously to expect from Shakespearean comedy, Trevor Nunn's 1968 revival went a long way towards supplying the lack. This was after a curiously long gap for such a popular play – perhaps the RSC directorship felt that it had been overexposed in the 1950s, that it was a text exhausted by the popular idea that it was all 'style' (the apogee of the obsession with style was probably Zeffirelli's manic comic-Sicilian production at the National Theatre in 1965).

Set in an early version of designer Christopher Morley's 'great empty box',[5] dimly lit, and with the characters dressed for the most part in mottled reds and oranges, Nunn's production gave at times the impression of a dream, a return to the womb. 'The effect is to enclose and concentrate the action, certainly to darken the mood of the play', said Sheila Bannock (*Stratford Herald*, 17 October 1968). This was a play very much about sexual attraction: the Elizabethan-style costumes allowed the men to swagger in tight breeches and the women to show a great deal of bosom. One of its most striking moments early on was the military masque, danced by the men with clashing swords and huge phallic-nosed red masks.[6] The bawdy lines were given their full value (and more – I still recall Alan Howard's suggestive pause on 'fetch you the length of Prester John's … foot'). There was much more physical contact between all the characters than there had been in previous productions, hampered as they were by nineteenth-century costume and notions of style which came down to little more than 'elegant' movement. (Gielgud, objecting to nineteenth-century costuming, had perceptively commented, 'I do not think those fashions can ever suit a play which is so full of Elizabethan sex jokes. The jokes are hardly credible when set in a period in which everybody was ashamed to show so much as an ankle'.[7]) This physicality was particularly noticeable in the performances of Beatrice and Benedick (Janet Suzman and Alan Howard): they stayed close to each other, in smiling and delighted eye-contact, in the early scenes, as though held by invisible threads. In the church scene they began their duet apart, behind separate pews, and finally moved together to hug, kneeling; at the happy conclusion to Act V, scene ii, 'Benedick lifts Beatrice off bench and holds her in his arms'.[8] This is unequivocally the body language of modern youth (contrast the self-consciously 'modern' behaviour of Plummer and McEwan), and the audience was delighted to recognise it, both at Stratford where the production opened in October 1968, and then at its transfer to the Aldwych in July 1969 after a twelve-week tour in the US: 'it went very well with an audience containing a lot of young people', reported Philip Hope-Wallace (*Guardian*, 30 July 1969).

The critics were less whole-hearted in their enjoyment than the ordinary members of the audience, and one wonders if their response is that of defensive middle age against the growing assertiveness of the young, who were seeing the play with the eyes of the 1968 generation. The production had begun rehearsal soon after the student protests of May 1968; its director was the newly-appointed *wunderkind*, 28-year-old Trevor Nunn, and its principal quartet were of a similar age. Nunn's battlecry, which was to find an echo in many theatrical undertakings in the late 1960s and early 1970s (perhaps most notably in *Hair* [1968–73]) rang out proudly: 'what we have to do through the theatre is to lead and make a contact with the audience now through JOY, ENERGY AND AFFIRMATION' (*Daily Mail*, 16 October 1968).

The costumes, one critic reported, were 'Tudor executed in psychedelic chiffon prints, violet and pink, red and orange – the vigorous, exhibitionist colours of youth' (*Leamington Spa Courier*, 21 October 1968). B. A. Young's rather middle-aged carping about the production's style (or lack of it) is typical: 'Miss Suzman seems not altogether to have got over her Katharina in last year's *Shrew*. She wears an untidy straw-coloured wig, and looks, even at Hero's wedding, as if she had just hurriedly got out of bed' (*Financial Times*, 15 October 1968). Similarly, but more tolerantly, John Barber:

> The young players choose a homely English rather than a brilliantly courtly style of behaviour. Alan Howard's Benedick is tousled and charmingly gauche, while Janet Suzman makes a bubbling, almost boisterous Beatrice. ... In short, a cheerful rather than an inspiring production, with a number of good things and strong on spectacle and horseplay, but without the dancing intelligence of Shakespeare's conception.
>
> (*Daily Telegraph*, 15 October 1968)

The shibboleth of 'Shakespeare's conception' is brought up once again in defence of a conservative performance style. Nunn, however, made it clear in his extensive programme notes that his production had strong claims to intellectual respectability (his own biographical note begins, 'Studied under Dr Leavis at Cambridge'). The programme included quotations from literary critics regarding Beatrice and Benedick; lines from other comedies of courtship – *The Way of the World, The Importance of Being Earnest, Man and Superman*; five stanzas from Sir John Davies's *Orchestra*; and Nunn's own scholarly notes on the noting/nothing and semblance/reality tropes. The play, according to Nunn, is a serious comedy of ideas concerning the wholeness and regeneration of the community, most strikingly presented in the youthful Beatrice and Benedick's vitality and nonconformity. Even the Friar (Julian Curry) was young, an embodiment of the new belief in the power and wisdom of youth.

Some reviewers did see the serious intent underlying the production's energetic performance:

> It takes on a warmth and coherence which show up sharply the bogusness of Zeffirelli's attempt at the National Theatre to impose these from outside. ... The alignment of male against female, townsfolk against military, have the strength of a vanished community life.
> (Ronald Bryden, *Observer*, 20 October 1968)

'The production firmly reveals the play's theme of regeneration', said Gareth Lloyd Evans (*Guardian*, 16 October 1968). 'Even Don John' (Terence Hardiman), noted Wardle, 'is finally absorbed into the pattern as a mere carnival monster; and the production prepares for this by showing him earlier as an irresolute tippling malcontent who is led into villainy by Borachio' (*The Times*, 15 October 1968).

In this intellectual scheme Hero and Claudio become rather more than simple foils to the sparring Beatrice and Benedick. A number of critics were struck with Helen Mirren's 'pert teenage Hero', who hinted at a less than pure mind and by Bernard Lloyd's 'unpleasant' Claudio: 'He is consistently the calculating poseur, who has the good fortune to fall in love with an heiress and is sadistically determined to punish her to the utmost when he believes her to be untrue' (*Evesham Journal*, 16 October 1968). Harold Hobson, who did not much like the production, nevertheless found its lack of elegance 'consistent and defensible':

> it is unlike any 'Much Ado' I have seen before. Mr Nunn builds up his production to the church scene, the emphasis of which he places,

not on Beatrice's injunction to Benedick to kill Claudio, but on Claudio's terrible assassination of Hero's character. Bernard Lloyd sets about this with a venom that makes the episode, which is anyway one of the most disgusting in Shakespeare, the penetrating point of the evening.

(*Sunday Times*, 20 October 1968)

Hobson also disliked the unladylike forthrightness of Janet Suzman's Beatrice: 'Where Shakespeare says that Beatrice enters like a lapwing, Miss Suzman's giant leap seems more consonant with Mexico City and the lively buffalo.' But most found her sparky 'bluestocking' (she played several scenes in spectacles) enchanting and delightful, despite her caustic tongue:

> Miss Suzman's Beatrice has evidently been in love with Benedick in the past. A bright girl, scholarly ... she has despaired – like Shakespeare's harsher shrew Kate – of meeting a man of her intellectual level who isn't a sugar-candy courtier.
>
> (Jeremy Kingston, *Punch*, 6 August 1969)

It is interesting to contrast Kingston's comments with Suzman's own feminist recollection and assessment of the role twelve years later:

> I love her defiance. She's *damned* if she's going to admit she loves the man. She's got something so crystalline, so witty, so tough, yet underneath she's soft and vulnerable. She is one of the many women in Shakespeare who shows incredible loyalty and friendship for another woman.[9]

Such terms of evaluation for a female role were simply not part of the vocabulary of the complacently patriarchal critics of the 1960s.

Alan Howard as Benedick impressed most critics with his 'zany' impersonation, thus eschewing, as Jacobi and others were to do after him, the stereotypical masculine misogyny often given to the role. Jeremy Kingston commented that this Benedick was 'honest and engaging, a nice companion, very appealing in his crestfallen expressions and gleefully confident glances at the audience' – in short, a young man who seemed to belong to the contemporary community.

When the production was revived at the Aldwych in 1969 a number of authoritative reviewers found themselves having to revise their opinions; B. A. Young, for instance:

Beside its Stratford version of last October, this new incarnation of Trevor Nunn's production of *Much Ado* is a revelation. All the aggregation of rococo foolery, and all the superfluous slapstick that concealed the pleasures of Shakespeare's wit in this most witty play, have been ruthlessly clipped away. ... A new spirit of intelligence has spread through the whole thing. Janet Suzman's Beatrice ... is witty and confident, and her lines come sizzling across. ... [On 'Kill Claudio':] she does it with a break in her voice [rather than her previous shout] that makes you aware of the terrible nature of her request. And Alan Howard as Benedick, instead of replying with a shouted refusal, pauses for what seems an infinity of time before telling her, firmly but gently, that he cannot.

(*Financial Times*, 30 July 1969)[10]

If there was general agreement that Nunn and his actors were 'trying too hard' in the Stratford performances of what was almost literally a revolutionary new view of the play, it seems that by the time the production arrived in London the actors had become more confident, less aggressive in their presentation; and also that the critics had begun to accept the production on its own terms: Trewin and Wardle were two more who gracefully withdrew their earlier objections and heaped praise on the 'sheer amplitude of life' of this youthful, sexually-aware production (Wardle, *The Times*, 30 July 1969; Trewin, *Birmingham Post*, 30 July 1969).

1971–6

Other readings of *Much Ado About Nothing* emerged in the 1970s, among them a feminist one which suggests that not only *young* women experience sexual desire or are sexually desirable. Ronald Eyre's 1971 revival, which was mounted for the 41-year-old Elizabeth Spriggs partnered by a middle-aged Derek Godfrey, was once again set in the safe world of nineteenth-century decorum. Eyre followed Nunn in providing a programme full of thought-provoking quotations – a page each on 'Adam and Eve' and 'A Woman's World' – but offered no insights of his own, nor did the quotations seem to have much to do with what Michael Billington (*The Times*, 28 May 1971) called 'this amiable lightweight revival ... everything conspires to suggest a leisurely, sunlit, aristocratic society'. The set (by Voytek), an early Victorian conservatory, and the extravagant military costumes and gentlemen's summer country wear set the tone of the production. Much comment was made on the constant business with period-establishing props – cigars, fishing-rods, bird-watching apparatus, painting easels: 'No one is allowed merely to speak for long; he or she must be given something to do: fill a pipe, sign the Visitors' Book, or, frequently, light a cheroot' (*Stage*, 3 June 1971) – or engage in a round of glee-singing ('Sigh No More, Ladies', a charming Victorian pastiche by Carl Davis, was reprinted in the programme for the audience's further pleasure). The contrast between Nunn's military masque of 1968, with its aggressive sexuality, and Eyre's clowning dance by the gentry in masks made of frying-pans and other kitchen implements points up the difference between the two productions:

> although this is a very elegant and even spirited production, it does seem at the moment to lack passion ... the emotional involvement between Beatrice and Benedick – and indeed, between other characters of the play – is very muted: one does not sense the tug between inclination and instinct, and the comedy, though it is witty, remains rather heartless.
> (Sarah Elly Wood, *Stratford Herald*, 4 June 1971)

The period setting, remarked the Birmingham *Sunday Mercury* (30 May 1971), 'constrains the natural airs of the play and identifies too strongly with a period of our history which was not memorable for its easy-going ways or flirtatious habits'. Or an acceptance of women engaging in bawdy banter (in fact much of the bawdy talk was excised, allowing the play to appear even more 'Victorian'); the *Stage* commented:

> Beatrice is made to look too well brought up to speak her mind, or even to speak at all to a man ... on the brink of each dagger-sharp taunt, [she] hesitates as if wondering if she dare. Then she adds warmth to daring.
> (*Stage*, 3 June 1971)

Michael Billington nevertheless found the pair's romance touching:

> Elizabeth Spriggs ... a friendly, bustling spinster, pushing forty, who invents numerous little household tasks to disguise her starved emotional life ... in the later scenes she quietly suggests Beatrice has acquired a second youthfulness through the transforming power of love. Derek Godfrey's Benedick undergoes a similar metamorphosis from bovine hearty and born clubman ... to emotionally mature lover. But in his case the contrast is a shade too explicit.
> (*The Times*, 28 May 1971)

B. A. Young's opinion was that their performance lacked sexual excitement, and therefore the sense of potential renewal for the community: 'that marriage of theirs is no romantic union. They may become a popular party-going host and hostess; but they're no more likely to raise a family than the host and hostess in *Who's Afraid of Virginia Woolf*' (*Financial Times*, 28 May 1971).

The fact that the production was so deliberately lightweight meant that it also lacked a sense of evil in the Hero–Claudio plot. Billington commented:

> the element of public-school prankishness in all the plotting and counterplotting is really underlined. ... [However] the operatically villainous plot against Hero seems slightly out of place in this sun-dappled, country-house setting. You feel the worst that could happen here is that someone might get caught cheating at croquet ... one is left hungering for a much stronger realisation of the play's darker, melodramatic constituents.
>
> (*The Times*, 28 May 1971)

Eyre's one innovative touch was to give Richard Pasco's Don John a homosexual motivation. The *Birmingham Post* (31 May 1971) reported that Eyre told Pasco 'Don John loves Claudio', and Pasco's performance was by all accounts brilliant. Even the veteran Trewin thought that 'Richard Pasco, more than any man I recall, persuades us of the canker at the heart of that often inexplicable villain, Don John' (*Birmingham Post*, 28 May 1971). *The Observer*'s critic (30 May 1971) noted in him 'a discontent so powerful that it's like a deformity'. The development of the figure of Don John as an outsider, a dramatic critique of the fragility of the community's image of itself, is a notable feature of productions of the last twenty years; more recently, he has even been joined by his brother, Don Pedro, as another who cannot acquiesce in comedy's optimistic vision of the healing power of marriage. Pasco's Don John, however, was not enough by himself to add moral or emotional weight to the production, and audiences left the theatre finally unmoved.

John Barton's famous 'British Raj' 1976 production, still revered by many critics, wrung hearts *and* induced howls of laughter from the audience, owing to three factors: the underlying sadness of Judi Dench's Beatrice, the comic mastery of Donald Sinden's Benedick; and the hilarious antics of the Watch, played as an Indian *Dad's Army*, complete with funny 'babu' accents and Indian body-language ill-adapted to the conventions of the British Army. As a member of the audience I found this clever notion totally offensive – racist and patronising, even though I did find myself smiling at the comic performance of John Woodvine's Dogberry, which certainly put new life into those old jokes which critics almost unceasingly complain are never funny enough. It is significant that Barton had to go back to the early 1950s and 1960s humour of the Goons (Spike Milligan and Peter Sellers) for a source for his comic Watch. The 1970s laughed at Monty Python, a much more inward-looking, self-critical English satire. But Barton was not a young man in 1976 (he was 48) and his production was (again) about a middle-aged Beatrice and Benedick.

Critical opinion was largely complimentary about the production, particularly as it was brought off with such panache by a company of superb actors. Two or three voices were raised in objection, the most percipient Harold Hobson's:

> Mr Barton's premise is that a coloured man is funny merely by being coloured. Ridicule his salaams, comic ways of sitting down, and too precise forms of speech, and you have something that sends audiences into paroxysms of delight. Personally, I found this racial joke offensive, but it clearly filled the theatre with a comforting sense that if the British have lost an Empire they can at least jeer at those who have gained it. ... John Woodvine enters with enormous zest into his ignoble performance as Dogberry, and the degradation forced on him by Mr Barton is wildly applauded by the frustrated imperialist audience.
>
> (*Sunday Times*, 11 April 1976)

Similarly Benedict Nightingale remarked 'I'm not sure that [Dogberry's] earnest malapropisms were much appreciated by the lady in a sari sitting near me' (*New Statesman*, 16 April 1976), thus reminding his readers that the British audience was no longer as homogeneous as it had been in the 1950s, and that some of those Stratford visitors who come for a taste of Shakespeare might actually not be of Anglo-Saxon origin.

For John Barber of the *Daily Telegraph* (9 April 1976), who did not find the Indianisation offensive, the production offered the audience

> a fantastication on the play that is elaborate, ingenious, inventive and unnecessary. ... What is missing is the glitter of a sophisticated court, with two sensitive people at centre who conceal their feelings and display their intelligence by waging a merry war of words.

What Barton supplied in place of wit and 'style' was an elaborate realism; his forte, as Michael Billington pointed out, is that he 'has the rare knack among Shakespearean directors of endowing his characters with a complete past history' (*Guardian*, 10 April 1976). The 'Elizabethan' permanent set for the season, constructed of wooden slats, 'with just a piece or two of muslin, becomes a convincing hot, dry and dusty fort' (Peter Whitehouse, *Sunday Mercury*, 11 April 1976), in which bored and under-employed officers of Empire and their households fill in their time with idle jokes and petty domestic business (Beatrice, for instance, was seen shelling the peas for dinner, or aimlessly sweeping the dust around the floor). In this context, 'the decision of Claudio (Richard Durden, amiably chinless) to curse Hero at the altar on such slender evidence becomes the mindless reflex action of an officer, gentleman and twit' (*Punch*, 21 April 1976). 'They are a heartless lot, these officers', said B. A. Young: 'they will no doubt be moving to another station shortly; they continue as coldly frivolous after the interrupted wedding as before it, no doubt thinking themselves lucky to have got out of an embarrassing entanglement' (*Financial Times*, 9 April 1976).

Don John's character and motivation were also crystal clear: Ian McDiarmid presented him spindle-shanked, 'curly-haired and studious, obviously sent out to the Army against his will and bitterly resenting it' (Robert Cushman, *Observer*, 11 April 1976). Nightingale thought him 'a reedy milk-sop half-batty with sexual envy. When he calls Hero a "pretty lady", you feel he's verbally goosing her.' He added,

> the setting suits the play's atmosphere, but it does encourage a snooziness of pace – and perhaps also a certain staidness of manner. ... nor is it easy to believe that one of these Victorian misses, however spirited, would suddenly invite her swain to murder.

In fact Judi Dench's Beatrice was far from 'spirited'. Cherie Lunghi's Hero was much more likely unthinkingly to demand a man's death: she was, said the *Spectator* (17 April 1976),

> far less drearily virginal than usual and the tawdry report of her unchastity is thus, to take a cynical view, a shade more feasible. ... I can summon no confidence in [Hero and Claudio's] eventual union, which seems headed for a future of languid infidelities at country-house parties back home.

Dench's Beatrice was out of place in this heartless environment. Like Elizabeth Spriggs before her, she played the role as a woman fearing herself to be on the shelf (she was in fact 42 in 1976, though with her blonde gamine looks the Beatrice she presented seemed in her early thirties), and occupying her empty life with a succession of minor domestic tasks. But in contrast to Spriggs's cheerful bustle, Dench was sour and grumpy, in a much less pleasant situation than the nostalgic summer country-house England of Eyre's conception.

Remarking that 'Miss Dench is not, on the face of her, a plausible occupant of any shelf anywhere ... you could imagine her rejecting suitors, but never failing to attract them', Robert Cushman explained:

> Her strategy is, at first, to damp herself down; her dress is drab and her wit sour rather than sparkling. Her gibes at Benedick are meant to hurt, not to entertain; their first encounter is played, unusually, without spectators.

Noting, as many commentators did, the evidence of 'a previous, scarring involvement between the two protagonists', Cushman describes Dench's emotional exploration of the role: 'Miss Dench pulls this suggestion to the front of the play. We see what is gnawing her ... When she melts, the effect is breathtaking. ... We weep for happiness at Beatrice's conversion.' Peter Whitehouse confirmed Dench's ability to move an audience:

> [she] can turn on one of those needle sharp prickles of wit from a dazzling gaiety (with all the talents and timing of the comedienne) to expose, just for a second, a depth of sadness that makes a theatre full of people hold their breath. ... So compelling is she that when she eventually gets that kiss of love an uncontrollable 'ahhh' issues from the audience.

Details of Dench's performance indicate the particular stamp she put on the role. In the church scene, she distractedly 'falls to ... sweeping up the confetti; she must, instinctively, do something. Benedick has to fight hard to reclaim her; has in fact to declare his love to her unyielding back', reported Cushman. 'Miss Dench has prepared in everything she previously does the anguished indignation in which ... the peremptory demand "Kill Claudio!" is forced from her lips.' And at the end, Young noted, 'in the splendid final dance, she has got stuck with Benedick's sword and stands awkwardly in the middle of the rejoicings'. This final touch is indicative of the profound difference between Judi Dench's Beatrice and Donald Sinden's Benedick. She remained, for all her new-found happiness, an outsider to this conventionally-divided society of flighty young women and macho men; and although Sinden exited with her, on the opposite side of the stage from the rest of the company (thus, says Michael Greenwald, 'deliberately set[ting] themselves apart from the social shallowness of their peers'),[11] the rest of Sinden's performance hardly prepared us for this conclusion.

His Benedick was the regimental eccentric, the butt of the men's jokes, though also comfortably aware of his intellectual superiority. It was a great comic performance, played, said John Barber, 'with his familiar *batterie de cuisine*: the pursed mouth, the stressed sibilants, the pop-eyed indignation, the rotund declamation'. 'I suddenly remembered Mr Sinden's own Malvolio [in Barton's production of 1969]. The devices are the same but they still get the laughs', wrote Peter Whitehouse (Birmingham *Sunday Mercury*, 11 April 1976). Unashamedly playing to the audience, wrote the critic of the *Sunday Telegraph* (11 April 1976), 'Donald Sinden's boisterously histrionic Benedick swims vigorously against the tide of his director's conception, but his detachment, though consistently amusing, undermines the credibility of the later serious passages.' Peter Lewis (*Daily Mail*, 9 April 1976) reported that '"Kill Claudio" brought him an unwanted laugh. He just didn't look capable of challenging a brother officer to a serious duel'; though, to be fair, the *Spectator* thought 'Sinden's stricken, low-toned "Not for the wide world" ... calculated as perfectly as I have ever heard it done'. The point remains, however, that the two performances by Dench and Sinden are consistently spoken of as distinct in their effects. There was little or no sexual chemistry between them: one felt that Sinden had merely been tricked out of his bachelorhood, not into love; and that Dench's Beatrice was condemned to remain emotionally alone, though she might have a husband. Because of their very different 'masculine' (egoistic) and 'feminine' (affective) acting styles – Sinden playing to the audience, Dench inviting the audience's sympathy with her hidden feelings – they did not body forth the optimistic formula of a recognisably modern marriage offered in Anne Barton's programme essay:

> At the conclusion of *Much Ado About Nothing*, Beatrice and Benedick remain within the flawed society which has fostered them and brought them together. Their relationship, however, is one that they have created for themselves and it suggests an alternative mode

of love to that of the 'model' couple Hero and Claudio: ragged, humorous, a bit undignified, demanding, but also individual and emotionally realised as the other is not.

Barton's production was generally considered very satisfying (always excepting those few critics and members of the audience who disliked its complacent racism); owing to excellent casting and a richly-detailed realistic conception it soon assumed the status of a classic interpretation, which critics still refer to fondly as a yardstick. John Peter's commendation is telling:

> behind all this harmless pantomime there's a first-rate rendering of the kernel of the play. Like Mr Barton's unforgettable 'Twelfth Night' nine years ago, this is a warm, spacious and perceptive production, its shifting moods cunningly underscored by the skilful use of music and off-stage noises [including – of course – a cricket match]. It is a bitter-sweet comedy of middle-aged immaturity.
>
> (*Sunday Times*, 3 July 1977)

If, however, this production were revived today, in a society now acknowledged to be multi-cultural, would the depiction of the foolish Indian servants be considered a 'harmless pantomime'? Can we not read between the lines of Peter's praise that this was, in Hobson's words, essentially a piece of middle-aged nostalgia for an Empire that was past? It is interesting to observe that when Judi Dench herself directed the play in 1988 for the Renaissance Theatre Company she opted for a young and spirited Beatrice and Benedick (Samantha Bond and Kenneth Branagh), though she set the play in the nineteenth-century context of the Napoleonic wars, wanting the recognisably 'masculine' sign of trousers (rather than doublet and hose) for the men.[12] Bond's Beatrice was still very much one who had been previously hurt by Benedick – as, indeed, what Beatrice has not been since Dench's great representation? – but the production focused on the trials of being young and in love, rather than on the director's loving re-creation of a vanished world.

1982–90

It was five years before Stratford saw another *Much Ado about Nothing*. Terry Hands, who had directed *Twelfth Night* in 1979 and *As You Like It* in 1980 here completed the trilogy of middle comedies with an elegaic Caroline production, as though saying farewell to the old 'Elizabethan' order and the organic community it represented in the mid-twentieth-century literary imagination. The lighting, which was designed by Hands with Clive Morris, was, throughout the play, variations of sunset or evening light thrown onto a huge cyclorama, against which Ralph Koltai's tall trees on perspex screens were beautifully silhouetted. The floor-tiles mirrored the sky, the trees, the few pieces of garden furniture, and the rich satin costumes of the actors. This was not a nostalgic re-creation of lost glory but a very clear indicator that such a narcissistic world had to come to an end – not even Beatrice and Benedick, finally absorbed in each other, could regenerate it for long.

For Michael Billington, the symbolic design concept was impressive, if not as comforting as Barton's naturalism:

> it is clear that we are in a hermetic, self-loving society dazzled by appearance and fashion. It is a brilliantly appropriate image and leads to many solicitous touches: whereas the extrovert Benedick, for instance, plays the scene in which he is gulled in front of the perspex wall, the tricked Beatrice is later seen, lost in wonderment, behind a haze of smoked glass. My only cavil would be that this over-powering design precludes the kind of social detail that can (as in John Barton's Indian Raj production) give a kind of truth to the play's preposterous events.
>
> (*Guardian*, 21 April 1982)

For most critics, and certainly for the enthusiastic audiences, both in England and in America, the production was a triumph. There was general rejoicing that at last Derek Jacobi, a major classical actor now in his prime, had been lured to Stratford. Jacobi has the beauty of voice and elegance of phrasing that remind many people of Gielgud, but he also has a very modern physicality and comic flair, which he used to great effect to present a capering ninny of a Benedick who discovers his masculinity in the course of the play. For Michael Coveney, noting how Benedick is the centre of attention in the play's opening scene, he is this escapist society's 'natural spokesman ... with a dashing but qualified smile and an ostentatiously limp wrist', and, one might add, a much more frilled and furbelowed costume than the women. This characterisation 'introduces an air of sexual adventure and discovery into Benedick's progress that is quite new to the part' (*Financial Times*, 21 April 1982). A somewhat more probing perception of Jacobi's Benedick would note that his 'campness' is one way of dealing with a society whose conventions he can't take seriously: at the end, in the final celebratory dance, he sent up its self-satisfaction by playing the 'female' role in an impromptu ballet pas-de-deux, in which Sinead Cusack's Beatrice cheerfully lifts him – he, however, could not do the same for her when the roles were reversed.[13]

Jacobi played a late-twentieth-century 'new sensitive man'. He eschewed martial posturing in the church scene, which was played quickly and with urgency, as though he was as much concerned about Beatrice's friend Hero as she herself was (the hysterical laughter with which he greeted 'Kill Claudio' was dropped quite early in the run). In Act V, scene ii's relaxed conversation, they stood together, quietly bantering like old friends, until he turned to ask, with genuine concern and friendly familiarity, 'And now, how do *you?*' His conclusion, 'Man is but a giddy thing' was met with a firm nod of assent from Beatrice, which gave her, although silenced by the play and Benedick's kiss, a final feminist utterance. Jacobi's assessment of the meaning of these two characters for the later twentieth century fits a recognisable modern paradigm: 'You feel it's never going to be roses, roses all the way for them, both still have their extraordinary intellects which will crash against each other, both are very independent, but they will survive. Their joint sense of humour is the great saving grace in their relationship.'[14]

Sinead Cusack's Beatrice began the play even more obviously isolated than Judi Dench's: she circled around the assembled company until she plunged in to offer herself for Benedick's universal hand-kissing of the ladies; he deliberately ignored her. She played 'Indeed, my lord ... a double heart for his single one' visibly upset by the memory, though she recovered herself quickly to rejoice at Hero and Claudio's engagement. Before the gulling of Benedick, she was seen wandering alone across the back of the set – and she left the scene of her own revelation in a slow, private dance, as though a dream was at last coming true. The fact that Cusack was also playing Katharina in the same season led many critics to notice the connection between the two roles: Billington noted that she 'really is a budding blonde termagant "possessed with a fury" ... who through love acquires emotional equilibrium. Instead of the usual Restoration wit, Ms Cusack's intriguing Beatrice is a self-taming shrew.' This is the first record I have found of an experienced critic being 'intrigued' by a performance of Beatrice; we might speculate that it is because Sinead Cusack broke the mould, playing neither the brilliant, confident young woman, nor the desperate almost-middle-aged one, but an emotionally isolated person, using her wit as defence against being hurt. 'Being a woman, and therefore more self-aware and grown-up than men, she knows from the very beginning of the play ... that she loves Benedick but doesn't dare trust that he reciprocates', commented the *Spectator* (28 May 1983). Cusack describes her own conception of the role:

> When Terry [Hands] cast me as Beatrice, what he saw in me was femininity – that's what he cast, that's what he used in his direction of me. But because of who I am, I showed him other areas of the character. A Beatrice who is very angry. A woman who has been damaged by society. ... Beatrice has a physical grace which I think is terribly important, so my movements as Beatrice were as fluid as Kate's were jagged.[15]

Young, capable of both anger and hurt, but at ease with her sexuality and her body: this was an image that the young women of the 1980s could identify with. The middle-aged, 'on the shelf' Beatrices of Judi Dench and Elizabeth Spriggs were images from a pre-feminist way of thinking about women in society. Spriggs had even pushed the role towards caricature by using the awkward gait of the comic games-mistress; Dench's social unease in the final dance, and elsewhere, has already been noted.

The play's final image, accompanied by Nigel Hess's unearthly tubular-bells music, showed Beatrice and Benedick alone on stage, cheerfully arguing: a 'Shavian couple', noted the critics. Hands's point, presumably, was that it has always been a relationship based on talking, however defensive at times – contrast the few stilted speeches of Hero and Claudio, in this production no more than a pair of conventional adolescents. As Beatrice and Benedick realised that they were alone, they went into a slow dancing embrace – an affirmation of the importance of mutual affection and support (even more important than sexual fulfilment) when society itself is disintegrating. It is this human warmth that the play's outcasts missed out on: John Carlisle's Don John was no more an outsider than his brother, played by Derek Godfrey – 'both black-clad siblings take a delight in plotting', wrote Robert Cushman (*Observer*, 25 April 1982). At the end Don Pedro, surrounded by the dancing community, but himself without a partner, put on his black hat and left the stage.

In the late 1980s the RSC at last began to allow more women directors to work on the main stage at Stratford. Di Trevis had had successes with tough modern works at the Glasgow Citizens' and elsewhere, and had worked on satires at Stratford but her first excursion into 'high' comedy, with *Much Ado* in 1988, was by most critical accounts a disaster. Possibly she was trying too hard to prove her fitness for the august position accorded her; possibly she felt some ambivalence about a play so implicated in patriarchal ideology. Fortunately we have the RSC's archival videotape at the Shakespeare Centre Library to check the critics' impressions against.

The 'look' of the production was the main stumbling-block for the reviewers. Designed by Mark Thompson, it was set in the 1950s, in some tropical haven of the rich, with the British Army not too far away: Malaya, South America, Cyprus presented themselves as possibilities – the last the most likely as the aborted wedding took place in a Greek Orthodox chapel. Most disconcerting was the gimmick of the arrival of the army men at the beginning of the play, dropped from helicopters in their jungle fatigues. Perhaps Trevis was trying to make an opening statement about the parasitism of the idle rich, whose life of gossip and shallow frivolity she then anatomised for the next three hours. If this was the case, she had a resisting audience, who simply refused to think about what they saw: 'The men consistently lack dignity ... dressed in tropical shorts, bell-hop jackets or dressing-gowns; the women, in a succession of strapless ball-gowns, look foolishly over-dressed rather than glamorous', opined Katherine Duncan-Jones (*Times Literary Supplement*, 28 April 1988). This response was presumably intended; Sheridan Morley thought the 'costumes designed all too clearly to get the laughs they seem unable to find in the text ... [but] the production has no real point of view' (*International Herald Tribune*, 20 April 1988). (Nostalgic evocation of the Indian Raj is an acceptable 'point of view', but satire of the pink-gin brigade of the last days of the British Empire is apparently not.)

The other visual problem was with the casting of Beatrice and Benedick, Maggie Steed and Clive Merrison. Once again a couple on the verge of middle-age, this Beatrice and Benedick were physically mismatched. Steed is a tall woman, made to look even bigger in the full skirts and high heels of the 1950s (significantly she was in flatties for the intimate conversation of Act, V, scene ii) – a confident socialite inclined to swoop upon people. Clive Merrison was the spindly joker to the company, small, thin and balding, looking ridiculous in the Bombay bloomers and floral shirt he habitually sported. Irving Wardle, whose review was relatively charitable – he thought that 'one aim of the production is to hold out some hope to nature's wallflowers ... the sexual outsiders' – commented sadly: 'What fails to materialise is any transformation of the lovers. They look as they looked to begin with, a mismatched pair' (*The Times*, 15 April 1988).

The two actors played their roles very much for laughs – and got them, despite the grumpiness of the critics. Merrison got most of his by exasperated shouting – according to Wardle, he 'gives the impression of gnashing his teeth even when in full satirical flow ... he is apt to explode in her face ("Harpy!") even in company'. Even his declaration of love in the church scene was shouted, as though unwillingly ripped from him; he was only momentarily shocked into quietness by 'Kill Claudio', then the shouting match continued, though the end of the scene was touching in its physical awkwardness – holding hands, they seemed to want to kiss, but couldn't quite work out how to manage it (in the last scene, he simply grabbed her without forethought). One felt, however, that if once he stopped shouting, Merrison's exasperated little man would become the hen-pecked husband of 1950s mythology.

Maggie Steed's Beatrice was a more complex portrayal. She drawled her banter, getting a good deal more humour out of it than previous Beatrices had done for some time. But she was also able to use the depths of her voice to suggest warmth and emotion, as in her emergence from her hiding-place (an ornamental pool) in Act III, scene i – with her dress dripping, she presented a comic figure, but she controlled the audience's response by her speech, low, obviously deeply shaken. 'Kill Claudio' had the same delivery, and got no laugh. While some reviewers found her physical impersonation off-putting (Mrs Thatcher and Dame Hilda Bracket were both mentioned as models), others lamented lost possibilities for the actress:

> Maggie Steed is an intelligent actress whose range ... displays desolate heartbreak, wit and sensuality – the ideal and rarely-found combination for Beatrice. In this production she has to get her laughs from funny walks, funny hats and hiding in a pond.
>
> In the outburst of grief after her slandered cousin's rejection, Miss Steed fills the theatre with raw passion; and there are signs that, when the lumpen direction can drag itself away from stale gags and corny whimsy, it can generate some tension.
>
> (Martin Hoyle, *Financial Times*, 15 April 1988)

Ralph Fiennes played a very romantic, innocent Claudio, and Julia Ford a spirited and likable Hero. Many critics found them interesting and involving by contrast with the 'caricatures' of Beatrice and Benedick, and Wardle commented, 'There is, perhaps, more substance in the production's feminist angle; as where Hero ... collapses in church and is immediately surrounded by a flock of sympathetic girls, while the men all retire to nurse their personal grievances.' Was it perhaps Trevis's 'feminist angle', or just a negation of any possibility of finding good in this proto-modern society (contrast this vision of the world after the Second World War with Gielgud's bright optimism), that dictated that everyone in the last scene should be wearing black, as though for a funeral? They did not change out of the clothes worn for Hero's 'memorial', despite the clear instruction in the text to do so ('Come, let us hence, and put on other weeds', says Don Pedro in Act V, scene iii). Nevertheless the audience laughed and cheered; in their perception, at any rate, love and forgiveness had once more triumphed.

Bill Alexander's 1990 production returned the play to the early seventeenth century, very close to its original period. Set in a topiary garden designed by Kit Surrey, the production established a credible society by careful use of detail in the Barton manner. At the soldiers' arrival, for instance, basins of water and towels were brought for them to wash off after a dusty march. Arrogant lords of creation, they dropped their soiled shirts and jackets on the ground and left them for the servants to pick up.

'The soldiers take off their armour, and ritually wash away the war, but they still maintain their group as comrades, while the young women range behind their "general", Beatrice, as the wary but fascinated other side' (Paul Lapworth, *Stratford Herald*, 20 April 1990). Thus the 'merry war' began again. But the most striking detail in the opening scene was the behaviour of Beatrice (Susan Fleetwood): as the curtain rose she was fencing, cheerfully and affectionately, with Leonato, and she held on to her sword, occasionally feinting at Benedick (Roger Allam) with it, all through Act I, scene i. Finally she cast down one of her fencing gloves in front of him; he picked it up and tucked it in his belt, where it remained until he threw it at her on 'I cannot endure my lady Tongue'. (Benedick finally reclaimed it gently from her lap in Act V, scene ii.) This visual metaphor strongly established two things for the audience: Beatrice's unconventionality – her behaviour anything but ladylike, despite her gorgeous dress; and her passion for Benedick.

She could barely take her eyes off him for a second, and the sword-play seemed an almost desperate signal that she wished to engage in sexual encounter with him. In fact the production's foregrounding of the body was a striking characteristic (an emphasis not seen since 1968): beginning with the careless public stripping of the returning soldiers, and concluding with an extravagantly long luxurious kiss between Beatrice and Benedick, which left them both stunned; after a few lines she turned his face to her and kissed him again. In the church scene, also, after an intense, tearful exchange, their hands intertwined convulsively at Benedick's farewell; Beatrice kissed his clasping hands, and then touched his face as though brushing tears from it. The protagonists' physical and emotional need for each other had never been so strikingly presented. Fleetwood commented, 'Beatrice and Benedick are fearful of admitting to their love for each other. Full of defences. The near tragedy is that they almost lose one another and the joy is their voyage of self-discovery and final unity' (RSC publicity release).

'The heart of this production', Paul Lapworth wrote, 'was a powerful projection of real emotion', and he found it also in 'the reality of the behaviour of Don Pedro and Claudio rather than the malevolence of Don John ... there is a subtler and more disturbing villainy in the so-called "honourable" men, Don Pedro and Claudio'. John Carlisle as a brooding Don Pedro (developing a kinship suggested in his own Don John in the 1982 production), 'create[d] a character where on the page one barely exists':

> This is no princely cipher but an ageing Cavalier shrouded in solitude and hungry for emotional contact. Mr Carlisle enters into the proxy wooing of Hero with suspicious enthusiasm and proposes to Beatrice with direct urgency.
>
> (Michael Billington, *Guardian*, 12 April 1990)

By contrast, the affair between Claudio and Hero was that of callow youth, who did not seem to know much of sexual desire (Beatrice and Benedick looked in their thirties, both still in their sexual prime). Alex Kingston's Hero was all silly giggles, John McAndrew's Claudio an immature young man who thinks that first Don Pedro (by pulling rank and stealing his girl) and then Hero (by playing the whore) are out to insult and injure him.

The programme carried a solid essay by Lisa Jardine on the 'social conventions of the play ... recognisably those of early seventeenth-century England', particularly as they concerned 'marriage and courtship', 'reputation and honour'. It also had, as a number of programmes for previous productions had done, extracts from books describing the male camaraderie of military life, and the threat to it posed by emotional involvement with women. Alexander's psychological reading of the play as a text based in social reality allowed its characters' emotions to register directly with the audience: these were not comic or melodramatic types but 'real people' in 'real situations'. Nor was the audience distracted by a directorially-imposed historical period whose relevance might not be immediately obvious – 'There are no suffragettes in it, no cara- binieri, no Anglo-Indian colonels. Nobody enters riding a bicycle or exits eating an ice-cream; nobody wears sunglasses or Bermuda shorts', said John Gross with undisguised relief (*Daily Telegraph*, 15 April 1990).

The audience was 'ecstatic', reported Billington, though he himself and several other critics were more 'temperately enthusias- tic': he 'never quite felt this Beatrice and Benedick were one of nature's inevitable partnerships'. Others did, however – or at least they recognised a modern, rather than an idealised partnership: John Peter commented,

> Susan Fleetwood presents a brittle but earthy Beatrice: you sense that in her marriage to Benedick she will provide the solid psychological foundations and he will provide the imagination.
>
> How easy it would be to play Benedick as a shallow, witty fop! ... Allam does not take the easy path. His performance is articulated with delicacy and precision.
>
> (*Sunday Times*, 15 April 1990)

Roger Allam's 'thin-skinned Benedick' (Irving Wardle's phrase), despite his defensive bravado, was a characterisation along the lines established by Jacobi: the course of the play reveals his sensitivity as well as releasing his sexuality from the confines of male bonhomie. This, for late-twentieth-century audiences, is a profoundly-held fantasy (how often it is the basic material of the television sitcom romance); its complementary image is that of the witty and inde- pendent woman (sword-wielding Beatrice) whose libido is high but whose emotions run deep. Thus Beatrice in the eavesdropping scene:

> She has nowhere to hide. She flattens herself against the wall and listens in appalled recognition as Hero and Margaret [*sic*; actually

Ursula] take her character to pieces. When she is alone, Fleetwood's
emotional resources take over and the comic mask disappears.
(Irving Wardle, *Independent on Sunday*, 15 April 1990)

The audience heard a totally 'new' voice – the voice of profound
and passionate feeling – and the lights faded for the interval as
Beatrice stood, her hands clasped as if in prayer. The moment prepared us for the extremes of emotion of the church scene; however,
some of the older male critics still found Fleetwood's Beatrice a
little problematic:

> One cannot see [Allam's Benedick] surviving marriage to someone
> with Fleetwood's 'wild heart'. ... [On 'Kill Claudio':] Seconds before,
> Fleetwood has been exuding a touching tenderness. Now, all is femi-
> nist indignation rising to feral rage. In each case the actress is per-
> fectly plausible. She fails to reconcile lover and avenger.
> (Benedict Nightingale, *The Times*, 14 April 1990)

'Unfeminine' behaviour?

> It may seem perverse to complain about Susan Fleetwood, since she
> is probably the most gifted member of the cast. But that doesn't nec-
> essarily mean that she is an ideal Beatrice, and I can only say that I
> found a certain rawness in her acting – I could have done with a little
> more elegance and poise.
> (John Gross, *Sunday Telegraph*, 15 April 1990)

One wonders in what olde-worlde establishment these critics pursue
their 'ideals' – certainly not in the modern world, where at least in
the arts, the feminist revolution has established images of women
which accurately reflect their passion, their anger, their energy – all
of which Fleetwood presented, using only the Shakespearean text.
Beatrice, said Fleetwood, using a superbly unfeminine set of epi-
thets, is

> a wonderfully eruptive person, an oddball, like Benedick, they don't
> quite fit into their society. Beatrice is fascinating, quick-witted, vul-
> nerable, feels deeply and covers it up, has moments of pure joy and
> wants to fly just for the hell of it. She is delicious and courageous.[16]

The profound hunger for each other exhibited by this Beatrice and
Benedick did, ultimately, signal their marginal rather than their
central status in their society (in this respect there was no change
from Hands's 1982 production). *Their* marriage will succeed,

because of who they are, but it is a private bliss, rather than a public ceremony which will regenerate the community, as the extravagant final kiss paradoxically demonstrated. In fact the image of the community was distinctly shaky at the end of the play, despite a superficial air of festivity. Claudio and Hero remained children; or rather, had arrived at a mistrustful adolescence. Social contracts, whether of marriage or male comradeship, had been demonstrated to be hollow: Claudio was petulantly reluctant to take Benedick's hand on 'Come, come, we are friends'.[17] The final dance was performed to a lusty choral reprise of 'Sigh no more, ladies': it was an imposition of communal harmony which Susan Fleetwood thought inappropriate – the song 'says that men will always be unfaithful, and it completely negates what's gone before'.[18] Whether it was a deliberate irony on Alexander's part or an unthinking attempt to provide the traditional up-beat ending to a comedy, it failed finally to convince: the play itself, in this embodiment, was about a society's loss of faith in the conventions it had created and lived by for so long.

From Penny Gay, *As She Likes It: Shakespeare's Unruly Women* (London, 1994), pp. 143–77.

NOTES

[Penny Gay's consideration of *Much Ado About Nothing* is taken from her book, *As She Likes It: Shakespeare's Unruly Women* (London, 1994) in which she focuses on the way in which productions of Shakespeare's canon have altered over the last 50 years. It is a fascinating and pro-feminist account, especially in her recordings of interviews with the actresses themselves; there are also informative production stills which, unfortunately, it has not been possible to reproduce here. Ed.]

1. Pamela Mason, *Much Ado About Nothing: Text and Performance* (London, 1992), pp. 48, 50.

2. Robert Tanitch, *Ashcroft* (London, 1975). Ashcroft's voice famously retained its youthful lightness well into middle age.

3. John Gielgud, *An Actor and his Time* (1979; Harmondsworth, 1981), pp. 135, 136.

4. Ibid., p. 135.

5. Sally Beauman, *The Royal Shakespeare Company: a History of Ten Decades* (Oxford, 1982), p. 301: in 1969 'Christopher Morley created

a new permanent set that, with adaptations, was used for all the plays. It was a conscious stripping away of everything extraneous, creating a stage that was like a great empty box', lit in appropriate mood colours.

6. Pamela Mason recalls the masque as threatening: 'The stage was dimly lit and the soldiers wore threatening half-face visors with long, viciously pointed noses – their individuality was genuinely masked. They brandished drawn swords which were clashed menacingly at the end of the masque. While the military were welcomed for the colour, splendour and diversion they brought to Messina, bound up inextricably with this was a potential for evil' (*Much Ado About Nothing*, p. 57). Mason clearly agrees with my recollection of the masque as aggressively phallic; it seems somewhat unfair, however, to locate the source of the play's 'evil' in this display of gender difference, when the play itself is specific about the villainous motivations of Don John and his henchmen.

7. Gielgud, *An Actor and his Time*, p. 136.

8. Notes in the promptbook for the 1968 production, Shakespeare Centre Library.

9. Janet Suzman in Judith Cook, *Women in Shakespeare* (London, 1980), p. 33.

10. Suzman commented interestingly on this moment in different performances in London and Los Angeles: 'Here [London] everybody waits for it with baited [*sic*] breath. You can feel it and it makes you nervous. ... But in Los Angeles, they didn't know the story, and *Kill Claudio* when it happened was an absolute shock. Usually there was an audible gasp, which was terribly exciting. And you kind of yearn for that state of innocence in an audience, when they don't actually know what is going to happen' (*Plays & Players*, June 1973). A history of the performance of this critical moment can be found in J. F. Cox, 'The stage representation of the "Kill Claudio" sequence in *Much Ado About Nothing*', *Shakespeare Survey*, 32 (1979), 27–36.

11. Michael L. Greenwald, *Directions by Indirections: a Profile of John Barton* (London, 1985), p. 148. Judi Dench, commenting on her own conception of the role, said that she had found Barton's choice of period difficult because of the inappropriate 'racy' language of the girls – 'but I overcame it because John did create a terribly real household' (Cook, *Women in Shakespeare*, p. 33).

12. Judi Dench, interview Judith Cook, *Director's Theatre* (London, 1989) p. 127.

13. The programme included quotations about the 'officers' code' and an essay by Barbara Everett on the differing 'codes' of men and women: 'this is the first play, I think, in which the clash of these two worlds is

treated with a degree of seriousness, and in which the woman's world dominates': Barbara Everett, 'Something of great constancy' (first pub. 1961), repr. in John Russell Brown (ed.), *Much Ado About Nothing and As You Like It: A Casebook* (London, 1979), p. 95. [Barbara Everett's more recent essay on *Much Ado* is reprinted in this volume; see above pp. 51–68. – Ed.]

14. Derek Jacobi quoted in Judith Cook, *Shakespeare's Players* (London, 1983), p. 32.

15. Sinead Cusack in Carol Rutter, *Clamorous Voices: Shakespeare's Women Today* (London, 1988), pp. xvi–xvii.

16. Interview with Susan Fleetwood from an unidentified newspaper clipping, Shakespeare Centre Library.

17. Peter Holland, in his review for *Shakespeare Survey*, 44 (1992), 'Shakespeare performances in England, 1989–90', pp. 157–90, comments that in his opinion the production thought women 'of far less importance than male-bonding and an awareness of social hierarchies ... By the end of this production the relationship of Beatrice and Benedick mattered much less than Claudio and Benedick ... the play's climax was effectively the reconciliation of the two men with a handshake' (p. 171). I cannot agree with this assessment, as I thought Fleetwood's and Allam's performance together very strong and absolutely central, but our two responses are a good example of the way a critic reads the objective signs of a production from the point of view of what he/she finds interesting in its depiction of a society.

18. 'I just know that Beatrice would take that on board, and I can't look at Benedick while we're singing it, because then it would seem as if I were endorsing it' (Fleetwood interviewed by Vera Lustig, *Plays & Players*, February 1991).

5

Antitheatricality Staged: The Workings of Ideology in Shakespeare's *Much Ado About Nothing*

JEAN E. HOWARD

How a literary text relates to a context, whether verbal or social, is one of the many issues rethought in the last several decades of literary study. In the past, contextualising a literary work often meant turning it into an illustration of something assumed to be prior to the text, whether that something were an idea, a political event, or a phenomenon such as social mobility. This reading strategy had several problematic consequences. First, it seemed to suggest that texts had one primary determining context and that textual meaning could be stabilised by aligning a text with its 'proper' context. Second, it seemed to suggest that literary texts were always responses to, reflectors of, something prior to and more privileged than themselves by which they could be explained. This denied literature an initiatory role in cultural transformations or social struggles, and it seemed to foreclose the possibility that literature could have an effect on other aspects of the social formation, as well as being altered by them. Third, using literature as illustration of a context invited a flattening of that text, a denial of its plurality and contradictions in favour of a univocal reading of its relation to a particular contextual ground.[1]

I am now going to look at a Renaissance play that involves the representation of dramatic practices. That I do so following a discussion of the antitheatrical tracts [in the previous chapter of her book – Ed.] may seem to imply that I view these tracts as providing the context that will explain the plays with which I am concerned. It is not so simple. Plays, tracts, courtesy books – all are informed by a discourse of theatricality that does not by itself exhaust the meaning of any of these texts and is often deployed quite differently in each. I began with the antitheatrical tracts because they are so palpably political and selective in their condemnation of the theatre and of theatricality. Even though fissured by contradictions, these are unmistakably partisan documents aimed at intervening in the social struggles of the time. Most early modern plays operated somewhat differently, partly because they were part of an emergent commercial entertainment industry and usually did not announce themselves as having interested stakes in current social conflicts.[2] Consequently, it is not always easy to see that these plays were also implicated in the ideological and material struggles of their moment of production, especially because subsequent literary criticism has often turned them into 'timeless' objects above history and ideology. Talking about how playtexts participated in early modern conflicts over the theatre and theatricality is complicated, of course, by the fact that the performed plays were *embodiments* of theatricality as well as vehicles for *representing* the theatricality of fictional characters. In this chapter I am primarily going to deal with the representational level of these dramas, with their complex participation in antitheatrical discourse at the level of the dramatic narrative.

As part of a burgeoning entertainment industry, Renaissance plays gradually, but never totally, separated themselves from the overt didacticism of a homiletic tradition. Of course, enemies of the theatre saw it teaching Satan's lessons, and defenders such as Heywood argued that its fictions instilled both morality and patriotism in its spectators. Even the great moraliser, Ben Jonson, had to admit that the marketplace largely determined what shapes his fictions would take; and a playwright such as Shakespeare openly espoused an aesthetic of pleasure-giving, of delivering to audiences what they liked, as they liked it. Feste's refrain, 'And we'll strive to please you every day' (*Twelfth Night*, V.i.408), aptly summarises the first imperative governing play production in the public theatre. This hardly meant, however, that plays did not perform the work of ideology: the circulation of constructions of the real which serve particular interests but seem merely to express the natural order of things. As Althusser has convincingly shown, ideology most effectively sutures social subjects into their proper places in the social order when its workings are invisible to those subjects, when, for example, ideology passes as common sense, objective truth, or 'mere entertainment'.[3] In a materialist understanding of the world, in which class and other forms of stratification are preserved in part by means of ideological interpellation, no discourse, not even those we mark as literary, lies outside the domain of the ideological.[4] Ideology critique, itself never unsituated, examines the interests served by particular textual representations and narratives. It is a double-edged practice – part of a hermeneutics of suspicion, certainly, in that it assumes texts, and reading of texts, serve unannounced and unrecognised political ends; but part, too, of an ameliorative project to interrupt those processes by which privileged cultural narratives are used simply to legitimate the common sense of dominant social groups.

In thinking about the relationship of the early modern public stage to the circulation of ideology within Tudor and Stuart culture [... it is apparent that Shakespeare's *Much Ado About Nothing* – Ed.] effectively performs the essential work of ideology, that is the naturalisation of interested representations of the real. In particular, it employs antitheatrical discourse in a way that advantages certain social groups without calling attention to that fact. Once one begins to count, one discovers that *Much Ado* is filled with staged shows, inner plays, actors, and interior dramatists. Don Pedro and Don John both devise pageants designed to deceive specific audiences; most of Messina pretends to be someone else at a masked ball at the outset of the play; and the work ends with two shows involving Claudio: in one he plays the role of mourner before an empty tomb he believes contains his betrothed; in the other he plays the groom to a woman – really Hero – whom he believes to be Hero's cousin. I am interested in two things in regard to these aspects of the play: how these representations of theatrical practice function within the Elizabethan context to produce and reproduce class and gender difference within a social order dependent on these differences to justify inequalities of power and privilege, and how modern commentators have depoliticised the play by moralising it, that is, by focusing on the distinction between good and evil theatricality in the play, thus displacing a political analysis of why particular social groups 'naturally' play the opprobrious part in this moral drama.[5]

Reading the play in relationship to the antitheatrical tracts makes its political dimensions more apparent, I think, though Shakespeare's play does not participate in the overtly polemical rantings of those tracts. Far from placing the work 'above ideology' however, its distance from overtly polemical intention is what makes it an effective producer and disseminator of ideology, that is, of understandings of relations to the real so effectively naturalised that their constructed and interested character is obscured. Consequently, the ideological work performed by the discourse of theatricality in the play has to be unearthed through the work of ideology critique, through a strategy of reading aimed at speaking the unspoken of the text and at pressuring its contradictions to reveal its mediations of social struggle.

In regard to its representations of theatricality, one might expect *Much Ado* to be unequivocally positive. After all, the work itself is a play. But, just as support for the theatricality of *certain* groups can be found in the antitheatrical tracts, making them speak, as it were, against themselves, so Shakespeare's play speaks against itself in several important senses. Although *Much Ado* is a play, and although it dramatises a world permeated with theatrical practices, it also eventually leaves 'the better sort' in charge of theatrical practices and disciplines upstarts who would illegitimately seize such power. Read in relationship to the antitheatrical tracts, the play thus appears to police its own pro-theatre tendencies by acknowledging the validity of much antitheatrical polemic and reproducing its writing of the social order, especially its fear of the dangerous duplicity of women and of those who aspire beyond their station.

And yet, even as it enacts the disciplining of upstarts and the policing of theatrical power advocated by the antitheatrical tracts, the play as a material phenomenon – as produced on the Elizabethan public stage, rather than a modern one – literally involved men of low estate assuming the garments of women, playing the parts of kings and aristocrats, and gaining economic power from the sale of dramatic illusions. This is a case where the ideological function of the dramatic narrative comes into clear, if unacknowledged, conflict with the ideological implications of the material conditions of Elizabethan theatre production. Moreover, the play also speaks against itself in regard to its presentation of the relationship between truth and illusion. While it circulates the idea that in some absolute sense a true reading of the world is possible, a reading which eludes the 'distortions' and mediations of dramatic illusion, that view is countered by the dramatisation of a world in which truth is discursively produced and authorised and so remains unknowable outside a set of practices, including theatrical practices, which secure one understanding of the world at the expense of another.[6] To tease out these contradictions and to consider their ideological implications is the purpose of what follows.

At its centre *Much Ado* seems to dramatise the social consequences of staging lies. Don John precipitates the play's crisis by having a servant, Margaret, impersonate her mistress, Hero, in a love encounter observed by Hero's husband-to-be and Don John's brother. These theatrics make Hero appear a whore and lead directly to her denunciation in the church. This deception is clearly coded as evil: it is engineered by a bastard, involves the transgressive act of a servant wearing the clothes of one of higher rank, and leads to the threat of death for several of the play's characters.

Before discussing this evil trick further, however, I want to note the changes Shakespeare made in his source material which radically compounded the amount of theatricality in the play as a whole. For example, while all the sources contain the trick at the window, none contains the Benedick and Beatrice subplot which depends on Don Pedro's theatrical deceptions of each of them.[7] Moreover, while the source stories have two men, usually friends, vying for the Hero figure, Shakespeare substitutes, instead, a rivalry between Don Pedro and his bastard brother – not for actual possession of the woman – but for power, though the control of women is a chief way of establishing masculine power in the play.[8] This rivalry is largely carried on through competing theatrical tricks. If Don Pedro, the seeming agent for comic union, uses theatrical deception to promote marriages, Don John uses it to thwart his brother's fictions and to contest his brother's power.

The result of these changes is a series of highly overdetermined theatrical situations which betray a deeply conflictual psychic-social zone. None of the play's impersonations and playlets is unproblematical. When Don Pedro impersonates Claudio at the masked ball, for example, he doesn't unproblematically further Claudio's desires. Instead, his action opens the door for Don John's meddling and for a number of 'mistakings.' Moreover, even Don Pedro, the initiator of so much of the play's disguise and theatrical cozenage, cannot see through the pageant staged at Hero's window.

In trying to make sense of the play's treatment of theatricality, twentieth-century humanist criticism has typically made two moves: one involves drawing clear moral distinctions between 'good' and 'bad' theatrical practices; the other involves reassuring readers that the play offers ways to cope with – to see through – omnipresent theatrical deception. Richard Henze typifies the dominant critical position in discriminating between one form of theatrical deception which 'leads to social peace, to marriage, to the end of deceit' and another which 'breeds conflict and distrust and leads even Beatrice to desire the heart of Claudio in the marketplace'.[9] Later I will examine the implicit assumptions lying behind the disappointed phrase, 'even Beatrice', but for the moment I wish simply to point out that most readings of the play use the two brothers to figure good and evil theatricality. Indeed, most readings of the play depend, crucially, on maintaining differences in the motives of the two men and in the social consequences of their practices. Similarly, many readings insist on Shakespeare's insistence that beneath the world of unstable appearances there is a world of essences to which man has access if he has, paradoxically, either faith or careful noting skills. Those possessing faith, an essentially mystified notion encompassing both intuition and religious belief, can comprehend the truth which can't be seen, but which lies behind the distortions produced by deceivers. Thus Beatrice sees beyond the appearance of Hero's guilt; and Dogberry and Verges, God's naturals, intuitively know a thief despite misunderstanding utterly his actual language. On the other hand, illusion can also be pierced by careful noting, a pragmatic and practical skill, one paradoxically more congruent with the dawning scientific age than the waning age of faith. Thus the Friar is said to take careful note of Hero in the church and by her blushes and behaviour is able to pierce the lies of Don John's fictions. Henze, again, presents a characteristic summation of the dominant critical position: 'This combination of intuitive trust and careful observation seems to be the one that the play recommends'.[10] I wish to challenge the focus of this criticism, first by substituting a political and social for a moral analysis of the play's theatrical practices and, second, by looking, not at how the individual subject can discern truth, but at the role of authority and authoritative discourses in delimiting what can be recognised as true.

It is easy to provide a moral reading of Don John. He is the play's designated villain, its exemplification of the evil dramatist; and his chief deception – the substitution of Margaret for Hero at the bedroom window – is clearly a malicious act. Yet a characterological focus on Don John as origin of evil can obscure the extent to which the assumptions about women upon which his trick depends are shared by other men in the play. The trick at the window silently assumes and further circulates the idea that women are universally prone to deception and impersonation. This is a cultural construction of the feminine, familiar from the antitheatrical tracts, which serves the political end of justifying men's control and repression of the volatile and duplicitous female. Don John depends on the currency of this construction of woman in Messina, and he is not disappointed. Faced with Don John's accusations, many men – including Hero's father – quickly conclude she has merely been impersonating virtue.[11] In short, Don John lies about Hero, but his lie works because it easily passes in Messina as a truthful reading of women.

Second, while Don John is the play's villain, he is also the bastard brother of the play's highest-ranking figure. This fact is ideologically significant because it locates the 'natural' origins of social disruption in those who do not legitimately occupy a place in the traditional social order. Certainly, in the ideological economy of the play it is useful that the dangerous and threatening aspects of theatricality be located in and exorcised by the punishment of a scapegoat figure. While many figures *within* the play make Hero the scapegoat for their fears, for the audience the scapegoat is Don John, illegitimate intruder among the ranks of the aristocracy. Thus, much as in the antitheatrical tracts, women and 'bastards' (those who have no legitimate social position or have forsaken that position) are figured as the natural and inevitable source of social disruption and evil. Moreover, the very fact that Don John is a bastard further implicates women in crime. As Harry Berger writes: 'The play's two scapegoats are a bastard named Trouble and a woman named Hero, and his bastardy tells us where the blame lies: like Edmund, no doubt, he is a testimony both to his father's prowess and to his mother's sin – a by-product of the frailty named Woman.'[12]

Thus Don John is both a testimony to woman's weakness and a social outsider, someone tolerated within Messina society only on the say-so of his legitimate brother. He is, moreover, punished for usurping an activity – the manipulation of the world through theatrical fictions – which is from first to last in this play associated with aristocratic male privilege. While women are characterised as deceivers, literally, as Balthasar's song more accurately declares, it is 'men [who] were deceivers ever' (II.iii.63), especially men in power.[13] Don Pedro is, after all, the play's chief dissembler. It is he who first employs theatrical deception in his plan to woo Hero for Claudio, and he who then goes on to arrange the playlets by which Benedick and Beatrice are made to fall in love. When Claudio first approaches Don Pedro about marrying Hero, for example, the Prince volunteers in his own person to negotiate the contract between his retainer and his old friend's daughter. Moreover, while the Hero figure in the sources is of humble origins, this is not true of Shakespeare's Hero.[14] Don Pedro is thus not in the ambiguous position of sanctioning a marriage across class lines, but instead promotes a union between social equals and so strengthens the existing social order.

His actions in regard to Benedick and Beatrice are more complex, and I will discuss them further below, but what they achieve is the disciplining of social renegades and their submission to the authority of Don Pedro and to the institution of marriage which it seems his special function to promote. Benedick, of course, openly scoffs at marriage throughout a good portion of the play; and Beatrice turns aside a marriage proposal – however seriously meant – from Don Pedro himself. Through his staged pageants, Don Pedro asserts control over these two renegades and checks the socially subversive impulse their refusal to marry implies. What Don John by his deceptions thus usurps is the prerogative of theatrical deception by which his legitimate brother controls Messina. If Don Pedro is the one first to make use of impersonation and theatrical tricks, Don John is the copycat who imitates the initial trick at the bedroom window. If Don Pedro exercises power by arranging marriages, Don John counters that power by spoiling marriages and does so using the very tools of theatrical deception employed by Don Pedro. The bastard's acts thus appropriate a power the play seeks to lodge with the legitimate brother. At play's end, it is this aggression for which the worst punishment is promised.

Further, the very *way* the various deceptions of the two brothers are materially represented on the stage has specific ideological consequences. Don John's crucial deception is his substitution of maid for mistress at the bedroom window. This trick involves a transgression against hierarchy in which, as on the public stage itself, an inferior assumes the borrowed robes of a social superior. This action is not dramatised. Consigned to the realm of the 'unseen', its consequences disappear utterly – like a bad dream – at play's end. By contrast, Don Pedro's two most elaborate deceptions, the playlets put on for Benedick and Beatrice, *are* dramatised and are presented as part of the prerogatives of Messina's highest-ranking visitor. Ironically, these presentational choices naturalise Don Pedro's practice so that, as in all ideological effects, the arbitrary passes as the inevitable. Moreover, the theatre audience, knowing of Don Pedro's plans and taking pleasure in the spectacle of Benedick and Beatrice's recantation of prior positions, is fully complicit with Don Pedro's trick, legitimating it by laughter. By contrast, the bastard's acts are represented as evil and as so outside the natural order that they are assigned to the unreality of the unseen. There is no opportunity for audience involvement in the unfolding of his plot. What results is the production of differences between similar activities in ways that obscure the social differences justified and held in place by moral categories. As in the theatrical tracts, a key question turns out to be: whose fiction-making activities are to be construed as legitimate? And, as in those tracts, the answer involves matters of gender and rank as much as moral motive. Much modern criticism of the play, by focusing so resolutely on the morality of deception, has been complicit in allowing to pass unnoted the function of moral categories in reproducing existing power relations and social arrangements.

This criticism has also been obsessed with the problem of how we can 'see through' the play's many theatrical practices to a truth not obscured by lies. This play, more than most, seems to engender in readers fears about never getting to 'the real', but of being trapped in competing and manipulative discursive constructions of it. Focusing on getting outside of discourse, through either the empiricism of careful noting or the transcendentalism of faith, shortcircuits a political analysis of how truth effects are produced through discourse, and of the social origins of those dissenting perspectives through which 'truth' is exposed as somebody's truth.

The utopian nature of the desire to escape discourse is perhaps best seen by looking at the play's handling of Dogberry and Verges who, with their apparently intuitive recognition of villainy, are crucial to any reading which insists on the ultimate transparency of the world to the faithful and/or the astute. First of all, there is something improbable about their rescue of Messina from illusion. For three-quarters of the play illusions seem impermeable. Don Pedro and Claudio fall victim to them as do the witty and sceptical

Beatrice and Benedick. The world is only righted by two lower-class figures who flounder mightily in the Queen's English, and who capture the villains virtually by instinct rather than by any rational understanding of what was overheard or said or done by anyone. Moreover, it seems that the gift of intuition is bought at the price of speech and rationality. Dogberry and Verges exist almost outside of language, and this placement denies them any real social power. Constructed as God's naturals, these lower-class figures conveniently solve society's problems without ever threatening its central values or power relations or providing an alternative understanding of the social order.[15] Pathetically eager to please their betters, they are obsessively preoccupied with that phantom, Deformed, whose chief crime, besides thievery, seems to be that he 'goes up and down like a gentleman' (III.iii.126–7) and spends money beyond his ability or desire to repay it (V.i.308–12). Dogberry and Verges are as concerned as their betters to discipline upstarts. Unlike the more rebellious, clever, and even dangerous lower-class figures in some of Shakespeare's plays – Pompey, Jack Cade, Feste, Pistol – Dogberry and Verges perform a sentimental, utopian function. They keep alive the dream of a world where good and evil are transparent to the eye of innocence and inferiors correct the 'mistakings' of their betters without ever threatening the essential beliefs of those betters.

The utopian impulse simply to escape the world of deception and mediation not only finds its logical end in the garbled speech of Dogberry and Verges, but is also strongly countered by other aspects of the play's action which point to the conclusion that in a thoroughly dramatistic universe one can escape neither from discourse nor from the play of power which authorises the truth of one construction of the world over another. In Elizabethan culture and in this play, a chief form of power is, of course, theatrical power. The role of theatrical fictions as instruments of power and as a means of compelling belief in a particular view of truth is most graphically shown in Don Pedro's successful manipulation of Benedick and Beatrice. Readers often point out that these two are depicted as showing a keen interest in one another from the play's opening moments and as, perhaps, having once been romantically involved. By contrast, I want to focus on the role of Don Pedro's pageants in producing their love. While a modern discourse of love understands it as, essentially, a private, inwardly produced emotion which serves as the motive for marriage, in the Renaissance many upper-class marriages had other motives, political, economic, or social. In *Much Ado*, through the actions of Don Pedro one can see the investment of established authority in using marriage to reproduce existing social relations (both gender and class relations) and to control threats to the social order. Far from *discovering* Benedick's and Beatrice's pre-existent love, Don Pedro works hard to *create* it. When the two of them 'fall in love', they do not so much obey a spontaneous, privately engendered emotion as reveal their successful interpellation into particular positions within a gendered social order.[16] In this play, Don Pedro is the agent of such interpellation. He never indicates that he sees a repressed attraction between Benedick and Beatrice, nor does he present his fictions as simply revealing that truth. Instead, his object is to create love where its existence seems impossible and thus to control the social world around him. He places both Benedick and Beatrice as subjects of a love discourse in which a role for each to play is clearly marked, the role of 'the normal' male and female.

The two playlets, however, though having the same general aim of making social renegades conform, also produce gender difference in the process. To be a 'normal' male is not the same as being a 'normal' female. In discussing Beatrice before Benedick, Leonato and his friends construct her as a vulnerable, pitiful victim. Her tears, her sleeplessness, her indecision – all are dwelt on in loving detail. The role mapped for Benedick is to be her rescuer, to become more 'manly' by accepting his duty to succour women as well as to fight wars. And Benedick takes up his assigned place in the gendered social order by vowing to put aside his pride and accept her love. He presents his change of heart as a species of 'growing up'. As he says, 'A man loves the meat in his youth that he cannot endure in his age' (II.iii.238–40), and the misogyny he had embraced is an example of such meat now displaced by the maturer pleasure of peopling the world and receiving a woman's adoration. By contrast, the conversation staged for Beatrice only briefly focuses on Benedick's suffering. He is presented as the good man any woman would be a fool to scorn, but most of the attention focuses on how unnatural her pride, her wit, and her independence are. Her great sin is to be 'so odd, and from all fashions' (III.i.72), that is, so quick in mocking men who are to be revered, not exposed to ridicule. Tellingly, Beatrice shows her successful interpellation into the gendered social order by vowing to tame her 'wild heart' to Benedick's 'loving hand' (III.i.112) – like a bird or an animal being domesticated. He becomes the protector and tamer and she the tamed repentant. And while Beatrice's character continues to show traces of the merry-shrew schema which served as Shakespeare's basic model, the two interior plays decisively mark the turn in the subplot toward marriage and the partial righting of the social order by the interpellation of social renegades into gendered and socially less iconoclastic subject positions.

The whole feat constitutes a remarkable display of power on Don Pedro's part. Using theatrical means, he offers Benedick and Beatrice understandings of self and other that serve his own ends. That Benedick and Beatrice accept his fictions as truth depends on a number of factors, including the authority of those promulgating this vision of truth. Benedick and Beatrice believe the lies being voiced in the two eavesdropping encounters first because it is their friends who speak these lies. And while the cynical Benedick can imagine his friends as deceivers, he cannot think this of the grave Leonato. 'I should think this a gull, but that the white-bearded fellow speaks it. Knavery cannot sure himself in such reverence' (II.iii.118–20). Age has authorising force. Further, Don Pedro's constructions are taken as true because they have the authority of cultural stereotypes. He writes Benedick and Beatrice for one another in terms that resonate, as I have argued, with cultural definitions of 'man-in-love' and 'woman-in-love'. Similarly, Don Pedro and Claudio believe the deception at Hero's window, not only because they trust the testimony of their eyes, but also because what Don John tells them has the truth of stereotype as well. Hero is the whore whose appetites are disguised by the illusion of virtue. Moreover, once Don Pedro and Claudio doubt Hero, it is their authority which plays a large part in making Leonato doubt his own daughter in the church. Those further down the social scale have less legitimating power. When in Act I, scene ii Antonio tells Leonato that a serving man has heard the Prince say he wants to marry Hero, Leonato asks at once: 'Hath the fellow any wit that told you this?' When Antonio replies 'A good sharp fellow' (I.ii.17–18), Leonato still decides to 'hold it [the report] as a dream till it appear itself' (ii.20–1). Nothing causes such scepticism in a play in which everyone is remarkably credulous so much as the lowly social status of the reporter.

Consequently, although critics have been quick to deny that theatrical fictions create Benedick and Beatrice's love, the work can be read otherwise as encoding the process by which the powerful determine truth, and revealing the way belief depends upon a fiction's congruence with the common sense of culture. Told by several people that Don Pedro wooed Hero for himself, Claudio responds: ''Tis certain so, the Prince woos for himself. / Friendship is constant in all other things / Save in the office and affairs of love' (II.i.174–6). This truism makes it easy to believe the truth of a particular tale of violated friendship. The more a fiction draws on conventional schemata, the more it appears true to life.

In such a context the play reveals how hard it is for marginal figures to counter common sense or to overturn the constructions of the powerful, though social marginality is more likely than either careful noting or faith to be the cause of one's ability to see the arbitrary nature of power's truths. In this play, women are clearly marginal to the male order. When Hero hears herself named whore at her wedding, she does not contest that construction of herself; she swoons beneath its weight. It is as if there were no voice with which to protest the forces inscribing her within the order of 'fallen' women. Even the Friar, another figure marginal to the real power in Messina, cannot directly contest the stories endorsed by Don Pedro. He must work by indirection, knowing all the while that his fictions may not alter the fixed views of Claudio and Don Pedro and that Hero may live out her life in a convent. In this context, when existing authority so clearly predetermines what will count as truth, the use of the powerless Dogberry and Verges to rescue the world seems all the more a kind of wish fulfilment or magical thinking: an attempt to reconcile the recognition of power's power to determine the truth with a worldview in which truth stands outside its discursive production in a social field.

Beatrice's role in the church is more complex. Drawn to the pattern of the witty shrew, Beatrice for much of the play does not see the world as others see it. Early in the play she is depicted as resisting the patriarchal dictum that the natural destiny of all women is marriage; similarly, her response to the revelations about Hero reveals that she does not accept the misogynist dictum that all women are whores. It is precisely Beatrice's iconoclasm that Don Pedro's playlet seems designed to contain. Iconoclastic voices such as hers need to be recuperated or silenced. In the church, however, no recuperation of her position seems possible. She refuses Don John's assimilation of Hero to the stereotype of whore, but she cannot by her voice triumph over Don Pedro's authority. This, of course, is why she is driven to demand that Benedick 'Kill Claudio'

(IV.i.289), a statement which has led to her denunciation in a good deal of criticism (recall Henze's 'even Beatrice' which, by implicitly constructing women as peacemakers and repositories of good sense, writes their anger as more transgressive than men's), but which can be read as an acknowledgement that in a world where power resides in the words of powerful men, the violence their speaking can do can be successfully countered – not by the speaking of women – but by the literal violence of the sword.

Of course, at this juncture another ideological fissure opens in the play. When Benedick and Beatrice are depicted as standing out against marriage, they figure a challenge to the social order. When led to confess love for one another, they take up their places within that gendered order. But pretty clearly for Don Pedro their doing so was not supposed to threaten the patriarchal system. The wife was to be the tamed bird, submissive to her husband's hand, and the bonds between men were not seriously to be disturbed, as we see in Claudio's offer to marry and then promptly to escort Don Pedro on the next stages of his journey. He may be about to become a husband, but that seems not to disturb the primacy of his role as attendant upon the Duke. But, ironically, the bond with a woman *does* disrupt Benedick's bonds to men. The subject position of 'lover' into which Don Pedro was so eager to manoeuvre his friend comes into conflict with the claims of male friendship, producing disequilibrium in the social order. At first, Benedick as lover offered no threat to Don Pedro. His perfume, his shaving, his seeking out of Beatrice's picture – all his actions reveal him very much the stereotypical and somewhat comic lover. He is exhibiting the appropriate masculine behaviour Don Pedro and Claudio both intended to elicit and undergoing a rite of passage which marks him as 'of the company of men' in a new way. Beatrice's 'Kill Claudio', however, forces the issues of competing loyalties, revealing the potential contradictions in Benedick's position. And when Benedick is depicted as choosing faith in Beatrice over loyalty to Claudio and Don Pedro, these former friends are at first simply incredulous. They cannot credit this disruption of the patriarchal order.

The ending of the play 'takes care' of this problem. As is the case with many of Shakespeare's comedies, the ending of *Much Ado* has a strongly recuperative function as it attempts to smooth over the contradictions or fissures that have opened in the course of the play. In several obvious ways the ending seems to affirm the 'naturalness' of a hierarchical, male-dominated social order and to treat challenges to that order, and to the privileges of its beneficiaries, as mere illusions or temporary aberrations. For example, the tension between male–male and male–female bonds simply disappears with Borachio's confession. There is no duel, and in the final scene the renewed friendship of Claudio and Benedick, affirmed by the exchange of cuckold jokes, is as prominent as their simultaneous marriages. In addition, the transgressive appropriation of theatrical power by the bastard Don John collapses with equal suddenness. He is, as we learn by report, captured and held for punishment, but he is allowed no moment on the stage, a fact once more contributing to our sense that the threat he poses has no ultimate reality.

Less obvious, but equally necessary to a conservative righting of the social order, is the process by which Act V of *Much Ado* relegitimates theatricality as a vehicle for the exercise, by aristocratic males, of power. When Don Pedro became the credulous audience to his brother's fictions, it is as though – in the play's economy of power – he loses the ability to control the world of Messina. Not only Benedick and Beatrice, but Antonio and Leonato, as well, slide outside his control. Violence threatens on several fronts, and the Friar's feeble fictions affect very little. Even with Borachio's confession, no marriages occur. It is as if the world of Messina cannot be 'well' until the power of fiction making has been relodged with duly constituted authority. This occurs when the patriarch, Leonato, takes up the task of righting the social order through a series of fictions to be enacted at Hero's tomb and at a second wedding. Hero, having died for the imagined crime of the independent use of her sexuality, is reborn when rewritten as the chaste servant of male desire. While it is often argued that through the second wedding Claudio is being taught to have faith in womankind, despite appearances,[17] I read the wedding as a lesson in having faith in the authority of social superiors, a lesson to which Claudio is already predisposed. He has always been ready to take Don Pedro's advice, especially about love,[18] and the gift of Hero at play's end implies simply that rewards will continue to flow from such obedience. What he gets is the still-silent Hero, the blank sheet upon which men write whore or goddess as their fears or desires dictate.[19] The figure of the compliant woman becomes the instrument through which men (Claudio, Don Pedro, Antonio, and Leonato) reconcile their differences.

But while Hero is regranted the status of goddess, the antifeminism which caused her original denigration surfaces again in the horn jokes that figure so prominently in the play's final moments. 'There is no staff more reverent than one tipped with horn' (V.iv.123–4). As the antitheatrical tracts insist, women are duplicitous; they marry men to make them cuckolds. Admittedly, Claudio also says Benedick may prove a 'double dealer' (V.iv.114), but from line 44, when Claudio first mentions Benedick's fear of horns tipped with gold, the scene returns again and again to the threat men face in entrusting their honour to women in marriage. At the same time that the play quietly revalorises the exercise of theatrical power by aristocratic males, it continues to locate – now less in bastards, but still in women – the threat of a dangerous and unsanctioned theatricality. Moreover, while Beatrice is not 'silenced' at the end of the scene, she is emphatically less in charge than in earlier scenes, and her mouth is finally stopped with Benedick's kiss. Thereafter it is he who dominates the dialogue and proposes the dance with which to 'lighten' the men's hearts before they marry, as if the prospect is one which has made those hearts heavy.

A final word about the scene and its legitimation of aristocratic, male theatricality. Crucial to this project, as I see it, is the erasure of any lingering suspicion that the fictions of a Don Pedro or a Leonato tamper with nature, rather than express it more fully. Only then can dramatistic and essentialist views of the world be held in tenuous reconciliation. In fact, the final moments of the play can be read as advancing the proposition that, while illusion is everywhere, good fictions merely reveal a pre-existent truth of nature (Beatrice's and Benedick's love, Hero's chastity), while evil fictions (Hero's promiscuity) which distort nature melt like manna in the sun and their perpetrators disappear. Consequently, Benedick and Beatrice must both learn of Don Pedro's tricks and also affirm, willingly and freely, the reality of their love for one another. At first they demur. What leads to their capitulation is the production of love sonnets each has written. What their hands have penned, their hearts must have engendered. And yet, of course, the sonnet form in the 1590s was the most highly conventional genre imaginable. In it one finds already written the text of love. Having been constructed by Don Pedro as lovers, Benedick and Beatrice *must* write sonnets, their production attesting less to the pre-existence of their love than to their successful interpellation into a gendered social order. And yet, by happy sleight of hand, what is their *destiny* within that order is made to seem their *choice*. This manoeuvre affords another instance of inter-class accommodation as the aristocratic ideology of arranged property marriages is made to appear seamlessly compatible with emergent middle-class ideologies of love and individual choice as preconditions for marital union.

Shakespeare's romantic comedies often provide such utopian resolutions to the strains and contradictions of the period. The comic form, however, was not to serve Shakespeare, or, more properly, his culture, much longer in the form apparent in the high or romantic comedies. In 1604, in writing *Measure for Measure*, he creates a comic authority figure, the Duke, who increasingly uses the arts of theatre to order a disordered society. Yet in the end no one is convinced that the Duke's visions merely reveal a pre-existing social reality. (Does Angelo love Mariana and just not know it?) The ending of that play makes much clearer than does *Much Ado* that when power's fictions fail to be persuasive, coercion will enforce their truth. Eventually, in a play like *Lear*, the potential moral bankruptcy of authority and its power to compel – if not belief – at least compliance, are openly acknowledged: 'a dog's obey'd in office' (IV.vi.158–9).

Much Ado hints at these things, but only obliquely. It polices its positive depiction of omnipresent theatrical practices by creating a villainous and illegitimate fiction maker who simply tells lies. The play thus seems irreproachably conservative in its insistence that the power of theatrical illusion-mongering belongs in the hands of the better sort and that their fictions simply reproduce the truths of nature. And yet, as I have argued, the play differs from itself in ways that allow other readings – readings which reveal the constituative, as opposed to the reflective, power of discursive practices, including theatrical practices, and the role of authority, not nature, in securing the precedence of one truth over other possible truths. Moreover under the pressure of a political analysis, the play's production of heroes and villains becomes visible as a strategy for holding in place certain inequalities of power and privilege.

But in approaching the self-divisions and contradictions of this work, the contemporary critic has in one respect less access to these features of the play than did the Elizabethan theatregoer. We watch *Much Ado* within institutions which are citadels of high culture and which by and large employ middle-class actors of both sexes. People sitting in the new and culturally contested institution of the Elizabethan public theatre on the one hand watched a fiction in which the theatrical practices of a bastard and a woman wearing her mistress's clothes were roundly castigated, even while on the other the agents of representation were most certainly men of mean estate who for their own profit assumed the clothes of women and of noblemen on the stage. As Robert Weimann has argued, a potential contradiction exists between what is being represented and who is doing the representing and under what material conditions.[20] For all its affinities with the antitheatrical tracts, *Much Ado* simply because it *is* a stage play, cannot occupy the same cultural space or produce exactly the same ideological effects.

From Jean E. Howard, *The Stage and Social Struggle in Early Modern England* (London, 1994), pp. 47–9 and 57–72.

NOTES

[This essay by Jean Howard is taken from a chapter in her book *The Stage and Social Struggle in Early Modern England* (London, 1994) in which she uses New Historicism as a starting point for the investigation of a range of Early Modern plays. Howard is also one of the critics who helped develop the theory of New Historicism; see, for example, 'The New Historicism in Renaissance Studies', *English Literary Renaissance*, 16 (1986), 13–43. The essay included here has been influential as a fine example of a radical and imaginative New Historicist reading of Shakespearean comedy. Ed.]

1. I discuss the relationship of text to context more fully in 'The New Historicism in Renaissance Studies', *English Literary Renaissance*, 16 (1986), pp. 13–43.

2. For an excellent discussion of the commercial imperatives governing theatrical production and the theatre's distance from social practices and from prescriptive literature see Kate McLuskie in *Renaissance Dramatists* (Atlantic Highlands, NJ, 1989), especially pp. 224–9.

3. Louis Althusser, 'Ideology and Ideological State Apparatuses (Notes Towards an Investigation)', in *Lenin and Philosophy and Other Essays* (New York, 1971), pp. 171–2.

4. T. Bennett, *Outside Literature* (London, 1990), pp. 117–42.

5. A. Rossiter, *Angel with Horns and Other Shakespeare Lectures* (London, 1961), p. 67 is typical of most of the play's thematic critics when he says: 'Deception by appearances in love is patently what most of *Much Ado* is "about".' Other critics take a metadramatic tack. J. D. Huston, *Shakespeare's Comedies of Play* (New York, 1981), p. 2, for example, sees many of Shakespeare's early comedies dramatising and celebrating the artist's playful ordering of the world through dramatic art. In *Much Ado*, however, Huston argues: 'Shakespeare may be

dramatising reservations he is beginning to feel about his art and about the relationship between it and reality. He may be dramatically confronting the problem of recognising that there are limits to his assimilative powers, that reality may sometimes successfully resist his attempts to play with it, even in art' (p. 142).

6. I am indebted throughout the ensuing discussion to Michel Foucault's investigations in *Power/Knowledge: Selected Interviews and Other Writings, 1972–77*, ed. Colin Gordon (New York, 1980) of the interconnections between power and knowledge.

7. C. Prouty, *The Sources of 'Much Ado About Nothing'* (New Haven, CT, 1950), p. 1.

8. Ibid., p. 34.

9. Richard Henze, 'Deception in *Much Ado About Nothing*', *Studies in English Literature*, 11 (1971), 187–201; 188.

10. Ibid., p. 194.

11. Harry Berger, 'Against the Sink-a-Pace: Sexual and Family Politics in *Much Ado About Nothing*', *Shakespeare Quarterly*, 32 (1982), 302–13; 306–7. [Berger's assay is reprinted in this volume; see above, pp. 13–30 – Ed.]

12. Ibid., p. 311.

13. All quotations from Shakespeare's plays are taken from *The Riverside Shakespeare*, ed. G. Blakemore Evans (New York, 1974).

14. Prouty, *The Sources*, pp. 43–4.

15. E. Kreiger, 'Social Relations and the Social Order in *Much Ado About Nothing*', *Shakespeare Survey*, 32 (1979), 49–61; p. 61.

16. For an important discussion of the discursive production of desire and of gendered subjectivities, see J. Henriques, W. Holloway, K. Urwin, C. Venn and V. Walkerdine (eds), *Changing the Subject: Psychology, Social Regulation and Subjectivity* (New York, 1984), pp. 203–63.

17. C. Dennis, 'Wit and Wisdom in *Much Ado About Nothing*', *Studies in English Literature*, 13 (1973), 223–37; 231–5.

18. Ralph Berry, *Shakespeare's Comedies: Explorations in Form* (Princeton, NJ, 1972), p. 169.

19. C. Cook in '"The Sign and Semblance of Her Honor": Reading Gender Difference in *Much Ado About Nothing*', *Proceedings of the Modern Language Association*, 101 (1986), 186–202; 192, argues that Hero's silence elicits male fears that women are not readable and calls forth their repeated rewritings of her. For a view of Beatrice quite different from my own, see the rest of Cook's article in which she pre-

sents Beatrice as inscribed within a male subject position and so posing no threat to the masculine social order.

20. R. Weimann, 'Towards a Literary Theory of Ideology: Mimesis, Representation, Authority', in *Shakespeare Reproduced: The Text in History and Ideology*, ed. Jean E. Howard and Marion F. O'Connor (London, 1987), pp. 265–72; p. 268.

6

The Turn of the Shrew

JOEL FINEMAN

> **Hortensio**   Now go thy ways, thou has tam'd a curst shrew.
> **Lucentio**   'Tis a wonder, by your leave, she will be tam'd so.
>   (V.ii.188–9)

In ways which are so traditional that they might be called proverbial, Shakespeare's *Taming of the Shrew* assumes – it turns out to
make no difference whether it does so ironically – that the language
of woman is at odds with the order and authority of man. At the
same time, again in ways which are nothing but traditional, the
play self-consciously associates this thematically subversive discourse of woman with its own literariness and theatricality. The
result, however, is a play that speaks neither for the language of
woman nor against the authority of man. Quite the contrary: at the
end of the play things are pretty much the same – which is to say,
patriarchally inflected – as they were at or before its beginning, the
only difference being that now, because there are more shrews than
ever, they are more so. It cannot be surprising that a major and
perennially popular play by Shakespeare, which is part of a corpus
that, at least in an English literary tradition, is synonymous with
what is understood to be canonical, begins and ends as something

orthodox. Nevertheless, there is reason to wonder – as my epigraph, the last lines of the play, suggests – how it happens that a discourse of subversion, explicitly presented as such, manages to resecure, equally explicitly, the very order to which it seems, at both first and second sight, to be opposed. This question, raised by the play in a thematic register, and posed practically by the play by virtue of the play's historical success, leads to another: is it possible to voice a language, whether of man or of woman, that does not speak, sooner or later, self-consciously or unconsciously, for the order and authority of man?

Formulated at considerably greater levels of generality, such questions have been advanced by much recent literary, and not only literary, theory, much of which finds it very difficult to sustain in any intelligible fashion an effective critical and adversary distance or difference between itself and any of a variety of master points of view, each of which claims special access to a global, universalising truth. It is, however, in the debates and polemics growing out of and centring upon the imperial claims of psychoanalysis that such questions have been raised in the very same terms and at precisely the level of generality proposed by *The Taming of the Shrew* – the level of generality measured by the specificity of rubrics as massive and as allegorically suggestive as Man, Woman, and Language – for it is psychoanalysis, especially the psychoanalysis associated with the name of Jacques Lacan, that has most coherently developed an account of human subjectivity which is based upon the fact that human beings speak. Very much taking this speech to heart, psychoanalysis has organised, in much the same ways as does *The Taming of the Shrew*, the relationship of generic Man to generic Woman by reference – to the apparently inescapable patriarchalism occasioned by the structuring effects of language – of Language, that is to say, which is also understood in broad genericising terms. In turn, the most forceful criticisms of psychoanalysis, responding to the psychoanalytic provocation with a proverbial response, have all been obliged, again repeating the thematics of *The Taming of the Shrew*, to speak against this Language for which the psychoanalytic speaks.

Thus it is not surprising, to take the most important and sophisticated example of this debate, that Jacques Derrida's (by comparison) very general critique of logocentric metaphysics, his deconstructive readings of what he calls the ontotheological ideology of presence in the history of the West, turns more specifically into a critique of phallogocentric erotics in the course of a series of rather pointed (and, for Derrida, unusually vociferous) attacks on Lacanian psychoanalysis. Lacan serves Derrida as a kind of limit case of such Western 'presence', to the extent that Lacan, centring the psychology of the human subject on a lack disclosed by language, deriving human desire out of a linguistic want, is prepared to make a presence even out of absence, and, therefore, as Derrida objects, a God out of a gap. As is well known, Derrida opposes to the determinate and determining logic of the language of Lacan – though with a dialectic that is of course more complicated than that of any simply polar opposition – an alternative logic of *différance* and writing, associating this a-logical logic with a 'question of style' whose status as an irreducible question keeps alive, by foreclosing any univocal answer, the deconstructive power of a corresponding 'question of woman'. Here again, however, it is possible to identify the formulaic ways in which this Derridean alternative to a psychoanalytic logos recapitulates, because it predicates itself as something Supplementary and Other, the general thematics of *The Taming of the Shrew*. And this recapitulation has remained remarkably consistent, we might add, in the more explicitly feminist extensions of the deconstructive line traced out by Derrida, all of which, for all the differences between them, attempt to speak up for, and even to speak, a different kind of language than that of psychoanalytic man (e.g., the preverbal, presymbolic 'semiotic' of Julia Kristeva, the *écriture féminine* of Hélène Cixous, the intentionally duplicitous or bilabial eroticism of Luce Irigaray, the Nietzschean narcissism of Sarah Kofman).[1]

This theoretical debate between psychoanalysis and the deconstructive feminisms that can be called, loosely speaking, its most significant other is in principle interminable to the extent that psychoanalysis can see in such resistance to its Language, as Freud did with Dora, a symptomatic confirmation of all psychoanalytic thought. In the context of this debate, *The Taming of the Shrew* initially possesses the interest of an exceptionally apt literary example, one to which the different claims of different theories – about language, desire, gender – might be fruitfully applied. On the other hand, to the extent that this debate appears itself to re-enact the action that is staged within *The Taming of the Shrew*, there exists the more than merely formal possibility that the play itself defines the context in which such debate about the play will necessarily take place. Understood in this way, the theoretical quarrel that might take place about *The Taming of the Shrew* would then emerge as nothing more than an unwitting reproduction of the thematic quarrel – between Man and Woman or between two different kinds of language – that already finds itself in motion in *The Taming of the Shrew*. If this were the case – and it remains to determine with what kind of language one might even say that this is the case – then the self-conscious literariness of *The Taming of the Shrew*, the reflexively recursive metatheatricality with which the play presents itself as an example of what it represents, would acquire its own explanatory, but not exactly theoretical, value. Glossing its own literariness, the play becomes the story of why it is the way it is, and this in turn becomes a performative account or self-example of the way a theoretical debate centred around the topoi of sexuality, gender, and language appears to do no more than once again repeat, to no apparent end, an old and still ongoing story.

That the story is in fact an old one is initially suggested by the ancient history attaching to the three stories joined within *The Taming of the Shrew*: the Christopher Sly framing plot, where a lord tricks a peasant into thinking himself a lord, which goes back at least as far as a fable in *The Arabian Nights*; the story of Lucentio's wooing of Bianca, which can be traced back, through Gascoigne and Ariosto, to Plautus or Menander; and the taming story proper, Petruchio's domestication of the shrewish Kate, which is built up out of innumerable literary and folklore analogues, all of which can claim an antique provenance. Correlated with each other by means of verbal, thematic, and structural cross-references, these three independent stories become in *The Taming of the Shrew* a single narrative of a kind whose twists and turns would seem familiar even on first hearing. Indeed, the only thing that is really novel about the plotting of *The Taming of the Shrew* is the way the play concatenates these three quite different stories so as to make it seem as though each one of them depends upon and is a necessary version of the other two.

Moreover, the play itself insists upon the fact that it retells a master plot of Western literary history. By alluding to previous dramatic, literary, and biblical texts, by quoting and misquoting familiar tags and phrases, by parodically citing or miming more serious literary modes (e.g., Ovidian narrative and Petrarchan lyric), the play situates itself within a literary tradition to which even its mockery remains both faithful and respectful. This is especially the case with regard to the taming subplot that gives the play its name. Soon after he enters, for example, Petruchio cites proverbial precursors for the cursing Kate, in one brief passage linking her not only to the alter ego of the Wife of Bath but also to the Cumaean Sibyl and Socrates' Xantippe (I.ii.69–71) (these references later to be counterbalanced by Kate's translation to 'a second Grissel, and Roman Lucrece' [II.i.295–6]).[2] Such women are all touchstones of misogynistic gynaecology. The commonplace way in which Petruchio evokes them here, drawing from a thesaurus of women whose voices will systematically contradict the dictates of male diction, is characteristic of the way, from beginning to end, the play works to give archetypal resonance and mythological significance to Kate's specifically female speech, locating it in the context of a perennial iconography for which the language of woman – prophetic and erotic, enigmatic and scolding, excessive and incessant – stands as continually nagging interference with, or as seductive and violent interruption of, or, finally, as loyally complicitous opposition to, the language of man.

What kind of language is it, therefore, that woman speaks, and in what way does it differ, always and forever, from the *language* of man? The first answer given by *The Taming of the Shrew* is that it is the kind of language Petruchio speaks when he sets out to teach to Kate the folly of her ways. 'He is more shrew than she' (IV.i.85) summarises the homeopathic logic of the taming strategy in accord with which Petruchio, assimilating to himself the attributes of Kate, will hold his own lunatic self up as mirror of Kate's unnatural nature. As perfect instance and reproving object lesson of his wife's excess, Petruchio thus finds 'a way to kill a wife with kindness' (IV.i.208). As an example which is simultaneously a counter-example, 'He kills her in her own humour' (IV.i.180). All Petruchio's odd behaviour – his paradoxical and contradictory assertions, his peremptory capriciousness, his 'lunacy', to use a word and image that is central to *The Taming of the Shrew* – presupposes this systematic and admonitory programme of an eye for an eye, or, as the play defines the principle: 'being mad herself, she's madly mated. / I warrant him, Petruchio is Kated' (III.ii.244–5; 'mated' here meaning 'amazed' as well as 'matched'). Moreover, all this madness bespeaks the language of woman, for Petruchio's lunatic behaviour, even when it is itself non-verbal, is understood to be a corollary function, a derivative example, of the shrewish voice of Kate, as when Petruchio's horrific marriage costume, a demonstrative insult to appropriate decorum – 'A monster, a very monster in apparel' (III.ii.69–70) – is taken as a statement filled with a didactic sense: 'He hath some meaning in his mad attire' (III.ii.124).

In Act I, scene ii, which is the first scene of the taming subplot, Grumio, Petruchio's servant, explains the meaning as well as the method of Petruchio's madness. At the same time, he suggests how this is to be related to all the action, especially the verbal action, of the play:

> A' my word, and she knew him as well as I do, she would think scolding would do little good upon him. She may perhaps call him half a score knaves or so. Why, that's nothing; and he begin once, he'll rail in his rope-tricks. I'll tell you what, sir, and she stand him but a little, he will throw a figure in her face, and so disfigure her with it that she shall have no more eyes to see withal than a cat.
>
> (I.ii.108–15)

This is an obscure passage, perhaps intentionally so, but 'the general sense', as the editor of the Oxford edition says, 'must be that Petruchio's railing will be more violent than Katherine's'.[3] Even so, it is the manner of the passage, more than its somewhat bewildering matter, that best conveys 'the general sense' of Petruchio's project, a point brought out by the apparently unanswerable puzzle posed by 'rope-tricks'. On 'rope-tricks' the Oxford editor says: 'If emendation is thought necessary, "rhetricks" is the best yet offered; but "rope-tricks" may well be correct and may mean tricks that can be punished adequately only by hanging.' The *Riverside* edition offers a similar answer to the 'rope-tricks' question, but does so with even more uncertainty, as evidenced by the parenthetical question-marks that interrupt the gloss: '*rope-tricks*: blunder for *rhetoric* (an interpretation supported by *figure* in line 114(?) or tricks that deserve hanging(?)'.

On the face of it, neither of these edgily tentative editorial comments is especially helpful in determining, one way or the other, whether Petruchio, when he 'rails in his rope-tricks', will be doing something with language or, instead, performing tricks for which he should be hanged. The 'interpretation', as the *Riverside* edition calls it, remains indeterminate. But such determination is of course not the point. The editors recognise – and so too, presumably, does an audience – that it is for what he does with language that Petruchio runs any risk with (bawdy) rope. Hence the special suitability of 'rope-tricks' as a term to describe the way in which Petruchio will respond to Kate in verbal kind. Playing on 'rhetoric' and on 'rope', but being neither, 'rope-tricks' simultaneously advances, one way *and* the other, both the crime (rape) and the punishment (rope) attaching to the extraordinary speech the play associates with Kate (rhetoric). 'Rope-tricks', moreover, is a uniquely performative word for rhetoric, since 'rope-tricks' *is* rhetoric precisely because it is not 'rhetoric', and thus discloses, by pointing to itself, a kind of necessary disjunction between itself as a verbal signifier and what, as a signifier, it means to signify. In this way, as a kind of self-remarking case of rhetoric in action, 'rope-tricks' becomes the general name not only for all the figurative language in the play but, also, for all the action in the play which seems literally to mean one thing but in fact means another: for prime example, the way in which Petruchio will speak the language of woman in order to silence Kate.

The point to notice about this is that, as far as the play is concerned, the 'interpretation' of 'rope-tricks', its meaning, is not altogether indeterminate or, rather, if it is indeterminate, this indeterminacy is itself very strictly determined. 'Rope-tricks' is a word that univocally insists upon its own equivocation, and this definitive indeterminacy is what defines its 'general sense'. In a way that is not at all paradoxical, and in terms which are in no sense uncertain, the question posed by 'rope-tricks' has as its answer the question of rhetoric, and the play uses this circularity – the circularity that makes the rhetoricity of a rhetorical question itself the answer to the question that it poses – as a paradigmatic model for the way in which, throughout the play, Petruchio will obsessively answer Kate with hysterical tit for hysterical tat.

Understood in this way, as 'rope-tricks', we can say that the words and actions of *The Taming of the Shrew* rehearse a familiar antagonism, not simply the battle between the sexes but, more specifically, though still rather generally, the battle between the determinate, literal language traditionally spoken by man and the figurative, indeterminate language traditionally spoken by woman. But by saying this we are only returned, once again, to the question with which we began, for if such indeterminacy is what rhetoric always means to say, if this is the literal significance of its 'general sense', why is it that this indeterminacy seems in *The Taming of the Shrew* so definitively to entail the domestication of Kate? Petruchio is never so patriarchal as when he speaks the language of woman – 'He is more shrew than she' – just as Kate's capitulation occurs at the moment when she obediently takes her husband at his lunatic, female, figurative word. This happens first when Petruchio forces Kate to call the sun the moon, and then when Petruchio forces Kate to address a reverend father as 'young budding virgin', a purely verbal mix-up of the sexes that leads an onlooker to remark: 'A will make the man mad, to make a woman of him' (IV.v.35–6). In accord with what asymmetrical quid pro quo does Petruchio propose to silence Kate by speaking the language she speaks, and why does the play assume that the orthodox order of the sexes for which it is the spokesman is reconfirmed when, madly translating a man into a mad woman, it gives explicit voice to such erotic paradox? Why, we can ask, do things not happen the other way around?

These are questions that bear on current theory. The editorial question-marks that punctuate the gloss on 'rope-tricks' mark the same site of rhetorico-sexual indeterminacy on which Derrida, for example, will hinge his correlation of 'the question of style' with 'the question of woman' (this is the same disruptive question-mark, we can note, that Dora dreams of when she dreams about her father's death).[4] But again, such questions are foregrounded *as* questions in *The Taming of the Shrew*, and in a far from naïve manner. We learn, for example, in the very first lines of the play performed for Christopher Sly that Lucentio has come 'to see fair Padua, the nursery of arts' (I.i.2), having left his father's 'Pisa, renowned for grave citizens' (I.i.10). Lucentio's purpose, he says, is to 'study / Virtue and that part of philosophy / ... that treats of happiness' (I.i.17–19). This purpose stated, and the crazy psycho-geography of Padua thus established by its opposition to sober Pisa, Tranio, Lucentio's servant, then rushes to caution his master against too single-minded a 'resolve / To suck the sweets of sweet philosophy' (ll.27–8): 'Let's be no Stoics nor no stocks', says Tranio, 'Or so devote to Aristotle's checks / As Ovid be an outcast quite abjur'd' (ll.31–2). Instead, Tranio advises his master to pursue his studies with a certain moderation. On the one hand, says Tranio, Lucentio should 'Balk logic with acquaintance that you have', but, on the other, he should also 'practice rhetoric in your common talk' (ll.34–5). This is the initial distinction to which all the subsequent action of the play consistently and quite explicitly refers, a distinction that starts out as the difference between logic and rhetoric, or between philosophy and poetry, or between Aristotle and Ovid, but which then becomes, through the rhetorical question raised by 'rope-tricks', the generalised and – for this is the point – quite *obviously* problematic difference between literal and figurative language on which the sexual difference between man and woman is seen to depend.

Tranio's pun on 'Stoics' / 'stocks', a pun which is a tired commonplace in Elizabethan comic literature, suggests both the nature of the problem and the way in which the play thematically exploits it. The pun puts the verbal difference between its two terms into question, into specifically rhetorical question, and so it happens that each term is sounded as the mimic simulation of the other. If language can do this to the difference between 'Stoics' and 'stocks', what can it do to the difference between 'man' and 'woman'? Is the one the mimic simulation of the other? This is a practical, as well as a rhetorical, question raised by the play, because the play gives countless demonstrations of the way in which the operation of stressedly rhetorical language puts into question the possibility of distinguishing between itself and the literal language it tropes. Petruchio, for example, when we first meet him, even before he hears of Kate, tells Grumio, his servant, to 'knock me at the gate' (I.ii.11). The predictable misunderstanding that thereupon ensues is then compounded further when a helpful intermediary offers to 'compound this quarrel' (l.27). These are trivial puns, the play on 'knock' and the play on 'compound', but their very triviality suggests the troubling way in which the problematic question raised by one word may eventually spread to, and be raised by, all. 'Knock at the gate', asks Grumio, 'O heavens! Spake you not these words plain?' (ll.39–40).

Given the apparently unavoidable ambiguity of language or, at least, the everpresent possibility of such ambiguity, it is precisely the question, the rhetorical question, of speaking plainly that Grumio raises, as though one cannot help but 'practice rhetoric' in one's 'common talk'. Moreover, as the play develops it, this argument between the master and his servant, an argument spawned by the rhetoricity of language, is made to seem the explanation of Kate's ongoing quarrel with the men who are her master. For example, the same kind of 'knocking' violence that leads Petruchio and Grumio to act out the rhetorical question that divides them is what later leads Kate to break her lute upon her music-master's head: 'I did but tell her she mistook her frets ... And with that word she strook me on the head' (II.i.149–53).

Such 'fretful' verbal confusions occur very frequently in the play, and every instance of them points up the way in which any given statement, however intended, can always mean something other than what its speaker means to say. For this reason, it is significant that, in almost the first lines of the play, Christopher Sly, after being threatened with 'a pair of stocks' (Ind.i.2), explains not only why this is possibly the case but, really, why this is necessarily the case, formulating, in a 'rope-trick' way, a general principle that accounts for the inevitability of such linguistic indeterminacy. '*Paucas pallabris*', says Christopher Sly, 'let the world slide' (Ind. i.5). The bad Spanish here is a misquotation from *The Spanish Tragedy*, Hieronimo's famous call for silence. An Elizabethan audience would have heard Sly's '*paucas pallabris*' as the comic application of an otherwise serious cliché, i.e., as an amusing deformation of a formulaic tag (analogous to Holofernes' '*pauca verba*' in *Love's Labour's Lost* [IV.ii.165]), whose 'disfiguring' corresponds to the troping way in which Sly mistakenly recalls Hieronimo by swearing by 'Saint Jeronimy' (Ind.i.9). So too with Sly's 'let the world slide', which is equally proverbial, and which is here invoked as something comically and ostentatiously familiar, as something novel just *because* it sounds passé, being half of a proverb whose other half Sly pronounces at the end of the frame, in the last line of the induction, which serves as introduction to the play within the play: 'Come madam wife, sit by my side, and let the world slip, we shall ne'er be younger' (Ind.ii.142–3).

Taken together, and recognising the register of self-parody on which, without Sly's knowing it, they seem to insist, the two phrases make a point about language that can serve as a motto for the rest of the play. There are always fewer words than there are meanings, because a multiplicity of meanings not only can but always will attach to any single utterance. Every word bears the burden of its hermeneutic history – the extended scope of its past, present, and future meanings – and for this reason every word carries with it a kind of surplus semiotic baggage, an excess of significance, whose looming, even if unspoken, presence cannot be kept quiet. Through inadvertent cognate homophonies, through uncontrollable etymological resonance, through unconscious allusions and citations, through unanticipatable effects of translation (*translatio* being the technical term for metaphor), through syntactic slips of the tongue, through unpredictable contextual transformations – in short, through the operation of 'rope-tricks', the Word (for example, Sly's 'world') will 'slide' over a plurality of significances, to no single one of which can it be unambiguously tied down. Sly's self-belying cry for silence is itself an instance of a speech which is confounded by its excess meaning, of literal speech which is beggared, despite its literal intention, by an embarrassment of unintended semiotic riches. But the play performed before Sly – with its many malapropisms, its comic language lesson, its mangled Latin and Italian, its dramatic vivifications of figurative play, as when Petruchio bandies puns with Kate – demonstrates repeatedly and almost heavy-handedly that the rhetorical question raised by Grumio is always in the polysemic air: 'Spake you not these words plain?'

It would be easy enough to relate the principle of '*paucas pallabris*' to Derrida's many characterisations of the way the ever present possibility of self-citation – not necessarily parodic citation – codes every utterance with an irreducible indeterminacy, leaving every utterance undecidably suspended, at least in principle, between its literal and figurative senses. Even more specifically, it would be possible to relate the many proverbial ways in which the 'wor(l)d' 'slides' in *The Taming of the Shrew* – '"He that is giddy thinks the world goes round"' (V.ii.26), a proverb that can lead, as Kate remarks, to 'A very mean meaning' (l.31) – to Lacan's various discussions of the not so freely floating signifier.[5] But, even if it is granted, on just these theoretical grounds, that the rhetoricity of language enforces this kind of general question about the possibility of a speaker's ever really being able to mean exactly what he means to say, and even if it is further granted that the 'practice' of 'rhetoric in common talk' is a self-conscious issue in *The Taming of the Shrew*, still, several other, perhaps more pressing, questions still remain. Why, for example, does the indeterminate question of rhetoric call forth the very determinate patriarchal narrative enacted in *The Taming of the Shrew*? Putting the same question in a theoretical register, we can ask why the question of rhetoric evokes from psychoanalysis the patriarchalism for which Lacan appears to be the most explicit mouthpiece, just as the same question provokes, instead, the antipatriarchal gender deconstructions – the chiasmically invaginated differences, the differentiated differences, between male and female – for which we might take Derrida to be the most outspoken spokesman. To begin to think about these questions, it is necessary first to recognise that *The Taming of the Shrew* is somewhat more specific in its account of female language than I have so far been suggesting. For there is of course another woman in the play whose voice is strictly counterposed to the 'scolding tongue' (I.i.252) of Kate, and if Kate, as shrew, is shown to speak a misanthropic, 'fretful' language, her sister, the ideal Bianca of the wooing story, quite clearly speaks, and sometimes even sings, another and, at least at first, a more inviting tune. There are, that is to say, at least two kinds of language that the play associates with women – one good, one bad – and the play invents two antithetical stereotypes of woman – again, one good, one bad – to be the voice of these two different kinds of female speech.

This is a distinction or an opposition whose specific content is often overlooked, perhaps because Bianca's voice, since it is initially identified with silence, seems to speak a language about which there is not that much to say. Nevertheless, this silence of Bianca has its own substantial nature, and it points up what is wrong with what, in contrast, is Kate's vocal or vociferating speech. In the first scene of the play within the play, which is where we first meet these two women, Lucentio is made to be a witness to the shrewish voice of Kate – 'That wench is stark mad or wonderful froward' (I.i.69) – and this loquacity of Kate is placed in pointed contrast to Bianca's virgin muteness: 'But in the other's silence do I see / Maid's mild behaviour and sobriety' (ll.70–1). This opposition, speech versus silence, is important, but even more important is the fact that it is developed in the play through the more inclusive opposition here suggested by the metaphorical way in which Lucentio 'sees' Bianca's 'silence'. For Bianca does in fact speak quite often in the play – she is not literally mute – but the play describes this speech, as it does Bianca, with a set of images and motifs, figures of speech, that give both to Bianca and to her speaking a specific phenomenality which is understood to be *equivalent* to silence. This quality, almost a physical materiality, can be generally summarised – indeed, generically summarised – in N terms of an essential visibility: that is to say, Bianca and her language both are silent because the two of them are something to be *seen*.

One way to illustrate this is to recall how the first scene repeatedly emphasises the fact that Lucentio falls in love with Bianca at first sight: 'let me be a slave, t'achieve that maid / Whose sudden sight hath thrall'd my wounded eye' (I.i.219–20). A good deal of Petrarchan imagery underlies the visuality of Lucentio's erotic vision: 'But see, while idly I stood looking on, / I found the effect of love in idleness' (I.i.150–1). More specifically, however, this modality of vision, this generic specularity, is made to seem the central point of difference between two different kinds of female language whose different natures then elicit in response two different kinds of male desire. There is, that is to say, a polar contrast, erotically inflected, between, on the one hand, the admirably dumb visual language of Bianca and, on the other, the objectionably noisy 'tongue' (I.i.89) of Kate:

> Tranio   Master, you look'd so longly on the maid ...
> Lucentio   O yes, I saw sweet beauty in her face ...
> Tranio   Saw you no more? Mark'd you not how her sister
>   Began to scold, and raise up such a storm
>   That mortal ears might hardly endure the din?
> Lucentio   Tranio, I saw her mortal lips to move,
>   And with her breath she did perfume the air.
>   Sacred and sweet was all I saw in her.
>
> (I.i.165–76)

In *The Taming of the Shrew* this opposition between vision and language – rather, between a language which is visual, of the eye, and therefore silent, and language which is vocal, of the tongue, and therefore heard – is very strong. Moreover, as the play develops it, this is a dynamic and a violent, not a static, opposition, for it is just such vision that the vocal or linguistic language of Kate is shown repeatedly to speak against. In the first scene this happens quite explicitly, when Kate says of Bianca, in what are almost the first words out of Kate's mouth, 'A pretty peat! It is best / Put a finger in the eye, and she knew why' (I.i.78–9). But this opposition runs throughout the play, governing its largest dramatic as well as its thematic movements. To take an example which is especially significant in the light of what has so far been said, we can recall that the 'rope-tricks' passage concludes when it prophetically imagines Kate's ultimate capitulation in terms of a blinding cognate with the name of Kate: 'She shall have no more eyes to see withal than a cat.' Again, it is in terms of just such (figurative) blindness that Kate will later act out her ultimate subjection, not only to man but to the language of man: 'Pardon old father, my mistaking eyes, / That have been so bedazzled with the sun ... Now I perceive thou art a reverent father. / Pardon, I pray thee, for my mad mistaking' (IV.v.45–9).

I have argued elsewhere that this conflict between visionary and verbal language is not only a very traditional one but one to which Shakespeare in his Sonnets gives a new subjective twist when he assimilates it to the psychology, and not only to the erotic psychology, of his first-person lyric voice.[6] In addition, I have also argued that Shakespeare's different manipulations of this vision/language opposition produce generically different characterological or subjectivity effects in Shakespearean comedy, tragedy, and romance. It is far from the case, however, that Shakespeare invents this conflict between visual and verbal speech, for it is also possible to demonstrate that the terms of this opposition very much inform the metaphorical language through which language is imagined and described in the philosophico-literary tradition that begins in antiquity and extends at least up through the Renaissance, if not farther. While it is not possible to develop in a brief essay such as this the detailed and coherent ways in which this visual/verbal conflict operates in traditionary texts, it is possible to indicate, very schematically, the general logic of this perennial opposition by discussing two rather well-known illustrations. The pictures are by Robert Fludd, the seventeenth-century hermeticist, and they employ a thoroughly conventional iconography.[7] A brief review of the two pictures will be worthwhile, for this will allow us to understand how it happens that a traditional question about rhetoric amounts to an answer to an equally traditional question about gender. This in turn will allow us to return not only to *The Taming of the Shrew* but also to the larger theoretical question with which we began, namely, whether it is possible to speak a Language, whether of Man or of Woman, that does not speak for the Language of Man.

The first picture is Fludd's illustration of the seventh verse of Psalm 63 (misnumbered in the picture as verse 8). '*In alarum tuarum umbra canam*', says or sings King David, and the picture shows precisely this. King David kneels in prayer beneath an eyeball sun, while from out of his mouth, in line with the rays of theophanic light which stream down on him, a verse of psalm ascends up to a brightness which is supported, shaded, and revealed by its extended wings. Because King David is the master psalmist, and because the picture employs perennial motifs, it would be fair to say that Fludd's picture is an illustration of psalmic speech per se. In the picture we see traditional figurations of the way a special kind of anagogic language does homage to an elevated referent. This referent, moreover, represented as an eye which is both seeing and seen, is itself a figure of a special kind of speech, as is indicated by the Hebrew letters inscribed upon its iris. These letters – *yod, he, vau, he* – spell out the name of God, '*Jehova*', which is the 'Name' in which, according to the fourth verse of the psalm, King David lifts up his hands: 'Thus wil I magnifie thee all my life, and lift up mine hands in the Name.'[8] However, though these letters spell out this holy name, nevertheless, in principle they do not sound it out, for these are letters whose literality, when combined in this famous Tetragrammaton, must never be pronounced. Instead, in accord with both orthodox and heterodox mystical prohibitions, this written name of god, which is the only proper name of God, will be properly articulated only through attributive periphrasis, with the letters vocalised either as *Adonai*, 'the Lord', or as *Ha Shem*, 'the Name' or even 'the Word'.

In Fludd's picture, where the verse of psalm and '*Jehova*' lie at oblique angles to each other, it is clearly the case that King David does not literally voice the name of God. It is possible, however, reading either up or down, to take inscribed '*Jehova*' as an unspoken part of David's praising speech, either as its apostrophised addressee or as the direct object of its '*canam*'. This syntactic, but still silent, link between the Latin and the Hebrew is significant, for unspeakable '*Jehova*' thus becomes the predicated precondition through which or across which what the psalmist says is translated into what the psalmist sees. The picture is concerned to illustrate the effect of this translation, showing David's verse to be the medium of his immediate vision of the sun, drawing David's verse as though it were itself a beam of holy light. In this way, because the verse is pictured as the very brightness that it promises to sing or speak about, Fludd's picture manages to motivate its portrait of a genuinely visionary speech. In the psalm, the reason why the psalmist praises is the very substance of his praise: 'For thy loving kindnes is better then life: therefore my lippes shal praise thee.' The same thing happens in the picture, where we see the future tense of '*canam*' rendered present, and where the promise of praise amounts to the fulfilment of the promise. But again, all this visionary predication depends upon the odd graphesis of unspeakable '*Jehova*', which is the signifier of all signifiers that even King David cannot bring himself to utter, just as it is the writing on his iris that even Jehova cannot read.

In an elementary etymological sense – remembering that 'ideal' comes from Greek '*idein*', 'to see' – Fludd's picture is a portrait of ideal language, of language that is at once ideal and idealising. As the picture shows it, King David speaks a visual speech, a language *of* vision that promotes a vision *of* language, a language which is of

the mouth only in so far as it is for the eye. This visual and visionary logos is nothing but familiar. Psalmic speech in particular and
the language of praise in general (and it should be recalled that up
through the Renaissance *all* poetry is understood to be a poetry of
praise) are regularly imagined through such visual imagery, just as
the referential object of such reverential praise is regularly conceived of as both agent and patient of sight. (Dante's vision of *luce
etterna* at the end of the *Paradiso* would be a good example, though
here again the height of vision is figured through a transcendental
darkness, when power fails the poet's '*alta fantasia*', and the poet's
'will and desire' then 'turn' ['*volgeva*'] with 'the love that moves the
sun and the other stars.')

In the second picture which is by no means a strictly Elizabethan
world picture (since its details go back at least to Macrobius and,
therefore, through Plotinus, to Plato) we see the idealist aesthetics,
metaphysics, and cosmology traditionally unpacked from and attaching to this visual idealism or visual idealisation of the Word. As
the title indicates, all arts are images of the specularity of integrated
nature because both art and nature reciprocally will simulate the
eidola or likenesses of beatific light. This commonplace eidetic reduction, which, by commutation, enables representation iconically
to replicate whatever it presents, is what makes both art and nature
into psalmic panegyric. Art becomes an art of nature just as nature
is itself a kind of art, because they both reflect, but do not speak,
the holy name which is the signifier and the signified of art and
nature both. From this phenomenologically mutual admiration,
which makes of art and nature each other's *special* (from *specere*,
'to look at') likeness, it is easy to derive the ontotheological imperatives that inform all visionary art, for example, the poetics of *ut
pictura poesis* and 'speaking picture'. Suspended from the hand of
God, the great chain of mimetic being (which Macrobius describes
as a series of successive and declensive mirrors) reaches down to
nature, and through her to man, the ape of nature, whose artful
calibration of a represented little world produces a demiurgic *mise
en abyme* that in no way disturbs – indeed, one whose recursive
reflections do nothing but confirm – the stability of the material
world on which the ape of nature squats.

Not surprisingly, Fludd's encyclopaedic picture of the hierarchic
cosmos also includes a representation of a corresponding gender hierarchy. We can see this by looking at the circle of animals where,
on the left, the picture illustrates generic man or *Homo* with his

arms unfolded towards the sun, in complementary contrast to the way that woman or *Mulier*, at the right of the circle of animals, looks instead up to the moon which is the pale reflection of the sun that shines above it. It is fair to say that this opposition, which makes woman the mimetic simulacrum of man, sketches out the horizontal gender opposition on which the vertical, metaphysical hierarchy of the cosmos perpendicularly depends. For this reason, however, it is important to notice that, as the picture shows it, this is not a simple or a simply polar contrast. Man is figured by the sun which is always the same as itself, whereas woman is figured by a waxing-waning-changing moon which is always other than itself, because its mimic light of likeness is what illuminates its difference from the sameness of the sun. Perhaps this constitutes a paradox, this lunar light which folds up likeness into difference. But if so, it is a paradox that stands in service of an orthodox erotics for which woman is the other to man, the hetero- to *Homo*, precisely because her essence is *to be* this lunatic difference between sameness and difference. In the same conventional way (conventional, certainly, at least up through Milton) that the difference between the sun and the moon *is* the moon, so too, and equally traditionally, the difference between man and woman is woman herself.[9] This is a piety, moreover, that we see fleshed out in the ornaments of nature, who sports, with all decorum, a sun on one breast, a moon on the other, and, as the castrated and castrating difference between them, a second fetishistic moon upon her beatific crotch. Such is the erotics that is called for by traditional metaphysics. The word whose solar brightness is revealed by that which clouds it bespeaks a female darkness which is veiled by lunar brightness. The sickle-crescent moon of nature, which is cut and cutting both at once, indicates a mystery beyond it which is complementary to the way the odd graphesis of '*Jehova*' is constitutively eccentric to the centred wholeness of the world.

I have put this point in this way so as to point up the fact that there is really only one way to read Fludd's picture, and this precisely because there are two ways to read it. As with 'rope-tricks', indeterminacy here again determines a specific story. On the one hand, given a set of assumptions about mimesis that go back at least to Plato, woman is the subordinate sub-version of originary man, in the same way that the moon is nothing more than an inferior reflection of the sun. In this sense, woman is nothing other than the likeness of a likeness. On the other hand, woman is equally the radical subversion of man, an insubordinate sub-version, because this system of mimesis inexorably calls forth a principle of difference which, as difference, is intrinsically excessive to such hierarchic likeness. In this sense, as the embodiment of difference – as, specifically, the difference *of* likeness – woman is nothing other than the other itself. The point to recognise, however, is not simply that these two hands go happily together – the logic of sub-version logically entailing its own subversion, the 'Mirror of Nature' already displaying what Luce Irigaray will call the *speculum de l'autre femme* – but, more important, that the necessity of this double reading is no esoteric piece of wisdom. Quite the contrary; what we see in Fludd's picture is that this is a profoundly orthodox paradox, one whose formal heterogeneity, whose essential duplicity, is regularly figured and expressed by commonplace placeholders of the difference between sameness and difference, as, for example, unspeakable '*Jehova*', whose circumlocutory logos tangentially straddles the inside and the outside of the universal wholeness, or the titillating hole between the legs of nature whose absent presence is highlighted by discretionary light.

What Fludd's picture shows us, therefore, is that traditional iconography regularly assumes, as though it goes necessarily without saying, that there cannot be a picture of visionary language which is not at the same time an emblem of the limits of vision. This limit, however, as a limit, is built into Fludd's Wittgensteinian picture theory of language, within it as precisely that which such a theory is without. '*Jehova*', for example, is a part of *because* it is apart from the ideal specularity of the praising integrated world, and so too with the secret private parts of nature, whose hole we here see integrated into the deep recesses of nature's integrated whole. Out of this internal contradiction, figured through such motivating motifs, there derives, therefore, a very traditional story about the way the language of ideal desire is correlated with a desire for an ideal language. We see this story outlined in the circle of minerals, where man is associated with *Plumbum*, lead, and where woman is associated with *Cuprum*, named for the copper mines in Cyprus, birthplace of Venus, the goddess of love. Here we are to assume an alchemical reaction whereby Venus, the 'Cyprian Queen', at once the object and the motive of desire, as a kind of catalytic converter, translates lead into gold, thereby supernaturally changing sub-nature into super-nature. And we can put this point more strongly by asserting that what Fludd's picture depicts is the

thoroughly conventional way in which a universe of logical sameness is built up *on* its logical contra-diction (or, as it is sometimes
written nowadays, as though this were a feminist gesture, its
'cuntra-diction', i.e., the language of woman) because it is the very
lunacy of discourse that returns both man and woman to the
golden, solar order of the patriarchal Word.

At this level of allegorical generality, we can very quickly turn
back to *The Taming of the Shrew* and understand how it happens
that Petruchio re-establishes the difference between the sexes by
speaking the lunatic language of woman. The language of woman *is*
the difference between the sexes, a difference Petruchio becomes
when, speaking 'rope-tricks', he is 'Kated'. And this translation is
dramatically persuasive because the play fleshes it out by invoking
the sub-versive, subversive terms and logic of traditional iconography. In the taming story, the first moment of Kate's capitulation
occurs when Petruchio, changing his mind, forces Kate first to call
the sun the moon and then again the sun: 'Then God be blest, it is
the blessed sun, / But sun it is not, when you say it is not; / And the
moon changes even as your mind. / What you will have it nam'd,
even that it is, / And so it shall be so for Katherine' (IV.v.18–22).
We can call Kate's articulation of 'change' the naming of the shrew
which is the instrument of her taming, for it is this transcendentalis-
ing, heliotropic, ontotheological paradox of 'change' – 'Then God
be blest' – that leads Kate then to beg a patriarchal pardon for her
blind confusion of the sexes: 'Pardon, old father, my mistaking
eyes, / That have been so bedazzled with the sun.' And the same
thing happens at the climax of the wooing story, when Lucentio,
until then disguised as Cambio, kneels down before his father and
reveals his proper self. 'Cambio is chang'd into Lucentio' (V.i.123)
is the line with which this revelation is theatrically announced. This
formula serves to return the father and his son, along with the
master and his servant, back to their proper order. But it also offers
us an economical example of the way in which the very operation
of rhetorical translation serves to change 'change' into light.

To say that this paradox is orthodox is not to say that it describes a complete logical circle. Quite the contrary, as is indicated
by the aporetic structure of Fludd's pictures, it is *as* a logical
problem for logic, as an everpresent, irreducible, and ongoing question raised by self-reflection, that the paradox acquires its effective
power. This is the question consistently raised by the insistent question of rhetoric, which is why, when Kate is tamed and order

restored, the heretofore silent and good women of the play immediately turn into shrews. The subversive language of woman with which the play begins, and in resistance to which the movement of the play is predicated, reappears at the end of the play so that its very sounding predicts the future as a repetition of the same old story. This is the final moral of *The Taming of the Shrew*: that it is not possible to close the story of closure, for the very idea and idealisation of closure, like the wholeness of Fludd's comprehensive cosmos, is thought through a logic and a logos whose internal disruption forever defers, even as this deferment elicits a desire for, a summary conclusion.

Hence, we can add, the function of the larger frame. Speaking very generally – and recalling, on the one hand, the Petrarchan idealism of the wooing story and, on the other, the parodic Petrarchanism, the Petruchioism, of the taming story – we can say that the two subplots of *The Taming of the Shrew* together present what in the Western literary tradition is the master plot of the relation between language and desire. Sly, however, to whom this story is presented, wishes that his entertainment soon were over, for only when the play is over will Sly get to go to bed with new-found wife. 'Would 'twere done!' (I.i.254), says Sly (these being the last words we hear from him), of a play which, as far as Sly is concerned, is nothing but foreplay. The joke here is surely on Sly, for the audience knows full well that the consummation Sly so devoutly desires will never be achieved; if ever it happens that Sly sleeps with his wife, he will soon enough discover that she is a he in drag disguise. This defines, perhaps, the ultimate perversity of the kinky lord who 'long[s] to hear' his pageboy 'call the drunkard husband' (Ind.i.133), and who arranges for Sly to be subjected in this tantalising way to what for Sly is nothing but the tedious unfolding of the play within the play. But it is not only Sly's desire that is thus seductively frustrated; and this suggests the presence, behind the play, of an even kinkier lord. I refer here to the ongoing editorial question regarding the absence of a final frame; for this response to the play's apparent omission of a formal conclusion to the Sly story is evidence enough that the audience for the entirety of the play is left at its conclusion with a desire for closure that the play calls forth *in order* to postpone. To say that this is a desire that leaves something to be desired – a desire, therefore, that will go on and on forever – goes a good way towards explaining the abiding popularity of *The Taming of the Shrew*.[10]

Perhaps this also explains why, at first glance, it looks as though the current theoretical controversy to which I have referred presents us with a lovers' quarrel in which psychoanalysis plays Petruchio to its critics' Kate. It is tempting to see in the debate between Lacan and Derrida, for example, a domestic and domesticating quarrel that re-enacts in an increasingly more sophisticated but, for this reason, an increasingly more hapless fashion a proverbial literary predicament. However, this is not the conclusion that I would like to draw from the fact that current theoretical polemic so faithfully shapes itself to traditional literary contours and so voraciously stuffs itself with traditional literary topoi. Again it would be possible to relate the logic of sub-versive subversion, as it appears in Fludd and Shakespeare, to Derrida's gnostic, a-logical logic of the copulating supplement. And again, and again even more specifically, it would be possible to relate all this to Lacan's account of 'The function and field of speech and language in psychoanalysis'. Lacan's characterisation of the relation of the imaginary to the symbolic very straightforwardly repeats the motifs of a traditional verbal/visual conflict, and it does so in a way that fully incorporates into itself its equally traditional intrinsic deconstruction, e.g., when Lacan says that the real is that which cannot be represented. When Lacan says, to take just a few examples, that the being of the woman is that she does not exist, or that the function of the universal quantifier, by means of which man becomes the all, is thought through its negation in woman's not-all, when he says that there is no sexual relation, or when he says that castration, the Φ is what allows us to count from 0 to 1, he is not only evoking the elementary paradox displayed in Fludd's picture – the class of all classes that do not classify themselves – he is also ornamenting this familiar paradox with its traditional figurative clothing.[11] Thus it is that Lacan, like Derrida, is a master of the commonplace, as when he says that there is no such thing as metalanguage, or that '*La femme n'existe pas*', or that '*Si j'ai dit que le langage est ce comme quoi l'inconscient est structuré, c'est bien parce que le langage, d'abord, ça n'existe pas. Le langage est ce qu'on essaye de savoir concernant la fonction de la langue.*'[12]

To recognise the fact that all of this is commonplace is to see that the argument between Lacan and Derrida, between psychoanalysis and its other (an argument that already takes place within Lacan and within psychoanalysis), repeats, not only in its structure but also in its thematic and illustrative details, a master plot of literature. To see this is also to recognise that coarse generic terms of a magnitude corresponding to that of man, woman, language historically carry with them an internal narrative logic which works to motivate a story in which every rubric gets to play and to explain its integrated role. At this level of generality it goes without saying that the language of woman inexorably speaks for the language of man, and it is therefore not surprising that a feminist critique of psychoanalysis which is conducted at this level of generality will necessarily recathect the story that is fleshed out in *The Taming of the Shrew*. If 'Cambio is chang'd into Lucentio', so too, for example, is 'Cambio' changed into Luce Irigaray.

It is, however, the great and exemplary value of both Lacan and Derrida that in their quarrel with each other they do more than scrupulously restrict their readings of the central topoi of Western self-reflexive language to the level of generality appropriate to the register of allegorical abstraction called for by such massive metaphoremes and motifs. In addition, they recognise this level of generality for what it is: the logic of the literary word in the West. Doing so, they open up the possibility of an extraliterary reading of literature. In a specifically literary context, Shakespeare is interesting because in Shakespeare's texts (from Freud's reading of which, we should recall, psychoanalysis originally derives) we see how, at a certain point in literary history, allegorical abstractions such as man, woman, language – formerly related to each other in accord with the psychomachian dynamics which are sketched out in Fludd's pictures – are introduced into a psychologistic literature, thereby initiating a recognisably modern literature of individuated, motivated character. But the relation to literature is not itself a literary relation, and there is no compelling reason, therefore, especially with the examples of Lacan and Derrida before them, why readers or critics of master literary texts should in their theory or their practice act out what they read.

From *Shakespeare and the Question of Theory*, ed. Patricia Parker and Geoffrey Hartman (New York and London, 1985), pp. 138–59.

NOTES

[Joel Fineman's essay was in the vanguard of a new trend in Shakespeare criticism that brought contemporary theory – psychoanalysis, deconstruction, feminism, Marxism – to bear on the Shakespearean canon. His essay was originally included in a collection which had this movement as its critical purpose, *Shakespeare and the Question of Theory*, ed. Patricia Parker and Geoffrey Hartman (London, 1985). Ed.]

1. Derrida's most explicit criticisms of Lacan can be found in 'The Purveyor of Truth', *Yale French Studies*, 52 (1975); and in *Positions*, trans. Alan Bass (Chicago, 1981). See also *Spurs: Nietzsche's Styles*, trans. Barbara Harlow (Chicago, 1979); *La carte postale* (Paris, 1980), which republishes and expands upon 'The Purveyor of Truth'; Julia Kristeva, *Desire in Language: A Semiotic Approach to Literature and Art* (New York, 1980); Hélène Cixous, *La Jeune Née* (with Catherine Clément) (Paris, 1975); 'The Laugh of the Medusa', trans. K. Cohen and P. Cohen, *Signs*, I (Summer 1976), 875–99; Luce Irigaray, *Speculum de l'autre femme* (Paris, 1974); *Ce sexe qui n'est pas un* (Paris, 1977); Sarah Kofman, 'The Narcissistic Woman: Freud and Girard', *Diacritics* (Fall 1980), 36–45; *Nietzsche et la scène philosophique* (Paris, 1979).

2. All Shakespeare references are to *The Riverside Shakespeare*, ed. G. B. Evans (Boston, 1974).

3. *The Taming of the Shrew*, ed. H. J. Oliver (Oxford, 1982), p. 124.

4. 'It was at this point that the addendum of there having been a question-mark after the word "like" occurred to Dora, and she then recognised these words as a quotation out of a letter from Frau K. which had contained the invitation to L —, the place by the lake. In that letter there had been a question mark placed, in a most unusual fashion, in the very middle of a sentence, after the intercalated words "if you would like to come"' (Sigmund Freud, *Dora: An Analysis of a Case of Hysteria* [1905], trans. J. Strachey [New York, 1963], p. 118). Dora dreams here, quite literally, of *écriture féminine*, but Frau K.'s peculiar question-mark, even if its interruption is taken as a signal of the lesbianism Freud insists on in the story, still marks the specifically Freudian question of female desire: 'what does woman want?' This question – not simply 'if you would like to come' but, instead, 'if you would like to like to come', i.e. do you desire desire? – remains a question at the end of the Dora case; and it seems clear enough that this enigma not only stimulates Freud's counter-transference to Dora's transference (Freud introduces the concept of transference in the Dora case), but also accounts for Freud's failure to analyse, on the one hand, his patient's relation to him and, on the other, his relation to his patient. This double failure explains why the Dora case, like *The Taming of the Shrew*, concludes inconclusively. As Freud reports it, the analysis of Dora amounts to a battle between doctor and patient wherein, in response to Freud's demand that Dora admit her desire for Herr K. – i.e. that she avow her Freudian desire – Dora refuses to say what she wants. This is a characteristic Freudian frustration. As in

Freud's dream of Irma's injection, where Freud looks into Irma's mouth for evidence of a specifically psychoanalytic sexuality that would prove Freud's psychoanalytic theory true, so Freud wants Dora to speak her desire so as thereby to satisfy Freud's desire for a confirmation of his theory of desire. In the Irma dream, Freud receives as enigmatic answer to this question the uncanny image of 'Trimethylamin' – not only a picture of a word, but a picture of the very word that formulates female sexuality – whereas in the Dora case the question is answered with the re-marked question-mark. In both cases, however, it is the question of female desire, staged as an essential and essentialising question, that leads Freud on in a seductive way. When Dora, manhandling Freud, breaks off her analysis, she leaves Freud with the question of woman, the answer to which Freud will pursue for the rest of his life, up through the late, again inconclusive, essays on gender, in all of which Freud argues for a determinate indeterminacy, a teleological interminability.

5. For example, 'The function and field of speech and language in psychoanalysis', in Jacques Lacan, *Ecrits*, trans. Alan Sheridan (New York, 1977), pp. 30–113.

6. Joel Fineman, *Shakespeare's Perjured Eye: The Invention of Poetic Subjectivity in the Sonnets* (Berkeley, CA, 1985).

7. The first picture comes from Fludd's *Tomi Secundi Tractatus Secundus: De Praeternaturali Utriusque Cosmi Majoris ...* (Oppenheim, 1621); the second picture comes from *Utriusque Cosmi Majoris ... (Oppenheim, 1617)*. There is a convenient collection of Fludd's illustrations in Joscelyn Godwin's *Robert Fludd* (London, 1979). [For reasons of cost the pictures have not been included here – Ed.]

8. All quotations from the psalm are from the Geneva translation.

9. See Milton, *Paradise Lost*, III, 722–32.

10. It is here that the affinities of *The Taming of the Shrew* with Henry James's *The Turn of the Screw*, to which I am of course alluding in my title, are most apparent. In both texts a specifically rhetorical 'turning', 'troping', 'versing', understood on the model of 'rope-tricks', generates an interpretative mystery which is then correlated with a sexual tropism towards, or an apotropaic aversion from, an uncanny, true-false, *female* admixture of male and female. In *The Taming of the Shrew* Sly's framing desire for the pageboy disguised as a woman is a metatheatrical filter that puts into question any univocal understanding of the coupling of Petruchio and Kate. Hence the continuing critical question as to whether the Pauline patriarchalism of Kate's final speech should be understood ironically, i.e. whether she is most a shrew when she is most submissive. This hermeneutic question with regard to Kate corresponds to the traditional duplicity of woman: Sly's

metatheatrical desire for the pageboy defines the essence of femininity as masquerade. So too with *The Turn of the Screw*, which shares with *The Taming of the Shrew* the same heavy-handed, play-within-play, *mise en abyme* structure, and which uses this reflexive literariness to invite and to excite a series of relevant but irresolvable, and therefore continuing, critical questions, for example, is the governess's story true or false? Is the governess crazy or sane? In *The Turn of the Screw* such interpretative questions find their objectification, their objectification as questions, in 'Peter Quint', a kind of verbal pageboy whose nominality invokes the primal scene – half-real, half-fantasy – that motivates the governess's hysterico-obsessive desire for Miles and Flora. Again the point to notice is the way in which rhetorical indeterminacy generates a determinate erotics. The name that couples male and female genitals, 'Peter' and 'Quint', produces a specifically *female* uncanny: the name is quaint – indeed, 'cunt' – because both 'Peter' and 'Quint'. So too, a master text such as *The Turn of the Screw* uses precisely this indeterminacy to resecure the place of the 'Master' in relation to his servants.

11. See especially, Jacques Lacan, *Encore* (Paris, 1975), pp. 49–94.

12. For Lacan's remarks on 'metalanguage', see, in *Ecrits*, 'On a question preliminary to any possible treatment of psychosis'. The concluding two quotations come, respectively, from *Télévision* (Paris, 1974), p. 60, and *Encore*, p. 126.

7

Renaissance Family Politics and Shakespeare's *The Taming of the Shrew*

KAREN NEWMAN

WETHERDEN, Suffolk. Plough Monday, 1604. A drunken tanner, Nicholas Rosyer, staggers home from the alehouse. On arriving at his door, he is greeted by his wife with 'dronken dogg, pisspott and other unseemly names'. When Rosyer tried to come to bed to her, she 'still raged against him and badd him out dronken dogg dronken pisspott. She struck him several times, clawed his face and arms, spit at him and beat him out of bed.' Rosyer retreated, returned to the alehouse, and drank until he could hardly stand up. Shortly thereafter, Thomas Quarry and others met and 'agreed amongest themselfs that the said Thomas Quarry who dwelt at the next howse ... should ... ryde abowt the towne upon a cowlestaff whereby not onley the woman which had offended might be shunned for her misdemeanors towards her husband but other women also by her shame might be admonished to offence in like sort'.[1] Domestic violence, far from being contained in the family, spills out into the neighbourhood, and the response of the community is an 'old country ceremony used in merriment upon such accidents'.

Quarry, wearing a kirtle or gown and apron, 'was carried to diverse places and as he rode did admonishe all wiefs to take heede how they did beate their husbands'. The Rosyers' neighbours re-enacted their troubled gender relations: the beating was repeated with Quarry in woman's clothes playing Rosyer's wife, the neighbours standing in for the 'abused' husband, and a rough music procession to the house of the transgressors. The result of this 'merriment' suggests its darker purpose and the anxiety about gender relations it displays: the offending couple left the village in shame. The skimmington, as it was sometimes called, served its purpose by its ritual scapegoating of the tanner, and more particularly, his wife. Rosyer vented his anger by bringing charges against his neighbours in which he complained not only of scandal and disgrace to himself, 'his wief and kyndred', but also of seditious 'tumult and discention in the said towne'.[2]

The entire incident figures the social anxiety about gender and power which characterises Elizabethan culture. Like Simon Forman's dream of wish-fulfilment with Queen Elizabeth, this incident, in Louis Montrose's words, 'epitomises the indissoluably political and sexual character of the cultural forms in which [such] tensions might be represented and addressed'.[3] The community's ritual action against the couple who transgress prevailing codes of gender behaviour seeks to re-establish those conventional modes of behaviour – it seeks to sanction patriarchal order. But at the same time, this 'old country ceremony' subverts, by its re-presentation, its masquerade of the very events it criticises by forcing the offending couple to recognise their transgression through its dramatic enactment. The skimmington seeks 'in merriment' to reassert traditional gender behaviours which are naturalised in Elizabethan culture as divinely ordained; but it also deconstructs that 'naturalisation' by its foregrounding of what is a humanly constructed cultural product – the displacement of gender roles in a dramatic representation.[4]

I   FAMILY POLITICS

The events of Plough Monday 1604 have an uncanny relation to Shakespeare's *The Taming of the Shrew* which might well be read as a theatrical realisation of such a community fantasy, the shaming and subjection of a shrewish wife. The so-called induction opens with the hostess railing at the drunken tinker Sly, and their interchange figures him as the inebriated tanner from Wetherden.[5] Sly is presented with two 'dreams', the dream he is a lord, a fantasy

which enacts traditional Elizabethan hierarchical and gender relations, and the 'dream' of Petruchio taming Kate. The first fantasy is
a series of artificially constructed power relationships figured first in
class relations, then in terms of gender. The lord exhorts his serv-
ingmen to offer Sly 'low submissive reverence' and traditional
lordly prerogatives and pursuits – music, painting, handwashing,
rich apparel, hunting, and finally a theatrical entertainment. In the
longer, more detailed speech which follows at Ind.i.100 ff., he
exhorts his page to 'bear himself with honourable action / Such as
he hath observ'd in noble ladies / Unto their lords'. Significantly, Sly
is only convinced of his lordly identity when he is told of his 'wife'.
His realisation of this newly discovered self involves calling for the
lady, demanding from her submission to his authority, and finally
seeking to exert his new power through his husbandly sexual prerogative: 'Madam, undress you and come now to bed' (Ind.ii. 118).
By enacting Sly's identity as a lord through his wife's social and
sexual, if deferred, submission, the Induction suggests ironically
how in this androcentric culture men depended on women to authorise their sexual and social masculine identities.[6] The Lord's
fantasy takes the drunken Sly who brawls with the hostess, and by
means of a 'play' brings him into line with traditional conceptions
of gender relations. But in the Induction, these relationships of
power and gender, which in Elizabethan treatises, sermons and
homilies, and behavioural handbooks and the like were figured as
natural and divinely ordained, are subverted by the metatheatrical
foregrounding of such roles and relations as culturally constructed.

The analogy between the events at Wetherden and Shakespeare's
play suggests a tempting homology between history and cultural artifacts. It figures patriarchy as a master narrative, the key to understanding certain historic events and dramatic plots. But as Louis
Althusser's critique of historicism epigrammatically has it, 'history
is a process without a *telos* or a subject'.[7] This Althusserian dictum
repudiates such master narratives, but as Fredric Jameson points
out, 'What Althusser's own insistence on history as an absent cause
makes clear, but what is missing from the formula as it is canoni-
cally worded, is that he does not at all draw the fashionable conclusion that because history is a text, the "referent" does not exist ...
history is *not* a narrative, master or otherwise, but that, as an
absent cause, it is inaccessible to us except in textual form, and
that our approach to it and to the Real itself necessarily passes
through its prior textualisation, its narrativisation in the political

unconscious.'[8] If we return to Nicholas Rosyer's complaint against his neighbours and consider its textualisation, how it is made accessible to us through narrative, we can make several observations. We notice immediately that Rosyer's wife, the subject of the complaint, lacks the status of a subject. She is unnamed and referred to only as the 'wief'. Rosyer's testimony, in fact, begins with a defence not of his wife but of his patrimony, an account of his background and history in the village in terms of male lineage. His wife has no voice; she never speaks in the complaint at all. Her husband brings charges against his neighbours presumably to clear his name and to affirm his identity as patriarch which the incident itself, from his wife's 'abuse' to the transvestite skimmington, endangers.

From the account of this case, we also get a powerful sense of life in early modern England, the close proximity of neighbours and the way in which intimate sexual relations present a scene before an audience. Quarry and the neighbours recount Rosyer's attempted assertion of his sexual 'prerogatives' over his wife, and her vehement refusal: 'She struck him several times, clawed his face and arms, spit at him and beat him out of bed.' There is evidently no place in the late Elizabethan 'sex/gender system'[9] for Rosyer's wife to complain of her husband's mistreatment, drunkenness and abuse, or even give voice to her point of view, her side of the story. The binary opposition between male and female in the Wetherden case and its figuration of patriarchy in early modern England generates the possible contradictions logically available to both terms: Rosyer speaks, his wife is silent; Rosyer is recognised as a subject before the law, his wife is solely its object; Rosyer's family must be defended against the insults of his neighbours, his wife has no family, but has become merely a part of his. In turning to *The Taming of the Shrew*, our task is to articulate the particular sexual/political fantasy or, in Jameson's Althusserian formulation, the 'libidinal apparatus' that the play projects as an imaginary resolution of contradictions which are never resolved in the Wetherden case, but which the formal structures of dramatic plot and character in Shakespeare's play present as seemingly reconciled.

II *A SHREW'S HISTORY*

Many readers of Shakespeare's *Shrew* have noted that both in the Induction and the play language is an index of identity. Sly is convinced of his lordly identity by language, by the lord's obsequious words and recital of his false history. Significantly, when he believes himself a lord, his language changes and he begins to speak the blank verse of his retainers. But in the opening scene of the play proper, Shakespeare emphasises not just the relationship between language and identity, but between women and language, and between control over language and patriarchal power. Kate's linguistic protest is against the role in patriarchal culture to which women are assigned, that of wife and object of exchange in the circulation of male desire. Her very first words make this point aggressively: she asks of her father 'I pray you, sir, is it your will / To make a stale of me amongst these mates?'[10] Punning on the meaning of stale as laughing stock and prostitute, on 'stalemate', and on mate as husband, Kate refuses her erotic destiny by exercising her linguistic wilfulness. Her shrewishness, always associated with women's revolt in words, testifies to her exclusion from social and political power. Bianca, by contrast, is throughout the play associated with silence (I.i.70–1).[11]

Kate's prayer to her father is motivated by Gremio's threat 'To cart her rather. She's too rough for me' (I.i.55). Although this line is usually glossed as 'drive around in an open cart (a punishment for prostitutes)', the case of Nicholas Rosyer and his unnamed wife provides a more complex commentary. During the period from 1560 until the English Civil War, in which many historians have recognised a 'crisis of order', the fear that women were rebelling against their traditional subservient role in patriarchal culture was widespread.[12] Popular works such as *The Two Angry Women of Abington* (1598), Middleton's *The Roaring Girl* (1611), *Hic Mulier*, or *The Man-Woman* (1620), and Joseph Swetnam's *Arraignment of lewd, idle, froward and inconstant women*, which went through ten editions between 1616 and 1634, all testify to a preoccupation with rebellious women.[13]

What literary historians have recognised in late Elizabethan and Jacobean writers as a preoccupation with female rebellion and independence, social historians have also observed in historical records. The period was fraught with anxiety about rebellious women. David Underdown observes that 'Women scolding and brawling with their neighbours, single women refusing to enter service, wives dominating or even beating their husbands: all seem to surface more frequently than in the periods immediately before or afterwards. It will not go unnoticed that this is also the period during which witchcraft accusations reach their peak.'[14] Underdown's account points out a preoccupation with women's rebellion through language. Although men were occasionally charged with scolding, it was predominantly a female offence usually associated with class as well as gender issues and revolt: 'women who were poor, social outcasts, widows or otherwise lacking in the protection of a family ... were the most common offenders'.[15] Underdown points out that in the few examples after the restoration, social disapproval shifts to 'mismatched couples, sexual offenders, and eventually ... husbands who beat their wives'.[16] Punishment for such offences and related ones involving 'domineering' wives who 'beat' or 'abused' their husbands often involved public shaming or charivari of the sort employed at Wetherden. The accused woman or her surrogate was put in a scold's collar or ridden in a cart accompanied by a rough musical procession of villagers banging pots and pans.

Louis Montrose attributes the incidence of troubled gender relations to female rule since 'all forms of public and domestic authority in Elizabethan England were vested in men: in fathers, husbands, masters, teachers, magistrates, lords. It was inevitable that the rule of a woman would generate peculiar tensions within such a "patriarchal" society'.[17] Instead of assigning the causes of such rebellion to the 'pervasive cultural presence' of the Queen, historians point to the social and economic factors which contributed to these troubled gender relations. Underdown observes a breakdown of community in fast-growing urban centres and scattered pasture/dairy parishes where effective means of social control such as compact nucleated village centres, resident squires, and strong manorial institutions were weak or non-existent. He observes the higher incidence of troubled gender relations in such communities as opposed to the arable parishes which 'tended to retain strong habits of neighbourhood and cooperation'. Both Montrose's reading of the Elizabethan sex/gender system in terms of 'female rule' and Underdown's explanation for this proliferation of accusations of witchcraft, shrewishness and husband domination are less important here than the clear connection between women's independent appropriation of discourse and a conceived threat to patriarchal authority contained through public shaming or spectacle – the ducking stool, usually called the cucking stool, or carting.[18]

From the outset of Shakespeare's play, Katherine's threat to male authority is posed through language; it is perceived as such by others and is linked to a claim larger than shrewishness – witchcraft – through the constant allusions to Katherine's kinship with the devil.[19] Control of women and particularly of Kate's revolt is from the outset attempted by inscribing women in a scopic economy.[20] Woman is represented as spectacle (Kate) or object to be desired and admired, a vision of beauty (Bianca). She is the site of visual pleasure, whether on the public stage, the village green, or the fantasy 'cart' with which Hortensio threatens Kate. The threat of being made a spectacle, here by carting, or later in the wedding scene by Petruchio's 'mad-brain rudesby', is an important aspect of shrew-taming.[21] Given the evidence of social history and of the play itself, discourse is power, both in Elizabethan and Jacobean England and in the fictional space of the *Shrew*.

The *Shrew* both demonstrated and produced the social facts of the patriarchal ideology which characterised Elizabethan England, but *representation* gives us a perspective on that patriarchal system which subverts its status as natural. The theatrically constructed frame in which Sly exercises patriarchal power and the dream in which Kate is tamed undermine the seemingly eternal nature of those structures by calling attention to the constructed character of the representation rather than veiling it through mimesis. The foregrounded female protagonist of the action and her powerful annexation of the traditionally male domain of discourse distances us from that system by exposing and displaying its contradictions. Representation undermines the ideology about women which the play presents and produces, both in the Induction and in the Kate/Petruchio plot: Sly disappears as lord, but Kate keeps talking.

III THE PRICE OF SILENCE

At Act II, scene i, in the spat between Bianca and Kate, the relationship between silence and women's place in the marriage market is made clear. Kate questions Bianca about her suitors, inquiring as to her preferences. Some critics have read her questions and her abuse of Bianca (in less than thirty lines, Kate binds her sister's hands behind her back, strikes her and chases after her calling for revenge) as revealing her secret desire for marriage and for the praise and recognition afforded her sister. Kate's behaviour may invite such an interpretation, but another view persistently presents itself as well. In her questions and badgering, Kate makes clear the relationship between Bianca's sweet sobriety and her success with men. Kate's abuse may begin as a jest, but her feelings are aroused to a different and more serious pitch when her father enters, taking as usual Bianca's part against her sister.[22] Baptista emphasises both Bianca's silence, 'When did she cross thee with a bitter word?' and Katherine's link with the devil, 'thou hilding of a devilish spirit' (II.i.28, 26). We should bear in mind here Underdown's observation that shrewishness is a class as well as gender issue – that women 'lacking in the protection of a family ... were the most common offenders'.[23] Kate is motherless, and to some degree fatherless as well, for Baptista consistently rejects her and favours her obedient sister. Kate's threat which follows, 'Her silence flouts me, and I'll be reveng'd' (II.i.29) is truer than we have heretofore recognised, for it is that silence which has ensured Bianca's place in the male economy of desire and exchange to which Kate pointedly refers in her last lines:

> What, will you not suffer me? Nay, now I see
> She is your treasure, she must have a husband,
> I must dance barefoot on her wedding day,
> And, for your love to her lead apes in hell.
> (II.i.31–4)

Here we recognise the relationship between father and husband, in which woman is the mediating third term, a treasure the exchange of which assures patriarchal hegemony. Throughout the play Bianca is a treasure, a jewel, an object of desire and possession. Although much has been made of the animal analogies between Kate and beasts, the metaphorical death of the courtly imagery associated with Bianca has been ignored as too conventional, if not natural, to warrant comment.[24] What seems at issue here is not so much Kate's lack of a husband, or indeed her desire for a marriage partner, but rather her distaste at those folk customs which make her otherness, her place outside that patriarchal system, a public fact, a spectacle for all to see and mock.

In the battle of words between Kate and Petruchio at Act II, scene i, lines 182ff., it is Kate who gets the best of her suitor. She takes the lead through puns which allow her to criticise Petruchio and the patriarchal system of wooing and marriage. Her sexual puns make explicit to the audience not so much her secret preoccupation with sex and marriage, but what is implicit in Petruchio's wooing – that marriage is a sexual exchange in which women are exploited for their use-value as producers. Significantly, Petruchio's language is linguistically similar to Kate's in its puns and wordplay. He also presents her, as many commentators have noted, with an imagined vision which makes her conform to the very order against which she rebels – he makes her a Bianca with words, shaping an identity for her which confirms the social expectations of the sex/gender system which informs the play. Their wooing can be interestingly compared with the next scene, also a wooing, between Bianca and her two suitors. Far from the imaginative use of language and linguistic play we find in Kate, Bianca repeats verbatim the Latin words Lucentio 'construes' to reveal his identity and his love. Her revelation of her feelings through a repetition of the Latin lines he quotes from Ovid are as close as possible to the silence we have come to expect from her.

In the altercation over staying for the wedding feast after their marriage, Kate again claims the importance of language and her use of it to women's place and independence in the world. But here it is Petruchio who controls language, who has the final word, for he creates through words a situation to justify his actions – he claims to be rescuing Kate from thieves. More precisely, he claims she asks for that rescue. Kate's annexation of language does not work unless her audience, and particularly her husband, accepts what she says as independent rebellion. By deliberately misunderstanding and reinterpreting her words to suit his own ends, Petruchio effectively refuses her the freedom of speech identified in the play with women's independence. Such is his strategy throughout this central portion of the action, in their arrival at his house and in the interchange with the tailor. Kate is figuratively killed with kin-dness, by her husband's rule over her not so much in material terms – the withholding of food, clothing and sleep – but the withholding of linguistic understanding. As the receiver of her messages, he simply refuses their meaning; since he also has material power to enforce his interpretations, it is his power over language that wins.

In the exchange between Petruchio and Kate with the tailor, Kate makes her strongest bid yet for linguistic freedom:

> Why, sir, I trust I may have leave to speak,
> And speak I will. I am no child, no babe.
> Your betters have endur'd me say my mind,
> And if you cannot, best you stop your ears.
> My tongue will tell the anger of my heart,
> Or else my heart concealing it will break,

And rather than it shall, I will be free
Even to the uttermost, as I please, in words.
(IV.iii.73–80)

When we next encounter Kate, however, on the journey to Padua, she finally admits to Petruchio: 'What you will have it nam'd, even that it is, / And so it shall be so for Katherine' (IV.v.21–2). On this journey Kate calls the sun the moon, an old man a budding virgin, and makes the world conform to the topsy-turvy of Petruchio's patriarchal whimsy. But we should look carefully at this scene before acquiescing in too easy a view of Kate's submission. Certainly she gives in to Petruchio's demands literally; but her playfulness and irony here are indisputable. As she says at Act IV, scene v, lines 44–8:

Pardon, old father, my mistaking eyes,
That have been so bedazzled with the sun
That everything I look on seemeth green.
Now I perceive thou art a reverend father.
Pardon, I pray thee, for my mad mistaking.

Given Kate's talent for puns, we must understand her line, 'bedazzled with the sun', as a pun on son and play with Petruchio's line earlier in the scene 'Now by my mother's son, and that's myself, / It shall be moon, or star, or what I list' (IV.v.6–7). 'Petruchio's bedazzlement' is exactly that, and Kate here makes clear the playfulness of their linguistic games.

In his paper 'Hysterical Phantasies and their Relation to Bi-Sexuality' (1908), Sigmund Freud observes that neurotic symptoms, particularly the hysterical symptom, have their origins in the day-dreams of adolescence.[25] 'In girls and women', Freud claims, 'they are invariably of an erotic nature, in men they may be either erotic or ambitious'.[26] A feminist characterological re-reading of Freud might suggest that Kate's ambitious fantasies, which her culture allows her to express only in erotic directions, motivate her shrewishness.[27] Such behaviour, which in a man would not be problematic, her family and peers interpret as 'hysterical' and/or diabolic. Her 'masculine' behaviour saves her, at least for a time, from her feminine erotic destiny.

Freud goes on to claim that hysterical symptoms are always bisexual, 'the expression of both a masculine and a feminine unconscious sexual phantasy'.[28] The example he gives is a patient who 'pressed her dress to her body with one hand (as the woman) while trying to tear it off with the other (as the man)'.[29] To continue our 'analysis' in the scene we are considering, we might claim that Kate's female masquerade obscures her continuing ambitious fantasies, now only manifest in her puns and ironic wordplay which suggest the distance between her character and the role she plays.[30] Even though she gives up her shrewishness and acquiesces to Petruchio's whims, she persists in her characteristic 'masculine' linguistic exuberance while masquerading as an obedient wife.[31]

Instead of using Freud to analyse Kate's character, a critical move of debatable interpretive power, we might consider the Freudian text instead as a reading of ideological or cultural patterns. The process Freud describes is suggestive for analysing the workings not of character, but of Shakespeare's text itself. No speech in the play has been more variously interpreted than Kate's final speech of women's submission. In a recent essay on the *Shrew*, John Bean has conveniently assigned to the two prevailing views the terms 'revisionist' for those who would take Kate's speech as ironic and her subservience as pretence, a way of living peaceably in patriarchal culture but with an unregenerate spirit, and the 'anti-revisionists' who argue that farce is the play's governing genre and that Kate's response to Petruchio's taming is that of an animal responding to 'the devices of a skilled trainer'.[32] Bean himself argues convincingly for a compromise position which admits the 'background of depersonalising farce unassimilated from the play's fabliau sources', but suggests that Kate's taming needs to be seen in terms of romantic comedy, as a spontaneous change of heart such as those of the later romantic comedies 'where characters lose themselves in chaos and emerge, as if from a dream, liberated into the bonds of love'.[33] Bean rightly points out the liberal elements of the final speech in which marriage is seen as a partnership as well as a hierarchy, citing the humanist writers on marriage and juxtaposing Kate's speech with the corresponding, and remarkably more mysogynist, lines in *The Taming of a Shrew* and other taming tales.[34]

Keeping in mind Bean's arguments for the content of the speech and its place in the intersection of farce and romantic love plot, I would like to turn instead to its significance as representation. What we find is Katherine as a strong, energetic female protagonist represented before us addressing not the onstage male audience, only too aware of its articulation of patriarchal power, but Bianca and the Widow, associated with silence throughout the play and finally arriving by means, as Petruchio calls it, of Kate's 'womanly persuasion'(V.ii.120).

Unlike any other of Shakespeare's comedies, we have here represented not simply marriage, with the final curtain a veiled mystification of the sexual and social results of that ritual, but a view, however brief and condensed, of that marriage over time.[35] And what we see is not a quiet and submissive Kate, but the same energetic and linguistically powerful Kate with which the play began. We know, then, in a way we never know about the other comedies, except perhaps *The Merchant of Venice*, and there our knowledge is complicated by Portia's male disguise, that Kate has continued to speak. She has not, of course, continued to speak her earlier language of revolt and anger. Instead she has adopted another strategy, a strategy which the French psychoanalyst Luce Irigaray calls mimeticism.[36] Irigaray argues that women are cut off from language by the patriarchal order in which they live, by their entry into the Symbolic which the Father represents in a Freudian/Lacanian model.[37] Women's only possible relation to the dominant discourse is mimetic:

> To play with mimesis is ... for a woman to try to recover the place of her exploitation by language, without allowing herself to be simply reduced to it. It is to resubmit herself ... to ideas – notably about her – elaborated in and through a masculine logic, but to 'bring out' by an effect of playful repetition what was to remain hidden: the recovery of a possible operation of the feminine in language. It is also to unveil the fact that if women mime so well they are not simply reabsorbed in this function. *They also remain elsewhere.*[38]

Whereas Irigaray goes on to locate this 'elsewhere' in sexual pleasure (*jouissance*), Nancy Miller has elaborated on this notion of 'mimeticism', describing it as a 'form of emphasis: an italicised version of what passes for the neutral ... Spoken or written, italics are a modality of intensity and stress; a way of marking what has already been said, of making a common text one's own.'[39]

Joel Fineman has recently observed the difficulty in distinguishing between man's and woman's speech in the *Shrew* by demonstrating how the rhetorical strategies Kate deploys are like Petruchio's.[40] But Kate's self-consciousness about the power of discourse, her punning and irony, and her techniques of linguistic masquerade, are strategies of italics, mimetic strategies, in Irigaray's sense of mimeticism. Instead of figuring a gender-marked woman's speech, they deform language by sub-verting it, that is, by turning it inside out so that metaphors, puns and other forms of wordplay manifest their veiled equivalences: the meaning of woman as treasure, of wooing as a civilised and acceptable disguise for sexual exploitation, of the objectification and exchange of women. Kate's having the last word contradicts the very sentiments she speaks; rather than resolve the play's action, her monologue simply displays the fundamental contradiction presented by a female dramatic protagonist, between woman as a sexually desirable, silent object and women of words, women with power over language who disrupt, or at least italicise, women's place and part in culture.

To dramatise action involving linguistically powerful women characters militates against patriarchal structures and evaluations of women in which their silence is most highly prized – which is why so many of Shakespeare's heroines, in order to maintain their status as desirable, must don male attire in order to speak: Rosalind, Portia, even the passive Viola. The conflict between the explicitly repressive content of Kate's speech and the implicit message of independence communicated by representing a powerful female protagonist speaking the play's longest speech at a moment of emphatic suspense is not unlike Freud's female patient who 'pressed her dress to her body with one hand (as the woman) while trying to tear it off with the other (as the man)'. We might even say that this conflict shares the bi-sexuality Freud claims for the hysterical symptom, that the text itself is sexually ambivalent, a view in keeping with the opposed readings of the play in which it is either conservative farce or subversive irony. Such a representation of gender, what I will call the 'female dramatisable',[41] is always at once patriarchally suspect and sexually ambivalent, clinging to Elizabethan patriarchal ideology and at the same time tearing it away by foregrounding or italicising its constructed character.

IV   MISSING FRAMES AND FEMALE SPECTACLES

Kate's final speech is 'an imaginary or formal solution to unresolvable social contradictions', but that appearance of resolution is an 'ideological mirage'.[42] On the level of plot, as many readers have noted, if one shrew is tamed two more reveal themselves. Bianca and the widow refuse to do their husbands' bidding, thereby undoing the sense of closure Kate's 'acquiescence' produces. By articulating the contradiction manifested in the scene's formal organisation and its social 'content' – between the 'headstrong women', now Bianca and the widow who refuse their duty, and Kate and her praise of women's submission – the seeming resolution of the play's ending is exploded and its *heterogeneity* rather than its unity is foregrounded. But can transgression of the law of women's silence be subversive? It has become a theoretical commonplace to argue that transgression presupposes norms or taboos. Therefore, the 'female dramatisable' is perhaps no more than a release mechanism, a means of managing troubled gender relations. By transgressing the law of women's silence, but far from subverting it, the *Shrew* reconfirms the law, if we remember that Kate, Bianca and the widow remain the object of the audience's gaze, specular images, represented female bodies on display, as on the cucking stool or in the cart, the traditional punishments for prostitutes and scolds. Representation contains female rebellion. And because the play has no final framing scene, no return to Sly, it could be argued that its artifice is relaxed, that the final scene is experienced naturalistically. The missing frame allows the audience to forget that Petruchio's taming of Kate is presented as a fiction.

Yet even with its missing frame and containment of woman through spectacle, the *Shrew* finally deconstructs its own mimetic effect if we remember the bisexual aspect of the representation of women on the Elizabethan and Jacobean stage. Kate would have been played by a boy whose transvestism, like Thomas Quarry's in the Wetherden skimmington, emblematically embodied the sexual contradictions manifest both in the play and Elizabethan culture. The very indeterminateness of the actor's sexuality, of the woman/man's body, the supplementarity of its titillating homoerotic play (Sly's desire for the page boy disguised as a woman, Petruchio's 'Come Kate, we'll to bed'), foregrounds its artifice and therefore subverts the play's patriarchal master narrative by exposing it as neither natural nor divinely ordained, but culturally constructed.

From *English Literary Renaissance*, 16 (1986), 131–45.

NOTES

[Karen Newman's essay was first published in the journal *English Literary Renaissance*, 16 (1986), and she has republished it as part of her book,

Fashioning Femininity and English Renaissance Drama (Chicago and London, 1991). In many ways Newman produces a classical piece of New Historicist criticism by locating the textual production of *The Taming of the Shrew* firmly within the ideologies of the period. But she is also concerned with gender and demonstrates the harsh realities of life for women in early modern England. Altogether the historical details are both illuminating and fascinating, allowing us to perceive Shakespeare's work in a radical new light. Ed.]

1. This would seem to be Rosyer's neighbour's duty. The OED cites Lupton's *Sivgila*, p. 50 (1580) as an early use of *cowlstaff*: 'If a woman beat hir husbande, the man that dwelleth next unto hir sha ride on a cowlstaffe.'

2. PRO STAC 8, 249/19. I am grateful to Susan Amussen for sharing her transcription of this case, and to David Underdown for the original reference. We do not know the result of Rosyer's complaint since only the testimony, not the judgment, is preserved.

3. Louis Montrose, '"Shaping Fantasies": Gender and Power in Elizabethan Culture', *Representations*, 1 (1983), 61–94.

4. See Natalie Z. Davis, 'Women on Top', in *Society and Culture In Early Modern France* (Stanford, CA, 1975); E. P. Thompson, 'Rough Music: "le Charivari Anglais"', *Annales ESC*, 27 (1972), 285–312.

5. In *The Taming of a Shrew*, the frame tale closes the action; Sly must return home after his 'bravest dreame' to a wife who 'will course you for dreaming here tonight', but he claims: 'Ile to my / Wife presently and tame her too'. See Geoffrey Bullough, *Narrative and Dramatic Sources of Shakespeare* (London, 1957), I, p. 108.

6. See Montrose's discussion of the Amazonian myth, '"Shaping Fantasies"', 66–7.

7. Louis Althusser, *Réponse à John Lewis* (Paris, 1973), pp. 91–8.

8. Fredric Jameson, *The Political Unconscious* (Ithaca, NY, 1981), p. 35.

9. Montrose, '"Shaping Fantasies"', 62, after Gayle Rubin.

10. (I.i.57–8); all references are to the New Arden edition, ed. Brian Morris (London, 1981).

11. See, for example, Robert Greene's *Penelope's Web* (1587) which presents the Renaissance ideal of womanhood – chastity, obedience and silence – through a series of exemplary tales; see also Ruth Kelso, *Doctrine for the Lady of the Renaissance* (Urbana, IL, 1956); Linda T. Fitz, '"What Says the Married Woman?": Marriage Theory and Feminism in the English Renaissance', *Mosaic*, 13 (1980), 1–22; the books Suzanne Hull examines in her *Chaste, Silent and Obedient*:

English Books for Women, 1475–1640 (San Marino, 1982); and most recently Lisa Jardine, *Still Harping on Daughters* (Sussex, 1983), pp. 103–40.

12. See, among others, Lawrence Stone's *The Crisis of the Aristocracy 1558–1641* (Oxford, 1965) and Keith Wrightson's *English Society 1580–1680* (New Brunswick, NJ; 1982), esp. chs 5 and 6. I am grateful to David Underdown for referring me to Wrightson.

13. Stone, *The Crisis of the Aristocracy*, cites Swetnam, *Family*, p. 137; for references to *Hic Mulier*, see David Underdown, 'The Taming of the Scold: the enforcement of patriarchal authority in Early Modern England', in *Order and Disorder in Early Modern England*, ed. by Anthony Fletcher and John Stevenson (Cambridge, 1985), pp. 116–36.

14. Underdown, 'The Taming of the Scold', p. 119.

15. Ibid., p. 120.

16. Ibid., p. 121, citing E. P. Thompson.

17. Montrose, '"Shaping Fantasies"', 64–5.

18. Ibid. See also Davis, 'Women on Top' and Thompson, 'Rough Music'.

19. See, for example, I.i.65, 105, 121, 123; II.i.26, 151; for the social context of witchcraft in England, see Alan Macfarlane, *Witchcraft in Tudor and Stuart England* (New York, 1970) and Keith Thomas, *Religion and the Decline of Magic* (London, 1971).

20. On the importance of the gaze in managing human behaviour, see Michel Foucault, *Surveiller et Punir* (Paris, 1975); see also Laura Mulvey's discussion of scopophilia in 'Visual Pleasure and Narrative Cinema', *Screen*, 16 (1975), 6–18, and Luce Irigaray's more philosophical *Speculum de l'autre femme* (Paris, 1974).

21. Kate's speech at III.ii.8, 18–20 makes clear this function of his lateness and his 'mad-brain rudesby'. 'She recognises that this shame falls not on her family, but on her alone: "No shame but mine ... Now must the world point at poor Katherine / 'Lo, there is made Petruchio's wife. If it would please him come and marry her"' (III.ii.8,18–20). Although Katherine to herself, she recognises that for others she will be 'Petruchio's wife'.

22. See Marianne Novy's discussion of the importance of the father and paternity in her essay 'Patriarchy and Play in *The Taming of the Shrew*', *English Literary Renaissance*, 9 (1979), 273–4.

23. Underdown, 'The Taming of the Scold', p. 120.

24. See Novy's detailed discussion of Kate's puns, animal imagery and sexual innuendoes in this scene, 'Patriarchy and Play', 264, and

Martha Andreson-Thom's 'Shrew-taming and other rituals of aggression: Baiting and bonding on the stage and in the wild', *Women's Studies*, 9 (1982), 121–43.

25. Sigmund Freud, *Collected Papers*. trans. Joan Riviere (London, 1948), II. pp. 51–9.

26. Ibid., II, p. 51.

27. For a discussion of female fantasy, see Nancy K. Miller, 'Emphasis Added: Plots and Plausibilities in Women's Fiction', *PMLA*, 97 (1981), 36–48.

28. *Collected Papers*, II, p. 57.

29. Ibid., II, p. 58.

30. See Joan Riviere's essay on female masquerade in *Psychoanalysis and Female Sexuality*, ed. H. Ruitenbeek (New Haven, CT, 1966); also of interest is Sir Thomas Elyot's *Defense of Good Women* in which Zenobia is allowed autonomy in relation to her husband, but exhorted to dissemble her disobedience. See Constance Jordan, 'Feminism and the Humanists: The Case of Thomas Elyot's *Defense of Good Women*', *Renaissance Quarterly*, 36 (1983), 195.

31. Freud describes a similar strategy of evasion in his essay, *Collected Papers*, II, p. 58.

32. John Bean, 'Comic Structure and the Humanizing of Kate in *The Taming of the Shrew*', in *The Woman's Part*, ed. Carolyn Ruth Swift Lenz, Gayle Greene, and Carol Thomas Neely (Urbana, IL, 1980). Bean quotes the anti-revisionist Robert Heilbrun, 'The *Taming* Untamed, or, the Return of the Shrew', *Modern Language Quarterly*, 27(1966), 147–61. For the revisionist view, see Coppélia Kahn's '*The Taming of the Shrew*: Shakespeare's Mirror of Marriage', *Modern Language Studies*, 5 (1975), 88–102.

33. Bean, 'Comic Structure', p. 66.

34. Ibid., pp. 67–70.

35. See Nancy K. Miller's discussion of the mystification of defloration and marriage in 'Writing (from) the Feminine: George Sand Amid the Novel of Female Pastoral', *The Representation of Women, English Institute Essays* (Cambridge, 1983).

36. Luce Irigaray, *Ce sexe qui n'en est pas un* (Paris, 1977), pp. 134ff.

37. Irigaray, *Speculum de l'autre femme*, particularly pp. 282–98. Contemporary handbooks often seem an uncanny description of woman as Other: the popular preacher Henry Smith, whose *Preparative to Marriage* was published in 1591, suggests that marriage is an equal partnership, but goes on to declare that 'the ornament of

women is silence; and therefore the Law was given to the man rather than to the woman, to shewe that he shoulde be the teacher, and she the hearer' (quoted in Novy, 'Patriarchy and Play', p. 278).

38. Irigaray, *Speculum*, p. 74, quoted and translated by Nancy Miller, 'Emphasis Added', 38.

39. Miller, 'Emphasis Added', 38.

40. Joel Fineman, 'The Turn of the *Shrew*', in *Shakespeare and the Question of Theory*, ed. Patricia Parker and Geoffrey Hartman (London, 1985), pp. 141–4 [Fineman's essay is included in this collection; see above, pp. 123–47 – Ed].

41. See D. A. Miller's discussion of the 'narratable' in *Narrative and its Discontents* (Princeton, NJ, 1981), especially the chapter on Austen.

42. Jameson, *The Political Unconscious*, pp. 79, 56.

8

Scolding Brides and Bridling Scolds: Taming the Woman's Unruly Member

LYNDA E. BOOSE

In the past fifteen years or so, historical scholarship has shifted away from its perennial concentration on the structures of authority and has begun to view history from the bottom up. What has emerged from approaching historical records in entirely new ways and proposing newly complex intersections of such data[1] is a picture of England that requires us to read the social text in terms of such phenomena as the widespread and quite dramatic rise in the years 1560–1640 in those crimes labelled as ones of 'interpersonal dispute', that is, ones involving sexual misconduct, scolding, slander, physical assault, defamation, and marital relations. Keith Wrightson and David Levine offer an instructive explanation of this phenomenon: the statistical increase during these years reflects less a 'real' increase in such crimes than a suddenly heightened official determination to regulate social behaviour through court prosecution.[2] This itself reflects the wider growth of a 'law and order consciousness', the increase of fundamental concern about social order that manifested itself in the growing severity of criminal statutes directed primarily against vagrants and female disorder. In other words, what had sprung into full operation was a social anxiety that came to locate the source of all disorder in society in its marginal and subordinate groups. And in the particular types of malfeasance that this society or any other seeks to proscribe and the specific groups it thereby implicitly seeks to stigmatise, time may read its ideology.[3]

For Tudor-Stuart England, in village and town, an obsessive energy was invested in exerting control over the unruly woman – the woman who was exercising either her sexuality or her tongue under her own control rather than under the rule of a man. As illogical as it may initially seem, the two crimes – being a scold and being a so-called whore – were frequently conflated. Accordingly, it was probably less a matter of local convenience than one of a felt congruity between offences that made the cucking stool the common instrument of punishment. And whether the term 'cucking stool' shares any actual etymological origins with 'cuckold' or not, the perceived equation between a scolding woman and a whore or 'quean' who cuckolded her husband probably accounts for the periodic use of 'coqueen' or 'cuckquean' for the cucking stool.[4] This particular collocation of female transgressions constructs women as creatures whose bodily margins and penetrable orifices provide culture with a locus for displaced anxieties about the vulnerability of the social community, the body politic. Thus Ferdinand, in saying that 'women like that part, which, like the lamprey, / Hath nev'r a bone in't. / ... I mean the tongue',[5] jealously betrays his own desire for rule over what he sees as the penetrable misrule of his Duchess-sister's body/state. In his discussion of the grotesque tropes that connect body and court, Peter Stallybrass comments on the frequency with which 'in the Jacobean theatre, genital differentiation tended to be subsumed within a problematically gendered orality'.[6] Within that subsumption the talkative woman is frequently imagined as synonymous with the sexually available woman, her open mouth the signifier for invited entrance elsewhere. Hence the dictum that associates 'silent' with 'chaste' and stigmatises women's public speech as a behaviour fraught with cultural signs resonating with a distinctly sexual kind of shame.[7]

Given these connections between body and state, control of women's speech becomes a massively important project. By being imagined as a defence of all the important institutions upon which the community depends, such a project could, in the minds of the magistrates and other local authorities, probably rationalise even such extreme measures as the strange instrument known as the 'scold's bridle' or 'brank'. Tracing the use of the scold's bridle is problematic because, according to [T.N.] Brushfield,

> Notwithstanding the existence at Chester of so many Scold's Bridles, no notice of their use is to be found in the Corporation [town or city] books, several of which have been specifically examined with that object in view. That they were not unfrequently called into requisition in times past cannot be doubted; but the Magistrates were doubtless fully aware that the punishment was illegal, and hence preferred that no record should remain of their having themselves transgressed the law.[8]

Since the bridle was never legitimate, it does not appear, nor would its use have been likely to be entered, in the various leet court records with the same unself-conscious frequency that is reflected in the codified use of the cucking stool. Because records are so scarce, we have no precise idea of how widespread the use of the bridle really was. What we can know is that during the early modern era this device of containment was first invented – or, more accurately, adapted – as a punishment for the scolding woman. It is a device that today we would call an instrument of torture, despite the fact – as English legal history is proud to boast – that in England torture was never legal. Thus, whereas the instrument openly shows up in the Glasgow court records of 1574 as a punishment meted out to two quarrelling women, if the item shows up at all in official English transactions, it is usually through an innocuous entry such as the one in the 1658 Worcester Corporation Records, which show that four shillings were 'Paid for mending the bridle for bridleinge of scoulds, and two cords for the same'.[9]

In the absence of what historians would rank as reliable documents, very little has been said by twentieth-century historians about the scold's bridle.[10] There are those who attempt by this lack of evidence to footnote it as an isolated phenomenon that originated around 1620, mainly in the north of England and one part of Scotland. I myself have some increasingly documented doubts. And while problems of documentation have made it possible for historians largely to ignore the scold's bridle even within their new 'bottom-up' histories of topics such as social crime, I would argue that its use and notoriety were widespread enough for it to have been an agent in the historical production of women's silence. As such, the bridle is both a material indicator of gender relations in the culture that devised it and a signifier crucial for reconstructing the buried narrative of women's history. Records substantiate its use in at least five English counties as well as in several disparate areas of Scotland; furthermore, likely pictorial allusions turn up, for example, in an eighteenth-century sampler handed down in an Irish family originally from Belfast,[11] or in the frontispiece of the 1612 edition of Hooker's Laws of Ecclesiastical Polity, where a woman kneels, a skull placed close by. and receives the Bible in one upstretched hand while in the other she holds a bridle, signifying discipline.[12] As I will argue below, the instrument is probably also signified in a raft of late sixteenth-century 'bridling' metaphors that have been understood previously as merely figurative; the item itself may well have appeared onstage as a prop in Part II of *Tamburlaine the Great* and Swetnam's *Woman-hater Arraigned by Women*. Moreover, it almost certainly appears as the explicit referent in several widely read seventeenth-century Protestant treatises published in London.

In Mr T. N. Brushfield's Cheshire County alone he was able to discover thirteen of these 200–250-year-old artifacts still lying about the county plus an appallingly large number of references to their use. In fact some eighteen months after he had presented his initial count in 1858, Mr Brushfield, with a dogged empiricism we can now be grateful for, informed the Society that he had come across three more specimens. There are, furthermore, apparently a number of extant bridles in various other parts of England, besides those in Chester County that Brushfield drew and wrote about,[13] and each one very likely carries with it its own detailed, local history. Nonetheless, so little has been written about them that had the industrious T. N. Brushfield not set about to report so exhaustively on scold's bridles and female torture, we would have known almost nothing about these instruments except for an improbable-sounding story or two. As it is, whenever the common metaphor of 'bridling a wife's tongue' turns up in the literature of this era the evidence should make us uncomfortably aware of a practice lurking behind that phrase that an original audience could well have heard as literal.

Scold's bridles are not directly mentioned as a means of taming the scold of Shakespeare's *Shrew* – and such a practice onstage would have been wholly antithetical to the play's desired romantic union as well as to the model of benevolent patriarchy that is insisted on here and elsewhere in Shakespeare.[14] What Shakespeare seems to have been doing in *Shrew* – in addition to shrewdly capitalising on the popularity of the contemporary '*hic mulier*' debate by giving it romantic life onstage – is conscientiously modelling a series of humane but effective methods for behavioural modification. The methods employed determinedly exclude the more brutal patriarchal practices that were circulating within popular jokes, village rituals, and in such ballads as 'A Merry Jest of a Shrewde and Curste Wyfe, Lapped in Morrelles Skin, for Her Good Behavyour', in which the husband tames his wife by first beating her and then wrapping her in the salted skin of the dead horse, 'Morel'. In 1594 or thereabout Shakespeare effectively pushes these practices off his stage. And in many ways his 'shrew' takes over the cultural discourse from this point on transforming the taming story from scenarios of physical brutality and reshaping the trope of the shrew/scold from an old, usually poor woman or a nagging wife into the newly romanticised vision of a beautiful, rich, and spirited young woman. But the sheer fact that the excluded brutalities lie suppressed in the margins of the shrew material also means that they travel as unseen partners, inside the more benevolent taming discourse that Shakespeare's play helps to mould. And, as Ann Thompson's synopsis of *Shrew*'s production history clearly demonstrates, such woman-battering although not part of Shakespeare's script, repeatedly leaks back in from the margins and turns up in subsequent productions and adaptations (including, for instance, the Burton–Taylor film version, to which director Franco Zeferelli added a spanking scene):

> In the late seventeenth century, John Lacey's *Sauny the Scott, or The Taming of the Shrew* (c. 1667), which supplanted Shakespeare's text on stage until it was replaced in 1754 by David Garrick's version called *Catherine and Petruchico*, inserts an additional scene in which the husband pretends to think that his wife's refusal to speak to him is due to toothache and sends for a surgeon to have her teeth drawn. This episode is repeated with relish in the eighteenth century in James Worsdale's adaptation *A Cure for a Scold* (1735).[15]

What turns up as the means to control rebellious women imagined by the play's seventeenth- and eighteenth-century versions is, essentially, the same form of violence as that suppressed in Shakespeare's playscript but available in the surrounding culture: the maiming/disfiguring of the mouth.

The scold's bridle is a practice tangled up in the cultural discourse about shrews. And while it is not materially present in the narrative of Shakespeare's play, horse references or horse representations – which are, oddly enough, an almost standard component of English folklore about unruly women – pervade the play.[16] The underlying literary 'low culture' trope of unruly horse/unruly woman seems likely to have been the connection that led first to a metaphoric idea of bridling women's tongues and eventually to the literal social practice. Inside that connection, even the verbs 'reign' and 'rein' come together in a fortuitous pun that reinforces male dominance. And there would no doubt have been additional metaphoric reinforcement for bridling from the bawdier use of the horse/rider metaphor and its connotations of male dominance. In this trope, to 'mount' and 'ride' a woman works both literally and metaphorically to exert control over the imagined disorder presumed to result from the 'woman on top'. Furthermore, the horse and rider are not only the standard components of the shrew-taming folk stories but are likewise the key feature of 'riding skimmington', which, unlike the French charivari customs of which it is a version, was intended to satirise marriages in which the wife was reputed to have beaten her husband (or was, in any case, considered the dominant partner).[17]

In shrew-taming folktale plots in general, the taming of the unruly wife is frequently coincident with the wedding trip home on horseback.[18] The trip, which is itself the traditional final stage to the 'bridal', is already the site of an unspoken pun on 'bridle' that gets foregrounded in Grumio's horse-heavy description of the journey home and the ruination of Kate's 'bridal' – 'how her horse fell, and she under her horse: ... how the horses ran away, how her bridle was burst' (IV.i.54, 59–60). By means of the syntactical elision of 'horse's', the phrase quite literally puts the bridle on Kate rather than her horse. What this suggests is that the scold's bridal/horse bridle/scold's bridle associations were available for resonant recall through the interaction of linguistic structures with narrative ones. The scold's bridle that Shakespeare did not literally include in his play is ultimately a form of violence that lives in the same location as the many offstage horses that are crowded into its non-representational space. The bridle is an artifact that exists in *Shrew*'s offstage margins – along with the fist-in-the-face that Petruchio does not use and the rape he does not enact in the offstage bedroom we do not see. Evoked into narrative possibility when Petruchio shares his taming strategy with the audience –

> This is a way to kill a wife with kindness,
> And thus I'll *curb* her mad and headstrong humour.
> He that knows better how to tame a shrew,

> Now let him speak – 'tis charity to show
>   (IV.i.179–82, my italics)

– the scold's bridle exists in this drama as a choice that has been deliberately excluded.

The antiquarians and few historians who have mentioned this instrument assign its initial appearance to the mid-1620s – a date that marks its first entry in a city record in northern England. There is, however, rather striking literary evidence to suggest that the scold's bridle not only existed some twenty to thirty years earlier but was apparently familiar to the playwrights and playgoers of London. The bridle turns up in Part II of Christopher Marlowe's *Tamburlaine the Great* (c. 1587) not as a metaphor but explicitly described as an extremely cruel instrument of torture that Tamburlaine devises for Orcanes and the three Egyptian kings who dare to protest when he kills his son, Calyphas, for being too womanish to fight. Demeaning their protest as dogs barking and scolds railing, Tamburlaine determines how he will punish their insolence:

> Well bark, ye dogs! I'll bridle all your tongues
> And bind them close with bits of burnished steel
> Down to the channels of your hateful throats;
> And, with the pains my rigor shall inflict,
> I'll make ye roar ...[19]

The scold's bridle is, furthermore, the key referent to understanding the condign nature of the punishment that the women jurors of the 1620 *Swetnam the Woman-hater Arraigned by Women* devise for the pamphlet writer, Joseph Swetnam, who had publicly declared himself the chief enemy to their sex. The dramatists, most probably women, dared – at a unique moment in English theatre history – to produce and have put on the stage at the Red Bull theatre a bold, political retaliation against the author of the notoriously misogynist pamphlet, *The Arraignment of Lewde, idle, froward, and unconstant women*. Having brought 'Misogynos' to trial, they order him to wear a 'Mouzell', be paraded in public, and be shown

> In every Street i'the Citie, and be bound
> In certaine places to Post or Stake,
> And bayted by all the honest women in the Parish.[20]

The above lines describe the standard humiliations involved in the bridling of a scold. Probably because so little has to date been said

about scolds' bridles, Simon Shepherd gives a tentative and parenthetical interpretation that '(presumably "Mouzell" alludes again to
[Rachel] Speght's pamphlet)'.[21] Unwittingly, the gloss obscures the
key point in the women dramatists' triumph. Onstage, their play
seeks poetic parity through condemning Swetnam to endure precisely the kinds of humiliation that women were sentenced to
undergo based on nothing more than the kinds of stereotyped accusations Swetnam's pamphlet reproduces.

Another pre-1620 allusion where the literal bridle seems once
again the likely referent occurs in the exchange Shakespeare earlier
wrote for his first 'shrew scene', the argument between Antipholus
the Ephesian's angry wife, Adriana, and her unmarried, dutiful, and
patriarchally correct sister, Luciana. Luciana's insistence that 'a
man is master of his liberty' and Adriana's feminist challenge, 'Why
should their liberty than ours be more?' provokes a dialogue that
seems to turn around a veiled warning about scolds' bridles from
Luciana and the furious rejection of that possibility from Adriana.

> Luciana O, know he is the bridle of your will.
> Adriana There's none but asses will be bridled so.
> Luciana Why, headstrong liberty is lash'd with woe...
> (*The Comedy of Errors*, II. i.13–15)

Another likely scold's bridle allusion turns up inside the shrew discourse in *Mundus Alter et Idem*, the strange voyage fantasy purportedly written by the traveller 'Mercurius Brittanicus' but actually
written by Joseph Hall and published (in Latin) in 1605. The work
– which Hall never publicly acknowledged but which went through
several printings and was even 'Englished' as *The Discovery of a
New World* in an unauthorised 1609 translation by John Healey[22] –
is accompanied by elaborate textual apparati that include a series of
Ortelius's maps, on top of which Hall has remapped his satiric
fantasy. In Hall's dystopia the narrator embarks in the ship
'Fantasia' and discovers the Antarctic continent, which is geograph-
ically the world upside down and therefore contains such travesties
of social organisation as a land of women. This is named 'New
Gynia, which others incorrectly call Guinea, [but which] I correctly
call Viraginia, located where European geographers depict the Land
of Parrots.'[23] The geography of Viraginia includes Gynaecopolis,
where Brittanicus is enslaved by its domineering women until he
reveals 'the name of my country (which is justly esteemed throughout the world as the "Paradise of Women")'.[24] In the province of

'Amazonia, or Gynandria', the fear of a society based on gender inversion emerges into full-blown nightmare: men wear petticoats and remain at home 'strenuously spinning and weaving' while women wear the breeches, attend to military matters and farming, pluck out their husband's beards and sport long beards themselves, imperiously enslave their husbands, beat them daily, and 'while the men work, the women ... quarrel and scold'.[25] What constitutes treason in this fantasised space is for any woman to treat her husband gently or with the slightest forbearance. As punishment for such treason, Hall's misogynistic satire adds one more twist to the shame-based model of gendered punishment by invoking a scenario of transvestite disguise similar to that which Shakespeare exploits in the boy-actor/Rosalind/Ganymede complications of *As You Like It*: the guilty wife 'must exchange clothes with her husband and dressed like this, head shaved, be brought to the forum to stand there an entire day in the pillory, exposed to the reproach and derisive laughter of the onlookers [until she] finally returns home stained with mud, urine, and all sorts of abuse ...'[26] Mercurius Britannicus is able to escape only because, since he is dressed in 'man's attire and ... in the first phase of an adolescent beard',[27] he is assumed to be female and thus enjoys a woman's freedom of movement.

Hall's Amazon fantasy – in which men may not select their dress, eat their food, conduct any business, go anywhere, speak to anyone, or ever speak up against their wives' opinions – is, of course, only an exaggeration of the lessons Kate is compelled to learn in Petruchio's taming school. The parallels derive from the fact that underlying both Hall's satire and Shakespeare's play is the same compulsive model that underwrites their culture – male fantasy of female dominance that is signified by the literary figure of the shrew/scold. Long before the Amazon fantasy emerges, the shrew story is implicit even in Mercurius Brittanicus's opening description of Viraginia's topographical features. In the region of Linguadocia (tongue), the society has ingeniously devised a means to control the enormous river called 'Sialon' (saliva) that flows through the city of 'Labriana' (lips). The overflow from Labriana could 'scarcely ... be contained even in such a vast channel, and indeed, ... the Menturnea Valley [chin] would be daily threatened by it had not the rather clever inhabitants carefully walled up the banks with bones.'[28] In the Healey translation the reference to scolds and the implied model of containing them is even clearer. In Healey almost

all provinces and cities are associated with women/excess
voicing/mouth through such names as 'Tattlingen', 'Scoldonna',
'Blubberick', 'Gigglottangir', 'Shrewes-bourg', 'Pratlingople',
'Gossipingoa', and 'Tales-borne'. To control the river 'Slauer' from
bursting out and overflowing 'Lypswagg', the 'countrimen haue
now deuised very strong rampires of bones and bend lether, to
keepe it from breaking out any more, but when they list to let it out
a little now & then for scouring of the channell'.[29]

Scolding is a verbal rebellion and controlling it was, in the instrument of the bridle, focused with condign exactitude on controlling a woman's tongue – the site of a nearly fetishised investment
that fills the discourse of the era with a true 'lingua franca', some
newly invented, some reprinted and repopularised in the late sixteenth to mid-seventeenth century. Among this didactic 'tongue literature' there is a quite amazing play by Thomas Tomkis that went
through five printings from 1607 to 1657 before its popularity
expired. In this play, called *Lingua: Or The Combat of the Tongue,
And the Five Senses For Superiority*, a female allegorical figure –
Lingua, dressed in purple and white – is finally brought to order by
the figures of the five senses who force her into compelled servitude
to 'Taste'.[30]

If – as I have speculated – the underlying idea for bridling a
woman comes initially from a 'low-culture' material association
between horse/woman, it was an association being simultaneously
coproduced on the 'high-culture' side within a religious discourse
that helped to legitimate such a literalisation. For in addition to a
number of repopularised theological treatises in Latin that dedicate
whole chapters to the sins of the tongue and emblem book pictures
that show models of the good wife pictured as a woman who is lit-
eralising the metaphoric by grasping her tongue between her
fingers, the era is stamped by that peculiarly Protestant literature of
self-purification in which the allegorical model of achieving interior
discipline by a 'bridling of the will' appears as an almost incessant
refrain. From the Protestant divines came a congeries of impassioned moral treatises that, as they linguistically test out their truths
by treading the extreme verge between literal and metaphoric, frequently move close to eliding any boundary between interior and
exterior application of self-discipline. Such suggestions occur in
works like *The Poysonous Tongue*, a 1615 sermon by John
Abernethy, Bishop of Cathnes, in which the personified tongue –
'one of the least members, most moueable, and least tyred' – is

ultimately imagined as an inflamed and poisonous enemy, especially to the other bodily members, and therefore the member most worthy to be severely, graphically punished.[31]

Discourse about the tongue is complexly invested with an ambivalent signification that marks it always as a discourse about gender and power – one in which the implied threat to male possession/male authority perhaps resolves itself only in the era's repeated evocation of the Philomela myth (a narrative that Shakespeare himself draws upon in a major way for three different works) – where a resolution to such gender contestation is achieved by the silencing of the woman, enacted as a cutting out – or castration – of her tongue. It was a male discourse that George Gascoigne had already taken to perhaps the furthest limits of aggression in 1593. Reduced to a court hack by the censorship of his master work, *A Hundreth Sundrie Flowers* (which he had retitled *The Posies* and tried without success to slip past the censors), Gasciogne in his last moralistic work *The Steel Glas* created a poetic persona who has been emasculated – hence depotentiated into the feminine – only to be raped and then have her tongue cut out by 'The Rayzor of Restraint'.[32]

A discourse that locates the tongue as the body's 'unruly member' situates female speech as a symbolic relocation of the male organ, an unlawful appropriation of phallic authority in which the symbolics of male castration are ominously complicit. If the chastity belt was an earlier design to prevent entrance into one aperture of the deceitfully open female body, the scold's bridle, preventing exit from another, might be imagined as a derivative inversion of that same obsession. Moreover, the very impetus to produce an instrument that actually bridled the tongue and bound it down into a woman's mouth suggests an even more complicated obsession about women's bodies/women's authority than does the chastity belt: in the obsession with the woman's tongue, the simple binary between presence and absence breaks down. Here, the obsession must directly acknowledge, even as it attempts to suppress, the presence in woman of the primary signifier of an authority presumed to be masculine. The tongue (at least in the governing assumptions about order) should always already have been possessed only by the male. Needless to say, theologians found ways of tracing these crimes of usurpation by the woman's unruly member back to the Garden, to speech, to Eve's seduction by the serpent, and thence to her seductive appropriation of Adam's rightful authority. Says the author of a sermon called *The Government of the Tongue*:

> Original sin came first out at the mouth by speaking, before it entered in by eating. The first use we find *Eve* to have made of her language, was to enter parly with the temter, and from that to become a temter to her husband. And immediately upon the fall, guilty *Adam* frames his tongue to a frivolous excuse, which was much less able to cover his sin than the fig-leaves were his naked-ness.[33]

Through Eve's open mouth, then, sin and disorder entered the world. Through her verbal and sexual seduction of Adam – through her use of that other open female bodily threshold – sin then became the inescapable curse of mankind. All rebellion is a form of usurpation of one sort or another, and if Eve's sin – her 'first use of language' through employment of her tongue – is likewise imagined as the usurpation of the male phallic instrument and the male signifier of language, the images of woman speaking and woman's tongue become freighted with heavy psychic baggage. Perpetually guilty, perpetually disorderly, perpetually seductive, Eve and her descendants become *the* problem that society must control.

In relation to scolds' bridles and the ways that the violent self-discipline urged by these treatises seeks to legitimate a literal practice, Thomas Adams's 1616 sermon, 'The Taming of the Tongue', is of particular interest. With a title suggestively close to that of Shakespeare's play, it envisions a future of brimstone and scalding fire for the untamable tongue and warns that the tongue is so intransigent that 'Man hath no bridle, not cage of brasse, nor barres of yron to *tame* it'.[34] Likewise, in a sermon by Thomas Watson, we are told that

> The Tongue, though it be a little Member, yet it hath a World of Sin in it. The tongue is an unruly Evil. We put *Bitts* in Horses mouths and rule them; but the Tongue is an unbridled Thing. It is hard to find a Curbing-bitt to rule the Tongue.[35]

Thus, when William Gearing dedicates his ominously titled treatise, *A Bridle for the Tongue: or, A Treatise of Ten Sins of the Tongue* to Sir Orlando Bridgman, Chief Justice of the Court of Common Pleas, his use of the bridle goes too far beyond the metaphoric to be construed as such. If anything, it seems prescriptive. In the dedication Gearing points out that the 'Tongue hath no Rein by nature, but hangeth loose in the midst of the mouth', and then invokes the Third Psalm to proclaim that the Lord will 'strike' those who scold 'on the cheekbone (jawbone), and break out their teeth'. Speaking here in an already gendered discourse, Gearing appears to invoke scriptural authority as justification for legalising the iron bridle as an instrument of official punishment.[36] In the process, his scriptural reference graphically suggests what could well have happened to the hapless women who were yanked through town, a lead rope attached to the metal bridle locked firmly around their heads, their tongues depressed by a two-to-three-inch metal piece called a 'gag'. Besides effecting the involuntary regurgitation that the term suggests, the gag could easily have slammed into their teeth with every pull, smashing their jawbones and breaking out their teeth, until finally the offending shrew would be tied up and made to stand in the town square, an object to be pissed on and further ridiculed at will.

There is one known account written by a woman who was bridled. We may infer from Dorothy Waugh's testimony that she experienced the bridling as a sexual violation. When her narrative reaches the moment of the gag being forced into her mouth, her embarrassment nearly overwhelms description and her words stumble as they confront the impossibility of finding a language for the tongue to repeat its own assault. Repeatedly, she brackets off references to the bridle with phrases like 'as they called it', as if to undermine its reality. Physically violated, made to stand bridled in the jail as an object of shame for citizens to pay twopence to view, and released still imprisoned in the bridle to be whipped from town to town in a manner that parallels the expulsion of a convicted whore, Dorothy Waugh several times asserts 'they had not any thing to lay to my Charge', as if the assertion of her innocence could frame her experience within the discourse of legality and extricate it from the one of sexual violation that it keeps slipping towards. Waugh's account of her *cruell usage by the Mayor of Carlile* occurs as the final piece of seven Quaker testimonies that comprise *The Lambs Defence against Lyes. And A True Testimony given concerning the Sufferings and Death of James Parnell* (1656). Originally haled off to prison after she had been 'moved of the Lord to goe into the market of *Carlile* to speake against all deceit & ungodly practices', Dorothy Waugh's implicit subversion of the local authority and substitution of biblical quotations as a source of self-authorisation is clearly what impelled the mayor into so implacable an antagonism. To the mayor's question from whence she came, Waugh responded:

> I said out of Egypt where thou lodgest; But after these words he was so violent & full of passion he scarce asked me any more Questions, but called to one of his followers to bring the bridle as he called it to put on me, and was to be on three houres, and that which they called so was like a steele cap and my hatt being violently pluckt off which was pinned to my head whereby they tare my Clothes to put on their bridles as they called it, which was a stone weight of Iron by the relation of their own Generation, & three barrs of Iron to come over my face, and a peece of it was put in my mouth, which was so unreasonable big a thing for that place as cannot be well related, which was locked to my head, and so I stood their time with my hands bound behind me with the stone weight of Iron upon my head and the bitt in my mouth to keep me from speaking; And The Mayor said he would make me an Example ... Afterwards it was taken off and they kept me in prison for a little season, and after a while the Mayor came up againe and caused it to be put on againe, and sent me out of the Citty with it on, and gave me very vile and unsavoury words, which were not fit to proceed out of any man's mouth, and charged the Officer to whip me out of the Towne, from Constable to Constable to send me, till I came to my owne home, when as they had not any thing to lay to my charge.[37]

If we may be thankful about anything connected with the scold's bridle, it is that so many were found in a county whose antiquarian groups were especially diligent in recording and preserving the local heritage. Mr T. N. Brushfield meticulously preserved all records he uncovered, even to the extent of making detailed drawings of the bridles he found in Cheshire and neighbouring areas. But in doing so, he also unwittingly managed to preserve some of the ideas and attitudes that had originally forged these instruments. Thus his own discourse, as he describes these appalling artifacts and instances of their use, stands smugly disjunct from its subject and seems disconcertingly inappropriate in its own investments and responses. As he opens his introduction of the scold's bridle, for instance, he rhetorically establishes a legitimating lineage for his authority by deferring to – without ever considering the implications of the text he invokes – the work of one of England's earliest antiquarians. He thus begins: 'In commencing a description of the Brank or Scold's Bridle, I cannot do better than quote a passage from Dr Plot's *Natural History of Staffordshire*' (1686). He then proceeds, without the slightest dismay or query, to pass along the following description from Dr Plot:

Lastly, we come to the *Arts* that respect *Mankind*, amongst which, as elsewhere, the civility of precedence must be allowed to the *women*, and that as well in punishments as favours. For the former whereof, they have such a peculiar *artifice* at *New Castle* (under Lyme) and *Walsall*, for correcting of *Scolds*; which it does, too, so effectually, and so very safely, that I look upon it as much to be preferred to the *Cucking Stoole*, which not only endangers the *health* of the party, but also gives the tongue liberty 'twixt every dipp; to neither of which is this at all lyable; it being such a *Bridle* for the tongue, as not only quite deprives them of speech, but brings shame for the transgression, and humility thereupon, before 'tis taken off ... which, being put upon the offender by order of the magistrate, and fastened with a *padlock* behind, she is lead round the towne by an *Officer* to her shame, nor is it taken off, till after the party begins to show all external signes imaginable of humiliation and amendment.[38]

To be released from the instrument that rendered them mute, the silenced shrews of Dr Plot's narrative were compelled to employ their bodies to plead the required degradation. Yet to imagine just what pantomimes of pain, guilt, obeisance to authority and self-abjection might have been entailed is almost as disturbing an exercise as is imagining the effects of the bridle itself.

Although Brushfield did unearth evidence that the scold's bridle had been used as late as the 1830s, it is clear that the use of such an instrument of torture at any time in England's history had managed to disappear beneath a convenient public amnesia until only a decade prior to his 1858 report. No longer used in public punishments, the bridles had been recycled behind the walls of state institutions; most turned up in places like women's workhouses, mental institutions, and other such establishments that, by the nineteenth century, had conveniently removed society's marginal people from public view. In the 1840s the scold's bridle seems to have caught the eye of the antiquarians, and Brushfield is therefore at pains to describe in detail the variety of bridles in the rich trove he has collected in Cheshire. Some, he tells us, are

contrived with hinged joints, as to admit of being readily adapted to the head of the scold. It was generally supplied with several connecting staples, so as to suit heads of different sizes, and was secured by a padlock. Affixed to the inner portion of the hoop was a piece of metal, which, when the instrument was properly fitted, pressed the tongue down, and effectually branked or bridled it. The length of the mouthpiece or gag varied from $1\frac{1}{2}$ inch to 3 inches – if more than $2\frac{1}{2}$ inches, the punishment would be much increased, – as, granting that the instrument was fitted moderately tight, it would not only arrest the action of the tongue, but also excite distressing symptoms of sickness, more especially if the wearer became at all unruly. The form of the gag was very diversified, the most simple being a mere flat piece of iron; in some the extremity was turned upwards, in others downwards; on many of the specimens both surfaces were covered with rasp-like elevations. The instrument was generally painted, and sometimes in variegated colours, in which case the gag was frequently red ... A staple usually existed at the back part of the instrument, to which was attached a short chain terminating in an iron ring: – any additional length required was supplied by a rope.

Wearing this effectual curb on her tongue, the silenced scold was sometimes fastened to a post in some conspicuous portion of the town – generally the market-place ...[39]

One bridle that was formerly used in Manchester Market 'to control the energetic tongues of the female stall-keepers', as Brushfield puts it, was found in the mid-nineteenth century still retaining its original coverings of alternating white and red cotton bands; its 'gag being large, with rasp-like surfaces; the leading-chain three feet long, and attached to the front part of the horizontal hoop'.[40] The spectacular red and white carnival festivity of the Manchester bridle would have no doubt been augmented not only by some appropriately carnivalesque parade and by the bridled woman comically resembling a horse in tournament trappings but likewise by the colourful if painful effects that almost any gag would have been likely to produce. Such effects are vividly illustrated in the account of a witness to, a 1653 bridling, who saw

One Ann Bidlestone, drove through the streets, by an officer of the same corporation [i.e., the city of Newcastle], holding a rope in his hand, the other end fastened to an engine, called the branks, which is like a crown, it being of iron which was musled, over the head and face, with a great gap [sic] or tongue of iron forced into her mouth, which forced the blood out; and that is the punishment which the magistrates do inflict upon chiding, and scoulding women.[41]

The same witness declared that he had 'often seen the like done to others'.

Brushfield – having described some six or seven variations of the bridle, including one 'very handsome specimen' that was 'surmounted with a decorated cross'[42] – leads up to his *tour de force*, the 'STOCKPORT Brank'. This 'perfectly unique specimen, ... by far the most remarkable in this county', currently belongs, he tells

us, to the corporate authorities of Stockport, whom he thanks effu-
sively for granting him the honour of being the very first person
privileged to sketch it:

> The extraordinary part of the instrument … is the gag, which com-
> mences flat at the hoop and terminates in a bulbous extremity, which
> is covered with *iron pins*, nine in number, there being three on the
> upper surface, three on the lower, and three pointing backwards; and
> it is scarcely possible to affix it in its destined position without
> wounding the tongue. To make matters still worse, the chain (which
> yet remains attached, and … measures two feet) is connected to the
> hoop in the fore part, as if to *pull* the wearer of the Bridle along on
> her unwilling tour of the streets; for it is very apparent that any
> motion of the gag must have lacerated the mouth very severely.
> Another specimen was formerly in the WORKHOUSE AT STOCK-
> PORT, and was sold, a few years ago, as old iron![43]

As he recounts the unauthorised sale of this extraordinary item as
scrap iron, Brushfield rises to outrage. He then launches into an in-
dignant description of how this bridle – which was originally and
legally the property of Brushfield's own Chester – had been given
away some thirty years before by the Chester jailer. Of this abuse of
property rights, Brushfield insists that, while 'The liberality of the
donor cannot perhaps be questioned … the right of transfer, on the
part of that official, is altogether another matter!' Therefore, 'An in-
ventory of these curious relics, taken once or twice a year under the
authority of the city magistrates, would', Brushfield exclaims, 'effectually curb these "fits of abstraction"'.[44] And as T. N. Brushfield's
disquisition on scolds' bridles devolves to issues of male ownership,
legitimate transmission, and proprietary rights, as his language
slides into a recommendation for curbing dangerous signs of liberality, and as he speaks forth his own authoritative proposals for insti-
tuting control over rights to own these brutal instruments that carry
with them a silenced women's history, it may well seem to the
stultified reader that 1858 is really still 1598 as far as any progress
in the complexly burdened history of women's space within culture
is concerned. Were we to shift the venue from sex to race, the assumption would be accurate. For while Mr T. N. Brushfield read
his paper on 'obsolete punishments' and registered genteel disapproval over his forefathers' use of such a barbaric control on the
fair sex of Chester County, on the other side of the Atlantic,
England's cultural heirs had carried this model of control one step
further. By 1858 – as readers of Toni Morrison's *Beloved* will recall

– the scold's bridle had been cycled over to the American South and the Caribbean, where in 1858 it was being used to punish unruly slaves.[45]

Among historians, 'scolds' or 'shrews' are commonly defined as a particular category of offender, almost without exception female. In David Underdown's descriptive scenario, 'women who were poor, social outcasts, widows or otherwise lacking in the protection of a family, or newcomers to their communities, were the most common offenders. Such women were likely to vent their frustration against the nearest symbols of authority.'[46] And, we might add, such women were also the most likely to have the community's frustration vented against them. But the evidence that T. N. Brushfield has left about the bridle suggests that this definition of scolds – which is derived mainly from various legal records, most of which are, in any case, documents of cucking-stool punishments – may be far too narrow.

From the rich evidence T. N. Brushfield compiled from a variety of archaeological journals, offbeat treatises, collective town memories, and information given him by senior citizens acting as quasi-official transmitters of oral history in towns and cities around Cheshire, we discover that the scold's bridle was apparently a symbol of mayoral office that passed from one city administration to the next, being delivered along with the mace and other recognised signs of officialdom into the keeping of the town jailer. The jailer's services, we learn,

> were not unfrequently called into requisition. In the old-fashioned, half-timbered houses in the Borough, there was generally fixed on one side of the large open fire-places, a hook; so that when a man's wife indulged her scolding the husband sent for the town Jailer to bring the Bridle, and had her bridled and chained to the hook until she promised to behave herself better for the future.[47]

One member of Brushfield's antiquary group was a former mayor of the town of Congleton, where hooks on the side of fireplaces still existed. According to his account, so chilling was the memory of this method of controlling domestic disputes that husbands in nineteenth-century Congleton could still induce instant obedience from their wives just by saying, 'If you don't rest with your tongue, I'll send for the Bridle, and hook you up'. The local bookseller at Macclesfield reported to Brushfield that he had frequently seen the bridle produced at petty sessions of the court '*in terrorem* to stay the volubility of a woman's tongue; and that a threat by a magistrate to order its appliance, had always proved sufficient to abate the garrulity of the most determined scold'.[48] By 1858, although the signified object had disappeared from social practice, it still existed within the culture as a powerful signifier of what had become a silenced history of women's silencing.

For evidence like the above we probably owe T. N. Brushfield a debt of gratitude. He preserved material that suggests a whole secondary, shadowed subtext to the history of women and the law – a history outside the law and yet one that took place inside England's much touted rule of law; a history that had no juries, no court trials, no official sentences, and that left few telltale records of itself; yet a history that was nonetheless passed down, circulated, and tacitly authorised in town after town, inside county court-houses, city jails, mayoral offices, corporate holdings, and authenticated by an entire set of legitimating signifiers. In the town of Congleton, not only was a husband 'thy lord, thy king, thy governor / ... thy life, thy keeper, / Thy head, thy sovereign' (*Shrew*, V.ii.138 and 146–7), he was also the law, and his tyrannies were supported by the existing legal institutions. And while such a grim history as that which is carried by the iron bridle may seem far indeed from Shakespeare's zesty comedy about the taming of shrews into conformable Kates, I would insist that it is not. For Kate the fictional shrew is but one of those women whose real history can all too easily be hidden behind and thus effectively erased by the romanticised version of her story that Shakespeare's play participates in creating.

Around 1640 the proverbial scold seems virtually to disappear from court documents. As Susan Amussen informs us, the 'formal mechanisms of control were rarely used after the Restoration'.[49]

> The prosecution of scolds was most common before 1640; while accusations of scolding, abusing neighbours, brawling in church and other forms of quarrelling usually make up between a tenth and a quarter of the offences in sample Act Books of the Archdeacons of Norwich and Norfolk before 1640, they do not appear in the samplebooks after 1660.[50]

Why did scolds apparently disappear? Were they always just the projection of an order-obsessed culture, who disappeared when life became more orderly? Or is the difference real and the behaviour of women in the early modern era indeed different from the norms of a later one? Did they really brawl, curse, scold, riot, and behave so abusively? Brushfield clearly assumes that they did, and thus is able to rationalise the otherwise disturbing fact that so many of these illegal instruments of torture turned up in good old Cheshire County, his own home space. As he says, 'if such a number of tongue-repressing Bridles were required', then they were so because the women must have been so disorderly as to have turned Cheshire into 'a riotous County indeed'. Benevolently, however, he then continues, forgiving England its disruptive foremothers and invoking the authority of the Bard himself to authorise his beatific vision of silent women:

> Suffice it, however, for us to say, – and I speak altogether on behalf of [all] the gentlemen, – that whatever it may have been in times gone by, yet it is certain that the gentleness and amiability of the ladies of the present generation make more than ample amends for the past; and Shakespeare, when he wrote those beautiful words,
>
> 'Her voice was ever soft, / Gentle and low; an excellent thing in woman',
>
> unintentionally, of course, yet fully anticipated the attributes of our modern Cheshire ladies.[51]

And it well may be that in his work on scolds' bridles, T. N. Brushfield may unwittingly have described the silent process of how gender is historicised. He may have recorded the social process by which the women of their generation – perhaps as rowdy, brawling, voluble, and outspoken as men have always been authorised to be – were shamed, tamed, and reconstituted by instruments like cucking stools and scolds' bridles, into the meek and amiable, softspoken ladies he so admires in his own time.[52] Perhaps the gentle and pleasing Stepford Wives of mid-nineteenth-century Chester are precisely the products that such a searing socialisation into gender would produce – and would continue to reproduce even long after the immediate agony of being bridled or of watching a daughter, mother, or sister being paraded through the streets and forced to endure that experience had passed from personal and recorded memory. The history of silencing is a history of internalising the literal, of erasing the signifier and interiorising a signified. The iron bridle is a part of that history. Its appropriate epigraph is a couplet from

Andrew Marvell's 'Last Instructions to a Painter'[53] – a couplet that could in fact have been written at exactly the moment that some curst and clamorous Kate in some English town was being bridled:

> Prudent Antiquity, that knew by Shame
> Better than Law, Domestic Crimes to tame.

From *Shakespeare Quarterly*, 42 (1991), 194–213.

NOTES

[Unfortunately, because of the constraints of space and finance I have been unable to include the whole of Lynda E. Boose's excellent essay in this collection. Brief notes on the first part of that essay will, I hope, both serve to elucidate the subsequent excerpt for the reader, as well as to do justice to the complex historicised argument Boose makes. She reasons that it is essential to historicise Shakespeare's plays and *The Taming of the Shrew* in particular, in order to comprehend the real-life social background which produced the texts. Ed.]

1. For an exemplum text on working with multiple documents coming from a variety of sources, including hitherto unused ones, see Alan Macfarlane, with Sarah Harrison, *The Justice and the Mare's Ale: Law and Disorder in Seventeenth-century England 1550–1750* (New York, 1981).

2. Keith Wrightson and David Levine, *Poverty and Piety in an English Village: Terling, 1525–1700* (New York, 1979). See also J. A. Sharpe, *Crime in Early Modern England 1550–1750* (London, 1984), p. 53; and 'Crime and Delinquency in an Essex Parish 1600–1649', in *Crime in England 1550–1800*, J. S. Cockburn (ed.), (London, 1977), pp. 90–109.

3. In the twentieth century the social offenders who had four centuries earlier been signified by whoring, witchcraft, scolding, and being masterless men and women have been replaced by those whose identity may be similarly inferred from the fetishised criminality the state currently attaches to abortion, AIDS, street drugs, and, most recently, subway-panhandling (read homelessness).

4. John Webster Spargo devotes considerable time to examining this and other etymological questions; see *Juridical Folklore in England: Illustrated by the Cucking Stool* (Durham, NC, 1944), esp. pp. 3–75. An exchange in Middleton's *The Family of Love* depends on the equation. In response to her husband's threat, 'I say you are a scold, and beware the cucking-stool', Mistress Glister snaps back, 'I say you are a ninnihammer, and beware the cuckoo' (*The Works of Thomas*

Middleton, ed. A. H. Bullen, 8 vols [London, 1885], V.i.25–8). My thanks to Sarah Lyons for this reference.

5. John Webster, *The Duchess of Malfi*, ed. Elizabeth M. Brennan (New York, 1983), I.ii.255–6, 257.

6. Peter Stallybrass, 'Reading the Body: *The Revenger's Tragedy* and the Jacobean Theater of Consumption', *Renaissance Drama*, 18 (1987), 121–48, esp. p. 122. See also Frank Whigham, 'Reading Social Conflict in the Ailmentary Tract: More on the Body in Renaissance Drama', *English Literary History*, 55 (1988), 333–50; and Patricia Parker, *Literary Fat Ladies: Rhetoric, Gender, Property* (London, 1987).

7. The stigma that joins these two signs is clearly a durable one, for even in the twentieth century, if a woman is known as 'loud mouthed' or is reputed to participate (especially in so-called 'mixed company') in the oral activities of joking, cursing, telling boisterous tales, drinking, and even eating – activities that are socially unstigmatised for males – she can still be signified negatively by meanings that derive from an entirely different register.

8. T. N. Brushfield, 'On Obsolete Punishments, With particular reference to those of Cheshire', *Chester Archaeological and Historic Society Journal*, 2 (1855–62), 31–48 and 203–34; p. 46. [In the full version of this essay Boose describes Brushfield's two-part paper which details the extant cucking stools and their earlier use in the Chester area – Ed.]

9. Brushfield, 'On Obsolete Punishments', p. 35 n.

10. David Underdown's 'The Taming of the Scold' is a notable exception. Literary essays that have brought the scold's bridle into focus and have included depictions of it include Joan Hartwig's 'Horses and Women in *The Taming of the Shrew*', *Huntington Library Quarterly*, 45 (1982), 285–94; Valerie Wayne's 'Refashioning the Shrew', *Shakespeare Studies*, 17 (1985), 159–88; and Patricia Parker, who calls the scold's bridle 'a kind of chastity belt for the tongue' (*Literary Fat Ladies*, p. 27).

11. The sampler is an heirloom in the family of Michael Neill, who provided this information.

12. My knowledge of this bridle comes from Deborah Shuger. In the frontispiece the woman with the bridle is only one figure in a quite complex visualisation of interior Protestant virtues, and it is impossible to know whether the bridle she holds intentionally depicts the instrument used on scolds or is purely an allegorical representation of interior discipline. But in a culture where the allegorical is simultaneously the literal and a bridle is being used to produce exterior discipline on

unruly women, the problem of signification is such that one representation cannot, it seems to me, remain uncontaminated from association with the other.

13. I am particularly indebted to Susan Warren for her invaluable research
in Cheshire County into this issue. Not only was she able to locate the
whereabouts of several of these items, but she discovered from an
overheard conversation between two women that the notion of a
woman 'needing to be bridled' was apparently still alive in the local
phrasing.

14. See especially Peter Erikson, *Patriarchal Structures in Shakespeare's
Drama* (Berkeley, CA, 1985).

15. Ann Thompson (ed.), *The Taming of the Shrew* (Cambridge, 1984),
pp. 18–19.

16. See especially Joan Hartwig (cited in n. 10. above) and Jeanne Addison
Roberts, 'Horses and Hermaphrodites: Metamorphoses in *The Taming
of the Shrew*', *Shakespeare Quarterly*, 34 (1983), 159–71, as well as
Linda Woodbridge, *Women and the English Renaissance: Literature
and the Nature of Womankind, 1540–1620* (Urbana, IL, 1984).

17. Antiquarian folklorist C. R. B. Barrett notes the first recorded skimmington at Charing Cross in 1562. See Barrett, '"Riding
Skimmington" and "Riding the Stang"', *Journal of the British
Archaeological Association*, 1 (1895), 58–68, esp. p. 63. Barrett discusses the way that a skimmington usually involved not the presentation of the erring couple themselves but the representation of them
acted out by their next-door neighbours, other substitutes, or even
effigies. Thomas Lupton's *Too Good to be True* (1580) includes a dialogue that comments acerbically upon the use of neighbours rather
than principals.
    As Martin Ingram notes, 'the characteristic pretext for such ridings
was when a wife beat her husband or in some other noteworthy way
proved that she wore the breeches' ('Ridings, Rough Music and
Mocking Rhymes in Early Modern England', in *Popular Culture in
Seventeenth-Century England*, ed. Barry Reay [New York, 1985],
pp. 166–97; p. 168). The skimmington derisions frequently incorpo-
rated the symbolics of cuckoldry – antlers or animal horned heads –
once again collapsing the two most pervasively fetishised signs of
female disorder into a collocation by which female dominance means
male cuckoldry.

18. See Thompson, *Shrew*, p. 12. All *Shrew* citations refer to this edition,
and quotations from other Shakespeare plays refer to *The Riverside
Shakespeare*, ed. G. Blakemore Evans (Boston, 1974); all references
will appear in the text.

19. *Tamburlaine the Great, Parts I and II*, ed. John D. Jump (Lincoln, NA, 1967), IV.i.180–4.

20. *Swetnam the Woman-hater: The Controversy and the Play*, ed. Coryl Crandall (Purdue, IN, 1969), V.ii.331–3. Given the impetus behind the writing of this play, it seems at least worth speculation that if women ever did dislodge the convention of boy actors during this period and appear onstage in women's roles themselves, this play would seem a prime location for such a possibility.

21. Simon Shepherd, *Amazons and Warrior Women: Varieties of Feminism on Seventeenth-Century Drama* (New York, 1981), p. 208.

22. Huntington Brown, ed. (Cambridge, MA, 1937).

23. *Another World and Yet the Same: Bishop Joseph Hall's* Mundus Alter et Idem, trans. and ed. John Millar Wands (New Haven and London, 1981): see 'Book Two: Viraginia or New Gynia', pp. 57–67, esp. p. 57.

24. Hall, *Another World*, p. 58.

25. Ibid., p. 64.

26. Ibid., p. 65.

27. Ibid., p. 66.

28. Ibid., p. 57.

29. Huntington Brown, *The Discovery*, pp. 64–5.

30. Catherine Belsey also refers to this play; see *The Subject of Tragedy: Ideology and Difference in Renaissance Drama* (London and New York, 1985) p. 181.

31. Other tongue treatises include an address by George Webbe, Bishop of Limerick, called *The Arraignement of an unruly Tongue Wherein the Faults of an euill Tongue are opened, the Danger Discouered, the Remedies prescribed, for the Taming of a Bad Tongue, the Right Ordering of the Tongue* ... (London. 1619); an offering by William Perkins in *A Direction for the Gouernment of the Tongue according to Gods Word* (Cambridge, 1593); a sermon by Thomas Adams on *The Taming of the Tongue* (London, 1616); a series of 'tongue' sermons by Jeremy Taylor (1653); and Edward Reyner's *Rules for the Government of the Tongue* (1656). The latter is accompanied by a prayer that the book shall prove 'effectuall to tame that unruly Member thy Tongue, and so make thee a good linguist in the School of Christ'. Spargo provides further data on the publication of all these treatises (*Juridical Folklore*, pp. 119–20).

32. In particular see Richard C. McCoy's essay, 'Gasciogne's "*Poemata castrata*": The Wages of Courtly Success', *Criticism*, 27 (1985), 29–55.

33. As quoted in Spargo, *Juridical Folklore*, pp. 118–19, n.28; Spargo notes that there has been considerable controversy over authorship.

34. Quoted here from Spargo, *Juridical Folklore*, p. 115, n. 21, the sermon was first printed in Adams's *The Sacrifice of Thankfulness* (London, 1616).

35. 'On the Government of the Tongue' appears in *A Body of Practical Divinity* (London, 1692), pp. 986–94.

36. Gearing, *A Bridle* (London, 1663); Spargo concurs with my reading (*Juridical Folklore*, p. 118. n. 26).

37. *The Lamb's Defence* (London, 1656), pp. 29–30. My thanks to Ann Blake for alerting me to the existence of this first-person account.

38. Quoted from Brushfield, 'On Obsolete Punishments', p. 33.

39. Ibid., p. 37.

40. Ibid., p. 269. This information was forwarded to the Chester Archaeological Society some eighteen months after Brushfield had read his paper and is included by the secretary in the 4 April (1860?) minutes. In the body of the paper he had earlier noted that bridles with their leading-chains attached to the nose-piece or front of the horizontal hoop – as is the chain on the Manchester bridle – were those designed to 'inflict the greatest lacerations to the wearer's tongue' (p. 37).

41. Ibid., p. 37.

42. Ibid., p. 44.

43. Ibid., p. 45.

44. Ibid.

45. In Morrison, Paul D. carries with him the memory of having 'had a bit in [his] mouth ... about how offended the tongue is, held down by iron, how the need too spit is so deep you cry for it. [Sethe] already knew about it, had seen it time after time ... Men, boys, little girls, women. The wildness that shot up into the eye the moment the lips were yanked back. Days after it was taken out, goose fat was rubbed on the corners of the mouth but nothing to soothe the tongue or take the wildness out of the eye' (*Beloved* [New York, 1987], pp. 69, 71).

46. David Underdown, 'The Taming of the Scold: the Enforcement of Patriarchal Authority in Early Modern England', in *Order and Disorder in Early Modern England*, ed. Anthony Fletcher and John Stevenson (Cambridge, 1985), p. 120. It was thought unseemly to duck or publicly punish women of higher status, primarily because in that class the status of the husband was invested in the wife, no doubt making officials reluctant to sentence such wives to punishments more harsh than a fine.

47. Brushfield, 'On Obsolete Punishments', p. 42.

48. Ibid.

49. Susan Amussen, *An Ordered Society: Gender and Class in Early Modern England* (London, 1988), p. 150.

50. Ibid., p. 122.

51. Brushfield, 'On Obsolete Punishments', p. 47. The Shakespeare lines Brushfield quotes are, of course, King Lear's words as he bends over the dead – and very silent – Cordelia.

52. Such a progress would complement the transformation Margaret George defines as 'From "Goodwife" to "Mistress": the transformation of the female in bourgeois culture', *Science and Society*, 37 (1973), 152–77.

53. I defer to David Underdown, who earlier used these lines as an epigraph to 'The Taming of the Scold'.

9

Household Kates: Domesticating Commodities in *The Taming of the Shrew*

NATASHA KORDA

Commentary on Shakespeare's *The Taming of the Shrew* has frequently noted that the play's novel taming strategy marks a departure from traditional shrew-taming tales. Unlike his predecessors, Petruchio does not use force to tame Kate; he does not simply beat his wife into submission.[1] Little attention has been paid, however, to the historical implications of the play's unorthodox methodology, which is conceived in specifically economic terms: 'I am he am born to tame you, Kate', Petruchio summarily declares, 'And bring you from a wild Kate to a Kate / Conformable as other household Kates' (II.i.269–71).[2] Petruchio likens Kate's planned domestication to a domestication of the emergent commodity form itself, whose name parallels the naming of the shrew. The *Oxford English Dictionary* defines *cates* as 'provisions or victuals bought (as distinguished from, and usually more delicate or dainty than, those of home production)'. The term is an aphetic form of *acate*, which derives from the Old French *achat*, meaning 'purchase'.[3] Cates are thus by definition exchange-values – commodities, properly speaking – as opposed to use-values, or objects of home production.[4] In order to grasp the historical implications of *Shrew's* unorthodox methodology and of the economic terms Shakespeare employs to shape its taming strategy, I would like first to situate precisely the form of its departure from previous shrew-taming tales. What differentiates *The Taming of the Shrew* from its precursors is not so much a concern with domestic economy – which has always been a central preoccupation of shrew-taming literature – but rather a shift in *modes of production* and thus in the very terms through which domestic economy is conceived. The coordinates of this shift are contained within the term *cates* itself, which, in distinguishing goods that are purchased from those that are produced within and for the home, may be said to map the historical shift from domestic use-value production to production for the market.

Prior to Shakespeare's play, shrews were typically portrayed as reluctant producers within the household economy, high-born wives who refused to engage in the forms of domestic labour expected of them by their humble tradesman husbands. In the ballad 'The Wife Wrapped in a Wether's Skin', for example, the shrew refuses to brew, bake, wash, card, or spin on account of her 'gentle kin' and delicate complexion:

> There was a wee cooper who lived in Fife,
> Nickety, nackity, noo, noo, noo
> And he has gotten a gentle wife ...
> Alane, quo Rushety, roue, roue, roue
>
> She wadna bake, nor she wadna brew,
> For the spoiling o her comely hue.
>
> She wadna card, nor she wadna spin,
> For the shaming o her gentle kin.
>
> She wadna wash, nor she wadna wring,
> For the spoiling o her gouden ring.[5]

The object of the tale was simply to put the shrew to work, to restore her (frequently through some gruesome form of punishment[6] to her proper productive place within the household economy. When the cooper from Fife, who cannot beat his ungentle wife due to her gentle kin, cleverly wraps her in a wether's skin and tames her by beating the hide instead, the shrew promises: 'Oh, I will bake, and I will brew, / And never mair think on my comely hue. / Oh, I will card, and I will spin, / And never mair think on my gentle kin', etc.[7] Within the tradition of shrew-taming literature prior to Shakespeare's play, the housewife's domestic responsibilities were broadly defined by a feudal economy based on household production, on the production of use-values for domestic consumption.[8]

With the decline of the family as an economic unit of production, however, the role of the housewife in late-sixteenth-century England was beginning to shift from that of skilled producer to savvy consumer. In this period household production was gradually being replaced by nascent capitalist industry, making it more economical for the housewife to purchase what she had once produced. Brewing and baking, for example, once a routine part of the housewife's activity, had begun to move from the home to the market, becoming the province of skilled (male) professionals.[9] Washing and spinning, while still considered 'women's work', were becoming unsuitable activities for middle-class housewives and were increasingly delegated to servants, paid laundresses, or spinsters.[10] The housewife's duties were thus gradually moving away from the production of use-values within and for the home and toward the consumption of market goods, or cates, commodities produced outside the home. The available range of commodities was also greatly increased in the period, so that goods once considered luxuries, available only to the wealthiest elites, were now being found in households at every level of society.[11] Even 'inferior artificers and many farmers', as William Harrison notes in his *Description of England*, had 'learned ... to garnish their cupboards with plate, their joint beds with tapestry and silk hangings, and their tables with carpets and fine napery'.[12] *The Taming of the Shrew* may be said both to reflect and to participate in this cultural redefinition by portraying Kate not as a reluctant producer but rather as an avid and sophisticated consumer of market goods. When she is shown shopping in Act IV, scene iii (a scene I will discuss at greater length below), she displays both her knowledge of and preference for the latest fashions in apparel. Petruchio's taming strategy is accordingly aimed not at his wife's productive capacity – he never asks Kate to brew, bake, wash, card, or spin – but at her consumption. He seeks to educate Kate in her new role as a consumer of household cates.

Before examining in precisely what way Petruchio seeks to tame Kate's consumption of cates, I would like to introduce a further complication into this rather schematic account of the shift from household production to consumption, being careful not to conflate material change with ideological change. The ideological redefinition of the home as a sphere of consumption rather than production in sixteenth-century England did not, of course, correspond to the lived reality of every early modern English housewife. Many women continued to work productively, both within and outside the home.[13] Yet the acceptance of this ideology, as Susan Cahn points out, became the 'price of upward social mobility' in the period and, as such, exerted a powerful influence on all social classes.[14] The early modern period marked a crucial change in the *cultural valuation* of housework, a change that is historically linked – as the body of feminist-materialist scholarship which Christine Delphy has termed 'housework theory'[15] reminds us – to the rise of capitalism and development of the commodity form.[16]

According to housework theory, domestic work under capitalism is not considered 'real' work because 'women's productive labour is confined to use-values while men produce for exchange'.[17] It is not that housework disappears with the rise of capitalism; rather, it becomes economically devalued. Because the housewife's labour has no exchange-value, it remains unremunerated and thus economically 'invisible'.[18] Read within this paradigm, *Shrew* seems to participate in the ideological erasure of housework by not representing it on the stage, by rendering it, quite literally, invisible. The weakness of this analysis of the play, however, is that it explains only what Kate does not do onstage and provides no explanation for what she actually does.

In continuing to define the housewife's domestic activity solely within a matrix of use-value production, housework theory – despite its claim to offer an historicised account of women's subjection under capitalism – treats housework as if it were itself, materially speaking, an unchanging, transhistorical entity, which is not, as we have seen, the historical case. For though the market commodity's infiltration of the home did not suddenly and magically absolve the housewife of the duty of housework, it did profoundly alter *both* the material form and the cultural function of such work insofar as it became an activity increasingly centred around the proper order, maintenance, and display of household cates – objects having, by definition, little or no use-value.

Privileging delicacy of form over domestic function, cates threaten to sever completely the bond linking exchange-value to any utilitarian end; they are commodities that unabashedly assert their own superfluousness. It is not simply that cates, as objects of exchange, are to be 'distinguished from' objects of home production, however, as the *OED* asserts. Rather, their very purpose is to signify this distinction, to signify their own distance from utility and economic necessity. What replaces the utilitarian value of cates is a symbolic or cultural value: cates are, above all, signifiers of social distinction or differentiation.[19] Housework theory cannot explain *Shrew's* recasting of the traditional shrew-taming narrative because it can find no place in its strictly economic analysis for the housewife's role within a *symbolic* economy based on the circulation, accumulation, and display of status objects, or what Pierre Bourdieu terms 'symbolic' (as distinct from 'economic') capital.[20] How did the presence of status objects, or cates, within the non-aristocratic household transform, both materially and ideologically, the 'domesticall duties' of the housewife? To what degree was her new role as a consumer and caretaker of household cates perceived as threatening? What new mechanisms of ideological defence were invented to assuage such perceived threats? I shall argue that it is precisely the cultural anxiety surrounding the housewife's new managerial role with respect to household cates which prompted Shakespeare to write a new kind of shrew-taming narrative.

To provide the framework for my analysis of Shakespeare's rewriting of the shrew-taming tradition, I would like to turn from housework theory to the theorisation of domestic leisure and consumption, beginning with Thorstein Veblen's *Theory of the Leisure Class*. Like the housework theorists, Veblen maintains that the housewife's transformation from 'the drudge and chattel of the man, both in fact and in theory, – the producer of goods for him to consume' – into 'the ceremonial consumer of goods which he produces' leaves her no less his drudge and chattel (if only 'in theory') than her predecessor.[21] For Veblen, however, the housewife's new form of drudgery is defined not by her unremunerated (and thus economically invisible) productivity but rather by her subsidised (and culturally conspicuous) non-productivity itself. The housewife's obligatory 'performance of leisure', Veblen maintains, is itself a form of labour or drudgery: 'the leisure of the lady ... is an occupation of an ostensibly laborious kind ... it is leisure only in the sense that little or no productive work is performed'.[22] Just as the housewife's leisure renders her no less a drudge of her husband, according to Veblen, her consumption of commodities likewise renders her no less his commodity, or chattel, insofar as she consumes for her husband's benefit and not her own.[23] The housewife's 'vicarious consumption' positions her as a status object, the value of which derives precisely from its lack of utility: 'She is useless and expensive', as Veblen puts it, 'and she is *consequently* valuable'.[24]

When it comes to describing what constitutes the housewife's non-productive activity, however, Veblen becomes rather vague, re-marking only in passing that it centres on 'the maintenance and elaboration of the household paraphernalia'.[25] Jean Baudrillard offers a somewhat more elaborated account in his *Critique of the Political Economy of the Sign*, a text strongly influenced by Veblen. With the advent of consumer culture, he asserts, the 'cultural status of the [household] object enters into direct contradiction with its practical status', and 'housekeeping has only secondarily a practical objective (keeping objects ready for use)'; rather, 'it is a manipula-tion of another order – symbolic – that sometimes totally eclipses practical use'.[26] Like Veblen, Baudrillard views the housewife's con-spicuous leisure and consumption as themselves laborious, though for the latter this new form of housework is more specifically de-scribed as the locus of a '*symbolic* labour', defined as the 'active manipulation of signs' or status objects.[27] The value of the house-wife's manipulation of the 'cultural status of the object', Baudrillard maintains, emerges not from an 'economic calculus' but from a 'symbolic and statutory calculus' dictated by 'relative social class configurations'.[28] For both Veblen and Baudrillard, then, the house-wife plays a crucial role in the production of cultural value in a consumer society.

It is in the early modern period that the housewife first assumes this vital new role within what I shall term the *symbolic order of things*.[29] The figure of 'Kate' represents a threat to this order, a threat that Petruchio seeks to tame by educating her for her role as a manipulator of status objects. To say that Kate poses a threat to the symbolic order of *things*, however, is to signal yet another de-parture from the traditional shrew-taming narrative, in which the shrew is characteristically represented as a threat to the symbolic order of *language*. This linguistic threat is not absent from Shakespeare's version of the narrative and has received substantial critical commentary. In order to compare this threat with that posed by her relationship to things, I will briefly consider two com-pelling accounts of the threat posed by Kate's words.

In Shakespeare's rendering of the traditional topos, Joel Fineman points out, the shrew's linguistic excess becomes a threat not of too many words but rather of too much meaning. Kate's speech under-scores the way in which language always 'carries with it a kind of surplus semiotic baggage, an excess of significance, whose looming, even if unspoken, presence cannot be kept quiet'.[30] The semantic superfluity of Kate's speech leads to a series of '"fretful" verbal confusions' in which the 'rhetoricity of language is made to seem the explanation of [her] ongoing quarrel with the men who are her master'.[31] The example Fineman cites is Kate's unhappy lute lesson, recounted by her hapless music master, Hortensio:

> **Baptista** Why then, thou canst not break her to the lute?
> **Hortensio** Why no, for she hath broke the lute to me.
> I did but tell her she mistook her frets. ...
> 'Frets, call you these?' quoth she, 'I'll fume with them.'
> And with that word she struck me on the head.
> (II.i.147–53)

Fineman sees Kate's shrewish 'fretting' as a direct result of the rhetorical excess of her speech – in this case, her pun on *frets*. Karen Newman adds that Kate's 'linguistic protest' is directed against 'the role in patriarchal culture to which women are assigned, that of wife and object of exchange in the circulation of male desire'.[32] Kate's excessive verbal fretting turns her into an unvendible commodity. Yet while Newman emphasises Kate's own position as an 'object of exchange' between men, she specifically discounts the importance of material objects elsewhere in the play. The role of things in Petruchio's taming lesson is subordinated in Newman's argument to the more 'significant' role of words: 'Kate is figuratively killed with kindness, by her husband's rule over her not so much in *material* terms – the withholding of food, clothing and sleep – but in the withholding of *linguistic* understanding.'[33]

In contrast to Newman, Lena Cowen Orlin, in a recent article on 'material culture theatrically represented', foregrounds the play's many 'references to and displays of objects, and especially household furnishings'. Orlin does not simply insist on the importance of *res* within the play at the expense of *verba*. She maintains that both material and linguistic forms of exchange, far from being opposed within the play, are repeatedly identified. Drawing on Lévi-Strauss, Orlin argues that the play 'synthesises' the three 'forms of exchange that constitute social life', namely, the exchange of wives, of goods, and of words.[34] While I agree with Orlin's claim that the play draws very explicit connections between its material and symbolic economies – particularly as these economies converge on what I have called the symbolic order of things – I resist the notion that

Kate's position with respect to this order is simply that of a passive object of exchange. Kate is not figured as one more cate exchanged between men within the play; rather, it is precisely her *unvendibility* as a commodity on the marriage market that creates the dramatic dilemma to be solved by the taming narrative. The question concerns the relation between Kate's own position as a cate and her role as a consumer of cates. For Kate's unvendibility is specifically attributed within the play to her untamed consumption of cates.

At the start of the play, Kate's consumption is represented as a threat that Petruchio, in his novel way, will seek to tame. Both Newman and Fineman take Petruchio's first encounter with Kate, perhaps the most 'fretful' instance of verbal sparring in the play, to demonstrate that the shrew-tamer chooses to fight his battle with the shrew 'in verbal kind'.[35] 'O, how I long to have some chat with her' (II.i.162), he utters, in anticipation of their meeting. The content of Petruchio's punning 'chat' with Kate, however, is principally preoccupied with determining her place within the symbolic order of things. The encounter begins with Petruchio stubbornly insisting on calling Katherina 'Kate':

> Petruchio Good morrow, Kate, for that's your name, I hear.
> Katherina Well have you heard, but something hard of hearing;
>   They call me Katherine that do talk of me.
> Petruchio You lie, in faith, for you are call'd plain Kate,
>   And bonny Kate, and sometimes Kate the curst;
>   But Kate, the prettiest Kate in Christendom,
>   Kate of Kate Hall, my super-dainty Kate,
>   For dainties are all Kates.
>
>   (II.i.182–9)

If Petruchio's punning appellation of Kate as a 'super-dainty' cate seems an obvious misnomer in one sense – she can hardly be called 'delicate' – in another it is quite apt, as his gloss makes clear. The substantive *dainty*, deriving from the Latin *dignitatem* (worthiness, worth, value), designates something that is 'estimable, sumptuous, or rare'.[36] In describing her as a 'dainty', Petruchio appears to be referring to her value as a commodity, or cate, on the marriage market (he has just discovered that her dowry is worth 'twenty thousand crowns' [II.i.122]).

Yet Petruchio's reference to Kate as 'super-dainty' refers to her not as a commodity or object of exchange between men but rather as a *consumer* of commodities. According to the *OED*, in its adjectival form the term *dainty* refers to someone who is 'nice, fastidious, particular; sometimes, over-nice' as to 'the quality of food, comforts, etc.'. In describing Kate as 'superdainty', Petruchio implies that she belongs to the latter category; she is 'over-nice', not so much discriminating as blindly obedient to the dictates of fashion. Sliding almost imperceptibly from Kate as a consumer of cates to her status as a cate, Petruchio's gloss ('For dainties are all Kates') elides the potential threat posed by the former by subsuming it under the aegis of the latter. His pun on *Kates/cates* dismisses the significance of Kate's role as a consumer (as does Newman's reading) by effectively reducing her to an object of exchange between men.

The pun on *Kates/cates* is repeated at the conclusion of Petruchio's 'chat' with Kate (in the pronouncement quoted at the beginning of this essay) and effects a similar reduction: 'And therefore, setting all this chat aside, / Thus in plain terms', Petruchio proclaims, summing up his unorthodox marriage proposal, 'I am he am born to tame you, Kate, / And bring you from a wild Kate to a Kate / Conformable as other household Kates' (II.i.261–2, 269–71). And yet, in spite of his desire to speak 'in plain terms', Petruchio cannot easily restrict or 'tame' the signifying potential of his own pun. For once it is articulated, the final pun on *Kates/cates* refuses to remain tied to its modifier, 'household', and insists instead upon voicing itself, shrewishly, where it shouldn't (i.e., each time Kate is named). In so doing, it retrospectively raises the possibility that cates themselves may be 'wild', that there is something unruly, something that must be made to conform, in the commodity form itself. This possibility in turn discovers an ambiguity in Petruchio's 'as', which may mean either 'as other household cates are conformable' or 'as I have brought other household cates into conformity'. The conformity of household cates cannot be taken for granted within the play because cates, unlike use-values, are not proper to or born of the domestic sphere but are produced outside the home by the market. They are by definition extra-domestic or to-be-domesticated. Yet insofar as cates obey the logic of exchange and of the market, they may be said to resist such domestication. Petruchio cannot restrict the movement of cates in his utterance, cannot set all 'chat' aside and speak 'in plain terms', because commodities, like words, tend to resist all attempts to restrict their circulation and exchange.

The latter assertion finds support – quite literally – in Petruchio's own chat. The term *chat*, as Brian Morris points out in a note to his Arden edition, was itself a variant spelling of *cate* in the early modern period (both forms descend from *achat*). The term *chat* thus instantiates, literally performs, the impossibility of restricting the semantic excess proper to language in general and epitomised by Kate's speech in particular. In so doing, however, it also links linguistic excess – via its etymological link with the signifier *cate* – to the economic excess associated with the commodity form in general and with cates, or luxury goods, in particular. Within the play, the term *chat* may thus be said to name both material and linguistic forms of excess as they converge on the figure of the shrew. It refers at once to Kate's 'chattering tongue' (IV.ii.58) and to her untamed consumption of cates.

Kate's verbal frettings are repeatedly linked within the play to her refusal to assume her proper place within the symbolic order of things: she cannot be broken to the lute but breaks it instead. It is not clear, however, that her place is simply that of passive exchange object. For to be broken to the frets of a lute is to become a skilled and 'active manipulator' (to recall Baudrillard's term) of a status object.[37] My argument thus departs from traditional accounts of the commodification of or traffic in women which maintain that women 'throughout history' have been passive objects of exchange circulating between men. Such accounts do little to explain the specific historical forms the domination of woman assumes with the rise of capitalism and development of the commodity form. They do not, for example, explain the housewife's emerging role as a manipulator of status objects, or household cates.

I would like to question as well the viability, in the present context, of Veblen's assertion that the housewife's 'manipulation of the household paraphernalia' does not render her any less a commodity, 'chattel', of her husband. The housewife's consumption of cates, which Veblen views as thoroughly domesticated, was in the early modern period thought to be something wild, unruly, and in urgent need of taming.[38] If *Shrew's* taming narrative positions Kate as a 'vicarious consumer' to ensure that her consumption and manipulation of household cates conforms to her husband's economic interests, it nevertheless points to a historical moment when the housewife's management of household property becomes potentially threatening to the symbolic order of things. Before attending to the ways in which the shrew-taming comedy seeks to elide this threat, we should take the threat itself seriously; only then will we be able to chart with any clarity Kate's passage from 'chat' (i.e., from the material and linguistic forms of excess characteristic of the shrew) to 'chattel'.

At the start of the play, as Newman asserts, Kate's fretting is represented as an obstacle to her successful commodification on the marriage market. When Baptista finally arranges Kate's match to the madcap Petruchio, Tranio remarks: ''Twas a commodity lay fretting by you, / 'Twill bring you gain, or perish on the seas' (II.i.321–2). Baptista's response, 'The gain I seek is quiet in the match' (II.i.323), underscores the economic dilemma posed by Kate's speech: her linguistic surplus translates into his financial lack and, consequently, her 'quiet' into his 'gain'. Yet Kate's fretting refers not only to what comes out of her mouth (to her excessive verbal fretting) but to what goes into it as well (to her excessive consumption). The verb *to fret*, which derives from the same root as the modern German *fressen*, means 'to eat, devour [of animals]; ... to gnaw, to consume, ... or wear away by gnawing' or, reflexively, 'to waste or wear away; to decay'.[39] Kate's untamed, animal-like consumption, Tranio's remark implies, wears away both at her father's resources and at her own value as well. In describing Kate as a 'fretting commodity', as a commodity that not only consumes but consumes itself, Tranio emphasises the tension between her position as a cate, or object of exchange, between men and her role as a consumer of cates.

To grasp the threat posed by the early modern housewife's consumption of cates, as this threat is embodied by Kate, however, we must first consider more closely what Baudrillard terms the 'relative social class configurations' at work within the play. For the discourse of objects in *The Taming of the Shrew* becomes intelligible only if read in the context of its 'class grammar' – that is to say, as it is inflected by the contradictions inherent in its appropriation by a particular social class or group.[40] In general terms *The Taming of the Shrew* represents an *embourgeoisement* of the traditional shrew-taming narrative: Petruchio is not a humble tradesman but an upwardly mobile landowner. Unlike the cooper's wife, Kate is not of 'gentle kin'; she is a wealthy merchant's daughter. The play casts the marriage of Petruchio and Kate as an alliance between the gentry and mercantile classes and thus between land and money, status and wealth, or what Bourdieu identifies as symbolic and economic capital.

Petruchio is straightforward about his mercenary motives for marrying Kate: 'Left solely heir to all his [father's] lands and goods', which he boastfully claims to 'have better'd rather than decreas'd' (II.i.117–18), Petruchio ventures into the 'maze' of mercantile Padua hoping to 'wive it wealthily ... / If wealthily, then happily in Padua' (I.ii.74–5). Likening his mission to a merchant voyage, he claims to have been blown in by 'such wind as scatters young men through the world / To seek their fortunes farther than at home' (I.ii.49–50). Petruchio's fortune-hunting bombast, together with his claim to have 'better'd' his inheritance, marks him as one of the new gentry, who continually sought to improve their estates through commerce, forays into business or overseas trade, or by contracting wealthy marriages.[41] If Petruchio seeks to obtain from his marriage to Baptista's mercantile household what is lacking in his own domestic economy, however, the same can be said of Baptista, who seeks to marry off his daughter to a member of the landed gentry. The nuptial bond between the two families promises a mutually beneficial exchange of values for the domestic economies of each: Petruchio hopes to obtain surplus capital (a dowry of 'twenty thousand crowns'), and Baptista the status or symbolic capital that comes with land (the jointure Petruchio offers in return [II.i.125]).[42]

Kate's commodification as a marriage-market cate thus proves beneficial to both her father's and her future husband's households. But it is also the case that her consumption of cates is represented, at least initially, as mutually detrimental. At the start of the play, as we have seen, Kate's excessive consumption renders her an unvendible commodity. Baptista is unable to 'rid the house' (I.i.145) of Kate and is consequently unwilling to wed his younger daughter, Bianca, to any of her many suitors. Kate's fretting represents perhaps an even greater threat to Petruchio's household, however, although one of a different order. To comprehend this difference, one must comprehend the place occupied by cates within the two domestic economies. Petruchio's parsimonious attitude toward cates, evidenced by the disrepair of his country house and the 'ragged, old, and beggarly' condition of his servants (IV.i.124), stands in stark contrast to the conspicuous consumption that characterises Padua's mercantile class.[43] Gremio, a wealthy Paduan merchant and suitor to Bianca, for example, describes his 'house within the city' as 'richly furnished with plate and gold' (II.i.339–40):

My hangings all of Tyrian tapestry.
In ivory coffers I have stuff'd my crowns,
In cypress chests my arras counterpoints,
Costly apparel, tents, and canopies,
Fine linen, Turkey cushions boss'd with pearl,
Valance of Venice gold in needlework,
Pewter and brass, and all things that belongs
To house or housekeeping.
                                    (II.i.342–49)

If housekeeping at Petruchio's country estate involves little more than keeping the 'rushes strewed' and the 'cobwebs swept' (IV.i.41), in Gremio's description of his city dwelling, it is an enterprise that centres on the elaborate arrangement and display of cates. Each of Gremio's 'things' bears testimony to his ability to afford superfluous expenditure and to his taste for imported luxuries: his tapestries are from Tyre (famous for its scarlet and purple dyes), his apparel 'costly', his linen 'fine', his 'Turkey cushions boss'd with pearl'. His household is invested, literally 'stuff'd', with capital.

The marked difference between the two men's respective notions of the 'things that belongs / To house or housekeeping' underscores the differing attitudes held by the minor gentry and mercantile classes in the period toward 'household cates'. For the mercantile classes conspicuous consumption served to compensate for what, borrowing Baudrillard's terminology, we might call a 'true social recognition' that otherwise evaded them; the accumulation of status objects served to supplement their 'thwarted legitimacy' in the social domain.[44] As Lawrence and Jeanne Fawtier Stone observe, however, for the upwardly mobile gentry 'the obligation to spend generously, even lavishly', as part of their newly acquired social status 'implied a radical break with the habits of frugality which had played an essential part in the[ir] ... upward climb'.[45] The lesser gentry could make it into the ranks of the elite only by being 'cautious, thrifty, canny, and grasping, creeping slowly, generation after generation, up the ladder of social and economic progress, and even at the end only barely indulging in a life-style and housing suitable to their dignity and income.'[46] For the mercantile classes conspicuous consumption functioned as a necessary (though not always sufficient) means to elite status; for the lesser gentry it was an unwished-for consequence of it.

Arriving at their wedding in tattered apparel and astride an old, diseased horse, Petruchio proclaims: 'To me she's married, not unto my clothes. / Could I repair what she will wear in me / As I can change these poor accoutrements, / 'Twere well for Kate and better for myself' (III.ii.115–18). As if to prove his point that Kate's extravagance will leave him a pauper, his self-consuming costume seems to wear itself out before our eyes: his 'old breeches' are 'thrice turned' (l. 42); his boots have been used as 'candlecases' (l. 43); his 'old rusty sword' has a 'broken hilt' (ll. 44–5). As for his horse: it is 'begnawn with the bots [parasitical worms or maggots]' (ll. 52–3) and, even more appropriately, 'infected' – as, he insinuates, is his future wife – 'with the fashions' (l. 50). The term *fashions* (or *farcin*, as it was more commonly spelled), which derives from the Latin *farcire*, meaning 'to stuff', denotes a contagious equine disease characterised by a swelling of the jaw. Kate's taste for fashionable cates is likened to this disease of excessive consumption, which threatens to gnaw away at her husband's estate.

Following the wedding ceremony, Kate's excessive consumption seems to result in her swift reduction to the status of 'chattel'. Petruchio whisks his bride away after announcing to the stunned onlookers:

> I will be master of what is mine own.
> She is my goods, my chattels, she is my house.
> My household stuff, my field, my barn,
> My horse, my ox, my ass, my any thing.
> And here she stands.
>
> (ll. 227–31)

Petruchio's blunt assertion of property rights over Kate performs the very act of domestication it declares; reduced to an object of exchange ('goods' and 'chattels'), Kate is abruptly yanked out of circulation and sequestered within the home, literally turned into a piece of furniture or 'household stuff'. The speech follows a domesticating trajectory not unlike that outlined by housework theory: it circumscribes Kate within a matrix of use-value production. The relationship between household stuff and household cates may be described as that between mere use-values and exchange-values, or commodities, properly speaking. The *OED* defines *stuff* as 'the substance or "material" … of which a thing is formed or consists, or out of which a thing may be fashioned'.[47] As such, it may be identified with the use-value of the object.[48] Entering into the process of exchange, commodities, 'ungilded and unsweetened, retaining their original home-grown shape', are split into the twofold form of use-value and value proper, a process Marx calls *'Stoffwechsel'* – literally the act of (ex)change (*Wechsel*) that transforms mere stuff (*Stoff*) into values, or cates.[49] In transforming Kate from an object of exchange into the home-grown materiality of mere stuff, into a thing defined by its sheer utility, a beast of burden ('my horse, my ox, my ass'), Petruchio's speech reverses the processes of commodification. Reducing Kate to a series of increasingly homely things, it finally strips her down to a seemingly irreducible substance whose static immobility ('here she stands') puts a stop to the slippage of exchange evoked by his list of goods. Her deictic presence seems to stand as the guarantee of an underlying, enduring use-value.

As a member of the gentry, Petruchio stands for the residual, land-based values of a domestic economy that purports to be 'all in all sufficient' (*Othello*, IV.i.265). The trajectory traced by his index of goods moves not only from exchange-value to use-value but from liquid capital, or 'movables',[50] to the more secure form of landed property ('house ... field ... barn'). Yet Petruchio's portrait of an ideally self-sufficient household economy, in which the value of things is taken to be self-evident and not subject to (ex)change, is belied by the straightforwardly mercenary motives he avows for marrying Kate. Paradoxically, in order to maintain his land-based values, Petruchio must embrace those of the marketplace.[51] In seeking to arrest the slippage of exchange, his speech implicates its speaker in an expanding network or maze of equivalent value-forms ('goods ... any thing') whose slide threatens to destabilise the hierarchy of values he would uphold. If Petruchio succeeds in mastering Kate, his position as master is nevertheless qualified by his own subjection to the exigencies and uncertainties of the new market economy. In his endeavour to domesticate the commodity form, one might say, Petruchio is himself commodified, himself subjected to the logic of commodity exchange. As Gremio so eloquently puts it: in taming Kate, Petruchio is himself 'Kated' (III.ii.243).

The contradictions inherent in Petruchio's class status make his task as shrew-tamer a complex one: he must restrict his wife's consumption without abolishing it entirely, must ensure that it adequately bears testimony to his own elite status without simultaneously leading him to financial ruin. The urgent requirement to maintain a proper balance between expenditure and thrift in the elite (or would-be elite) household and the perceived danger of delegating this task to the housewife are described in the following mid-seventeenth-century letter of advice, written by the Marquis of Halifax to his daughter:

> The Art of laying out Money wisely, is not attained to without a great deal of thought; and it is yet more difficult in the Case of a *Wife*, who is accountable to her *Husband* for her mistakes in it: It is not only his *Money*, his *Credit* too is at Stake, if what lyeth under the *Wife's* Care is managed, either with undecent *Thrift*, or too loose *Profusion*; you are therefore to keep the *Mean* between these two *Extreams* ... when you once break through those bounds, you launch into a wide Sea of *Extravagance*.[52]

At stake in the housewife's proper management of money or economic capital, Halifax suggests, is her husband's credit, or symbolic capital. 'Symbolic capital', Bourdieu maintains, 'is always *credit*, in the widest sense of the word, i.e. a sort of advance which the group alone can grant those who give it the best material and symbolic *guarantees*.'[53] It is not simply that economic capital serves to buttress symbolic capital when it is spent on 'material and symbolic guarantees' such as status objects. Symbolic capital in turn attracts economic capital: 'the exhibition of symbolic capital (which is always very expensive in economic terms) is one of the mechanisms which (no doubt universally) make capital go to capital'.[54] Yet symbolic and economic capital are not always mutually reinforcing. Indeed, insofar as 'symbolic capital can only be accumulated at the expense of the accumulation of economic capital', the two are often at odds.[55] In the case of the upwardly mobile gentry in early modern England, as the Stones make clear, the effort to balance the two was an ongoing struggle.

In this context the early modern housewife's new role in the symbolic ordering of household cates takes on its full importance. She was made responsible for maintaining the proper balance of economic and symbolic capital within the household economy. The early modern housewife had to learn to spend enough to ensure her husband's status or cultural credit without overspending his income or economic credit. Domestic manuals of the period repeatedly express anxiety over the housewife's ability to strike this balance and are intent on circumscribing her management of household expenditure within the bounds of her husband's authority. For example, in *Of Domesticall Dvties* William Gouge writes,

Wives cannot alwaies know their husbands ability: for their husbands may be much indebted, and yet to maintaine his credit, whereby he hopeth to raise his estate, may allow liberall maintenance for his house, if thereupon his wife shall gather that he is very rich, and accordingly be very bountifull in her gifts, she may soone goe beyond his ability, and so increase his debt, as he shall neuer be able to recouer himselfe.[56]

Gouge's warning is specifically concerned with the housewife's ability to distinguish symbolic from economic capital. Wives, he warns, are likely to be lured by symbolic capital, to believe that their husbands, because they spend freely on status objects, must be 'very rich'. The trick of good housewifery in this period, then, is knowing how to manipulate status objects for others and knowing how *not* to be taken in by them. It is precisely this trick, I maintain, that Petruchio teaches Kate. He seeks to unmask the lure of status objects for Kate while teaching her to deploy this lure skilfully for others.

Culminating in the play's final scene, in which Kate obeys Petruchio's command to take off her 'dainty' cap and throw it underfoot, Petruchio's strategy aims to tame Kate's consumption of cates. 'My falcon now is sharp [i.e., hungry] and passing empty', he explains, 'and till she stoop she must not be full-gorg'd, / For then she never looks upon her lure' (IV.i.177–9). Far from simply withholding cates from her, however, he continually offers them to her, only to find 'some undeserved fault' in their appearance (l. 186), which, he claims, will make them unworthy of her refined tastes. His taming thus succeeds not by destroying the lure of the commodity but rather by exploiting it, by combating Kate's daintiness with his own super-daintiness.

Arriving at his country estate at the beginning of Act IV, famished from their journey, Kate sits down to sup; but her dinner is sent back to the kitchen by Petruchio, who refuses it as 'burnt and dried away' (1.157). 'Better 'twere that both of us did fast', he assures her, than to eat 'such over-roasted flesh' (ll. 160–2). By the third scene Kate is ravenous and begs Petruchio's servant for something to eat: 'I prithee go and get me some repast, / I care not what, so it be wholesome food' (ll. 15–16). Momentarily forgetting the discriminations of taste, Kate is eager to fill her stomach with any wholesome stuff that will satisfy her appetite. Grumio does not simply ignore her request but perversely teases her with edible cates, offering her a 'neat's foot' (l. 17), a 'fat tripe finely broil'd' (l. 20),

and a 'piece of beef and mustard' (l. 23) – 'a dish', Kate acknowledges, 'that I do love to feed upon' (l. 24).[57] After listing all of the
delicacies on the menu, however, Grumio objects to each as being
'unwholesome'; like Kate, he gibes, they are 'too hot' and 'choleric'
(ll. 19, 25, 22). Her temper flaring at this, Kate begins to fret and
accuses Grumio of feeding her 'with the very name of meat' (l. 32).
Here Kate hits on the foundation of her husband's strategy:
Petruchio's object lesson in consumption centres on the *symbolic*
dimension of cates. By feeding her with nothing but the '*name* of
meat', with cates in their pure form as signifiers of taste and social
distinction, Petruchio aims to bring home to her their lack of substance, or stuff.

Following their abortive supper, Petruchio summons in the hab-
erdasher, commanding him to display his 'ruffling treasure' and 'ornaments' (ll. 60–1). When the latter produces the cap he has made
for Kate, Petruchio ridicules it, comparing it to an edible cate, or
'velvet dish' (an analogy that enables him to extend his lesson in
consumption from comestibles to other commodities):

> Why, this was moulded on a porringer!
> A velvet dish! Fie, fie! 'Tis lewd and filthy.
> Why, 'tis a cockle or a walnut-shell,
> A knack, a toy, a trick, a baby's cap.
> Away with it! Come, let me have a bigger.
> (ll. 64–8)

Petruchio objects to the cap on the grounds that it is unwholesome
and insubstantial – a cap, one might say, in name only. 'I'll have no
bigger', Kate responds. 'This doth fit the time, / And gentlewomen
wear such caps as these' (ll. 69–70), revealing that she has indeed
been seduced by the lure of the status object. Petruchio continues to
expand his list of edible trifles, insisting: 'It is a paltry cap, / A
custard-coffin, a bauble, a silken pie' (ll. 81–2). In likening the commodities that are brought in after supper to banqueting conceits,
commonly known as 'voids' or 'empty dishes', Petruchio again emphasises the commodity's lack of substance. To consume such cates
is to consume a void. It brings not satiety but only renewed want.

Banqueting conceits, Patricia Fumerton maintains, were made not
to satisfy the appetite (indeed, they were often made out of nothing
but paper) but rather to serve as signifiers of status and superfluous
expenditure.[58] This function was quite explicit in the case of
certain 'conceited dishes' that were actually made in the likeness of

expensive but 'trifling' luxury commodities, such as 'Buttons, Beades, Chaines ... Slippers ... [and] Gloues'.[59] As if to secure their purely superfluous status, the consumption of these 'empty dishes' took the form of conspicuous waste; at the banquet's end they were ceremonially smashed to pieces.[60] Through his taming lesson. Petruchio aims to separate the stuff of the commodity from its value as a cate. Status objects, he teaches, are not so much things as no-things.[61]

Petruchio continues the analogy, comparing the tailor's latest creation to a dainty dessert:

> What's this? A sleeve? 'Tis like a deini-cannon.
> What, up and down, carv'd like an apple-tart?
> Here's snip and nip and cut and slish and slash,
> Like to a censer in a barber's shop.
> Why, what a devil's name, tailor, call'st thou this?
> (ll. 88–92)

The dress is refused on account of its 'curiously cut' sleeves (l. 141), which are likened to the design of a dainty apple-tart, one that is 'carv'd' full of holes. When the tailor objects that the dress was designed 'according to the fashion and the time' (l. 95) and in accordance with Grumio's orders, the latter responds: 'I gave him no order, I gave him the stuff' (l. 119). Grumio follows his master in distinguishing between the 'stuff' of the dress in its 'ungilded and unsweetened' form and the labour that transforms it into a cate, a thing of value. 'I bid thy master cut out the gown', he says, 'but I did not bid him cut it to pieces' (ll. 127–8), further differentiating the utilitarian act of 'cut[ting] out' from the stylish 'cut[ting] ... to pieces' – the snipping, nipping, slishing, and slashing that creates its cultural value as an object of fashionable taste.

When the tailor reads out the 'note of the fashion' to show that it indeed specifies '"The sleeves curiously cut"', Grumio replies: 'Error i' th' bill, sir, error i' th' bill! I commanded the sleeves should be cut out, and sewed up again' (ll. 129, 141, 143–4). Grumio's remark suggests that, if Petruchio's taming strategy reveals the 'cut' that divides the commodity into its twofold form as use-value and status-value,[62] it does so only in order to sew it up again, to reduce the status-value, make it conform to the use-value. In a commodified world, however, to suture the cut of the commodity and thereby create the ruse that its value is inherent in its substance is to turn the commodity into a fetish.

Baudrillard's definition of commodity fetishism is particularly apt in this context. For what is fetishised, he maintains, is specifically 'the sign object, the object eviscerated of its substance ... and reduced to the state of marking a difference'.[63] Petruchio's taming lesson unmasks both the cut of the commodity, its function as a differentiating signifier of social distinction, and the lure that sutures this cut by dissimulating the lack of substance, or stuff, it conceals. It does so, however, in order to teach Kate both how better to distinguish and how to deploy them.

The success of this lesson is borne out by Kate's final gestures of obedience, the destruction of her dainty cap and her last speech, gestures that are performed as the final, sweet conceits of the play's concluding scene, which is, not coincidentally, set at a banquet. 'My banquet is to close our stomachs up', announces Lucentio, its host, to the play's three newlywed couples, 'For now we sit to chat as well as eat' (V.ii.9,11). The ensuing chat is an intricate verbal performance in which the bridegrooms argue over whose wife is the 'veriest shrew of all' (l. 64). To decide the matter, Petruchio proposes the test of obedience, which Kate wins when she unhesitatingly obeys his command to come. Although Kate's arrival wins the bet, Petruchio insists on 'show[ing] more sign' of his wife's 'new-built virtue and obedience' (ll. 118–19) by commanding her to destroy her dainty cap. That Kate should appear at the end of the play sporting a fashionable cap, much like (or, depending on the production, identical to) the one taken away when she was less obedient, confirms that Petruchio's taming strategy is aimed not at closing her stomach up, at abolishing her appetite for cates, but rather at harnessing that appetite, at making it conform to his own economic interests.

The destruction of Kate's confectionary cap, like that of a banqueting void, represents not a renunciation of the commodity but rather an affirmation of its power, of its new hold over the early modern household economy. 'Economic power', Bourdieu maintains, 'is first and foremost a power to keep economic necessity at arm's length. This is why it universally asserts itself by the destruction of riches.'[64] It is a gesture of conspicuous yet carefully controlled waste, demonstrating both Petruchio's ability to afford superfluous expenditure and his control over his wife's consumption. Unlike her earlier breaking of the lute, this destruction of riches demonstrates that Kate has been successfully broken to her proper place within the symbolic order of things.

While Kate's final gesture of obedience signals her readiness to assume an active managerial role in domestic affairs, we never in fact *see* her preside over the household economy or its property. This gesture itself, moreover, is peculiarly self-effacing. It seems that Kate can prove her readiness for this role only through a wholly *passive* gesture that displays her subordination to her husband's authority. She can prove herself a worthy caretaker of commodities only by destroying her own most cherished commodity, her fashionable cap. The self-consuming nature of the gesture reflects the contradictions inherent in the role of the 'vicarious consumer': it must appear wholly idle (efface its status as work); be ostensibly unproductive or superfluous (ideally, an act of conspicuous waste); and, most importantly, be executed vicariously (i.e., *for* another). The vicarious consumer consumes not for herself, in her own interest, but for that of her husband.

What distinguishes Kate from the other wives at the end of the play is not that she has learned how *not* to consume but that she has learned how to consume *nothings* (voids, empty dishes, insubstantial cates) for her husband's benefit. Failing to comprehend this novel form of duty, Bianca and the Widow express their abhorrence at the apparently useless waste of such a fine cap. Baptista, however, is won over by the signs of Kate's 'new-built' virtue and obedience, so much so that he awards Petruchio another twenty thousand crowns: 'Another dowry to another daughter', he announces, 'for she is chang'd, as she had never been' (ll. 115–16). By the end of the play, Kate has successfully learned to manipulate status objects and, in so doing, to bolster her husband's credit in a way that 'makes capital go to capital'.

If, as Baptista's act demonstrates, symbolic capital is but 'a transformed and thereby *disguised* form' of economic capital, it nevertheless produces its 'proper effect', according to Bourdieu, 'only inasmuch, as it conceals the fact that it originates in "material" forms of capital which are also, in the last analysis, the source of its effects'.[65] It becomes the ideological burden of Kate's final speech to conceal the economic underpinnings of her symbolic labour, to render them culturally invisible. The speech accomplishes this task by defining the housewife's (non-productive) activity as a form of leisure rather than labour:

> Thy husband is thy lord, thy life, thy keeper,
> Thy head, thy sovereign; one that cares for thee,

And for thy maintenance; commits his body
To painful labour both by sea and land,
To watch the night in storms, the day in cold,
Whilst thou liest warm at home, secure and safe;
And craves no other tribute at thy hands
But love, fair looks, and true obedience;
Too little payment for so great a debt.

(ll. 147–55)

Kate's speech inaugurates a new gendered division of labour, according to which husbands 'labour both by sea and land' while their wives luxuriate at home, their 'soft', 'weak' bodies being 'unapt to toil and trouble in the world' (ll. 166–7). It is this new division of labour that produces the economic invisibility and unremunerated status of housework described by housework theory. In erasing the status of housework as work, separate-sphere ideology renders the housewife perpetually indebted to her husband insofar as her 'love, fair looks, and true obedience' are insufficient 'payment' for the material comfort in which she is 'kept'.

Within the terms of the play, however, the unremunerated status of housework derives not from its circumscription within a matrix of use-value production but from the cultural necessity of concealing the economic origins of the housewife's symbolic labour. If *The Taming of the Shrew* may be said to map the market's infiltration of the household through the commodity form in late-sixteenth-century England, it also marks the emergence of the ideological separation of feminine and masculine spheres of labour (and with it the separation of home/market and housework/work), which masked this infiltration by constructing the household as a refuge *from* the market. Ironically, Kate's final speech renders invisible the housewife's managerial role as a consumer and caretaker of household cates – the very role for which Petruchio's 'taming-school' (IV.ii.54) seeks to prepare her. At the end of the play, she herself appears to stand idle, frozen within the domestic sphere, like a use-less household cate.

As Lena Cowen Orlin points out, 'the husband's political roles of lord, head, and sovereign are grounded economically' in Kate's speech in his role as her 'keeper'.[66] The speech ingeniously deploys the language of economic debt and indebtedness to secure a political analogy in which the household is figured as a microcosm of the state and the husband its sovereign or prince. Its aim is to restore the husband's 'rule, supremacy, and sway' (V.ii.164) within a domestic hierarchy that has been threatened by the housewife's managerial role in the household economy. The speech, as Orlin notes, shifts back and forth between political and economic forms of obligation; the husband's political sovereignty over his wife is immediately anchored in his role as her keeper. Once the marital relation is defined in economic terms ('one that cares for thee, / And for thy maintenance') and the wife's position within this relation defined as one of lack ('Too little payment for so great a debt'), the speech returns again to the political analogy, to what 'the subject owes the prince', as if the housewife's deficit in the former domain (her economic debt) entails her subjection in the latter (her political duty):

> Such duty as the subject owes the prince
> Even such a woman oweth to her husband.
> And when she is froward, peevish, sullen, sour,
> And not obedient to his honest will,
> What is she but a foul contending rebel,
> And graceless traitor to her loving lord?
> I am asham'd that women are so simple
> To offer war where they should kneel for peace,
> Or seek for rule, supremacy, and sway,
> When they are bound to serve, love, and obey.
>   (ll. 156–65)

The erasure of the economic value of the housewife's non-productive domestic activity in Kate's speech is thus employed to secure a political analogy that disarms the perceived threat posed by this activity.

The political analogy between 'the structure of authority in the family and the state' was not, of course, invented by Shakespeare. It was, as Susan Amussen points out, commonplace in both domestic manuals and political treatises of the period.[67] Yet there was, as Amussen also notes, a marked disparity between patriarchal theory and quotidian practice in the early modern household. Though 'theoretically, the husband ruled his wife, and she obeyed him in all things', Amussen asserts, in practice the wife 'was joined with him in the government of the household'.[68] The political analogy restores the husband's sovereignty or mastery over his wife by devaluing her role in the household economy. Moreover, insofar as it succeeds in domesticating the housewife's relation to household cates by subordinating it to her husband's authority, the speech may be said to circumscribe this relation within the safe boundaries of vicarious consumption. Kate's role as a consumer has by the end of the play been successfully adjusted, made to conform, to her position as chattel (perpetually indebted to her husband for the things he provides her with, she may be said to belong to him). As Orlin argues, the role of things in the final 'accommodation' that Petruchio and Kate reach is simply to 'purchase the consent that perpetuates the gendered social contract'; they serve merely to 'legitimate the social order'.[69]

In the commodious conclusion of the comedy, all 'jarring notes agree' (V.ii.1) and the cut of the commodity has been sutured, or sewn up again. What commodity fetishism seeks, according to Baudrillard, is 'the closed perfection of a system', a system that appears to know no lack.[70] Comedy is precisely such a system: 'suturing all contradictions and divisions', it 'gives ideology its power of fascination'.[71] The effect that Kate's final signs of obedience produce in her audience is indeed one of fascination: 'Here is a wonder, if you talk of a wonder', Lucentio utters. 'And so it is', Hortensio responds: 'I wonder what it bodes' (ll. 107–8). The 'wonder' produced by Kate's symbolic labour, I would argue, is nothing other than a fascination with a 'perfect closure effected by signs'.[72] Kate's final chat is fetishised as a 'labour of appearances and signs', as a symbolic labour that conceals its own economic motivation and erases all traces of the labour necessary to produce it.

I do not mean to suggest (following the play's so-called revisionist readers) that Kate's speech should be read ironically, as evidence of her deceit, any more than (with its anti-revisionist readers) as evidence of her 'true' submission.[73] Both readings, it seems to me, leave Kate squarely within the framework of the medieval shrew tradition. In the former she remains a duplicitous shrew, while in the latter she becomes 'a second Grissel' (II.i.288).[74] I maintain, rather, that *The Taming of the Shrew* recasts this tradition in entirely new terms, terms that map, through the commodity form itself, the market's infiltration and reorganisation of the household economy during the early modern period. From this perspective Kate's 'labour of signs' is of interest not because it marks her as a deep or complex subject but rather because it demonstrates the ways in which the housewife's subjectivity was constituted through its relation to status objects, or household cates.[75]

In the terms of this reading, it becomes less important to decide whether Petruchio succeeds in taming Kate than to point out, with Grumio, that in so doing, he is himself 'Kated'. Petruchio, no less than Kate, is subject to the logic of exchange, to the *perpetuum mobile* of commodity circulation. Grumio's insight also accounts for an ambiguity in my title: Are commodities in this play the subject or object of domestication? Slightly adapting Marx, we may answer this question as follows: The movement of subjects within the play takes the form of a movement made by things, and these things, far from being under their control, in fact control them.[76] Or we might choose to let Kate have the last word, recalling her answer to Petruchio's pronouncement that he has been 'mov'd' to make her his wife: 'Mov'd, in good time! Let him that mov'd you hither / Remove you hence. I knew you at the first / You were a movable' (II.i.195–7).

From *Shakespeare Quarterly*, 47 (1996), 109–131.

NOTES

[Natasha Korda's work on *Shrew* is particularly interesting in that it does not participate in the all-too-common debate about whether Kate speaks her submission speech with sincerity or irony. The question of the problematic final in *Shrew* has become overly formulaic and Korda's piece still stands as a perfect example of how feminist criticism can engage with the issues without playing to one side or the other of the gender debate. Ed.]

[The author] would like to thank Karen Bock, Krystian Czerniecki, John Guillory, Jonathan Gil Harris, and Jean Howard for their valuable comments on earlier drafts of this paper. I would also like to thank Heather Findlay for inviting me to present an abbreviated version of it for her panel, 'Shakespeare's Erotic Economies', at the 1994 meeting of the North East Modern Language Association in Pittsburgh, Pennsylvania.

1. See *The Taming of the Shrew*, ed. Brian Morris (London and New York, 1981), pp. 1–149; esp. p. 70; Richard Hosley, 'Sources and Analogues of *The Taming of the Shrew*', *Huntington Library Quarterly*, 27 (1963–64), 289–308; and John C. Bean, 'Comic Structure and the Humanizing of Kate in *The Taming of the Shrew*', in *The Woman's Part: Feminist Criticism of Shakespeare*, ed. Carolyn Ruth Swift Lenz, Gayle Greene, and Carol Thomas Neely (Urbana, Chicago, and London, 1980), pp. 65–78. See also n. 6, below.

2. Quotations from *The Taming of the Shrew* follow the Arden Shakespeare text, ed. Brian Morris.

3. *The Oxford English Dictionary*, 2d edn, prepared by J. A. Simpson and E. S. C. Weiner, 20 vols (Oxford, 1987), 2:978 and 1:66: hereafter cited simply as *OED*.

4. 'He who satisfies his own need with the product of his own labour admittedly creates use-values, but not commodities. ... In order to become a commodity, the product must be transferred to the other person ... through the medium of exchange' (Karl Marx, *Capital: A Critique of Political Economy, Volume One*, trans. Ben Fowkes [New York, 1977], p. 131).

5. Muriel Bradbrook cites this ballad as a possible source for *Shrew* in 'Dramatic Role as Social Image: a Study of *The Taming of the Shrew*', *Muriel Bradbrook on Shakespeare* (Sussex, UK and Totowa, NJ, 1984), pp. 57–71; esp. p. 60. Brian Morris discusses the ballad in his introduction to the Arden edition and in Appendix III, where he reprints several versions of it (pp. 75 and 310–16).

6. The prescribed method of shrew-taming prior to Shakespeare's play was typically violent. The more severe the punishment inflicted, the more complete the shrew's 'recovery' to the world of work seemed to be. In John Heywood's interlude *Johan Johan the Husband* (1533–34), cited by Bradbrook as an early Tudor source for *Shrew*, the eponymous Johan spends the first one hundred lines of the play elaborating how he will beat his wife. See Heywood, *Johan Johan the Husband*. The Malone Society Reprints (Oxford, 1972), sig. A1v; and Bradbrook, 'Dramatic Role', pp. 59–61. In the anonymous verse tale 'Here begynneth a merry Ieste of a shrewde and curste Wyfe, lapped in Morrelles Skin, for her good behauyour' (1550), the shrew is forced into a cellar by her husband, beaten mercilessly with birch rods until she faints, at which point he wraps her naked, bloody body in a salted hide, threatening to keep her there for the rest of her life. Thereafter she performs his commands humbly and meekly. See Morris, *The Taming of the Shrew*, p. 70.

7. In the Scottish tale titled 'The Handsome Lazy Lass', cited as a folktale source for *Shrew*, a farmer likewise tricks his wife, who 'will not do a hand's turn, she is so lazy', into offering to do 'the hardest and most exhausting work' on the farm; see Morris, *The Taming of the Shrew*, pp. 73–4. In Heywood's *Johan Johan the Husband* the protagonist points to his wife's reluctance to do housework as the reason for beating her: 'Whan she offendeth and doth a mys / And kepeth not her house / as her duetie is / Shall I not bete her if she do so / Yes by cokke blood that shall I do' (sig. A1v).

8. An interesting exception to this norm is the fifteenth-century cycle of mystery plays (in particular, the Towneley version) in which Noah's wife is portrayed as an overly zealous producer. She refuses to put aside her spinning and board the ark even as the flood waters reach

her feet: 'Full sharp ar thise showers / That renys aboute. / Therefor, wife, haue done; / Com into ship fast', Noah pleads. 'In fayth, yit will I spyn; / All in vayn ye carp', replies this industrious shrew (*The Towneley Plays*, ed. Martin Stevens and A. C. Cawley [Oxford, 1994]), pp. 506–9 and 519–20). Martha C. Howell speculates that Mistress Noah is spinning not solely for her own household but for the market, and that the play stigmatises the vital role many women played in late-medieval market production (*Women, Production, and Patriarchy in Late Medieval Cities* [Chicago and London, 1986], pp. 182. n. 19). See also n. 13, below.

9. See Susan Cahn, *Industry of Devotion: The Transformation of Women's Work in England, 1500–1660* (New York, 1987), esp. pp. 42–6. Cf. Alice Clark, *Working Life of Women in the Seventeenth Century* (New York, 1919); and Roberta Hamilton, *The Liberation of Women: A Study of Patriarchy and Capitalism* (London and Boston, 1978).

10. See Cahn, *Industry of Devotion*, pp. 53–6.

11. On conspicuous consumption in early modern England, see F. J. Fisher, *London and the English Economy, 1500–1700* (London and Ronceverte, 1990), pp. 105–18; Joan Thirsk, *Economic Policy and Projects: The Development of a Consumer Society in Early Modern England* (Oxford, 1978); Chandra Mukerji, *From Graven Images: Patterns of Modern Materialism* (New York, 1983); and *Consumption and the World of Goods*, ed. John Brewer and Roy Porter (London and New York, 1993).

12. William Harrison, *The Description of England: The Classic Contemporary Account of Tudor Social Life*, ed. Georges Edelen (New York, 1994), p. 200.

13. See Martha C. Howell's rich and complex account of the types of female labour that took place both within and outside the home, in late medieval and early modern northern European cities. Howell's book (*Women, Production, and Patriarchy*) resists the nostalgic over-valuation of female production in pre-capitalist society which has informed much of the earlier work on this subject and, in particular, that of the housework theorists.

14. See Cahn, *Industry of Devotion*, pp. 7 and 156.

15. In an article first published in 1978, Christine Delphy maintained: 'We owe to the new feminists ... the posing, for the first time in history, of the question of housework as a *theoretical* problem.' She asserted that no coherent 'theory of housework' had thus far been produced and offered her own preliminary attempt at such a systematic theorisation ('Housework or domestic work', in *Close to Home: A Materialist Analysis of Women's Oppression*, ed. and trans. Diana Leonard [Amherst, 1984], pp. 78–92; esp. p. 78).

16. As Annette Kuhn observes, feminist materialists of the 1970s 'seized upon [housework] as the key to an historically concrete understanding of women's oppression, ... as the central point at which women's specific subordination in capitalism is articulated' (*Feminism and Materialism: Women and Modes of Production*, ed. Annette Kuhn and AnnMarie Wolpe [London and Boston, 1978], p. 198).

17. See Karen Sachs, 'Engels Revisited', in *Women, Culture, and Society*, ed. Michelle Zimbalist Rosaldo and Louise Lamphere (Stanford, CA, 1974), pp. 221–2; and Kuhn, 'Structures of Patriarchy and Capital in the Family', in Kuhn and Wolpe, *Feminism and Materialism*, pp. 42–67; esp. p. 54. Housework theory is not so much a unified theory as a debate. Not all housework theorists view the unremunerated status of housework as resulting from its circumscription within a matrix of use-value production. Another, more radical strain of housework theory argues that the housewife does produce through her housework a commodity that is recognised and exchanged on the market – namely, the labour power of her husband and family – and that this work should therefore be paid or remunerated: see Mariarosa Dalla Costa and Selma James, *The Power of Women and the Subversion of the Community* (Bristol, 1972). For critiques of this notion, see Delphy, *Close to Home*, pp. 88–9; and Paul Smith, 'Domestic Labor and Marx's Theory of Value', in Kuhn and Wolpe, *Feminism and Materialism*, pp. 198–219; esp. p. 212.

18. On the economic invisibility of housework, see Delphy, *Close to Home*, p. 84.

19. On commodities as signs of distinction, see Pierre Bourdieu, *Distinction: A Social Critique of the Judgement of Taste* (Cambridge, 1984); and Jean Baudrillard, *For a Critique of the Political Economy of the Sign*, trans. Charles Levin (St Louis, MO, 1981).

20. Bourdieu, 'Symbolic capital', in *Outline of a Theory of Practice*, trans. Richard Nice (Cambridge, 1977), pp. 171–83.

21. Thorstein Veblen, *The Theory of the Leisure Class* (1899: rpt. New York, 1983), p. 83.

22. Ibid., pp. 57–8.

23. 'She still quite unmistakably remains his chattel in theory; for the habitual rendering of vicarious leisure and consumption is the abiding mark of the unfree servant' (Ibid., p. 83).

24. Ibid., p. 149 (my emphasis).

25. Ibid., pp. 57–8.

26. Baudrillard, *For a Critique*, pp. 45–6.

27. Ibid., pp. 33 and 5 (my emphasis).

28. Ibid., p. 46.

29. While it is conceptually closer to the work of Jean Baudrillard and Pierre Bourdieu, my phrase carries resonances of Jacques Lacan and Michel Foucault: see Lacan. *Ecrits: A Selection*, trans. Alan Sheridan (New York and London, 1977), pp. ix and 30–113; and Foucault, *The Order of Things: An Archaeology of the Human Sciences* (New York, 1970).

30. Joel Fineman, 'The Turn of the Shrew', in *The Subjectivity Effect in Western Literary Tradition* (Cambridge, MA, 1991), pp. 120–42; esp. p. 128. [Fineman's essay is reprinted in this collection, see above pp. 123–47 Ed.]

31. Ibid., p. 127.

32. Karen Newman, *Fashioning Femininity and English Renaissance Drama* (Chicago and London, 1991), pp. 39–40. [The essay referred to is reprinted in this collection, see above pp. 148–65 Ed.]

33. Ibid., p. 44 (my emphasis). In a book so strongly concerned with the relation of women to commodities in the early modern period, it is curious that Newman so emphatically denies the significance of the commodity's conspicuousness in *The Taming of the Shrew*. My reading of Kate's role with respect to household cates is greatly indebted to several chapters in this volume, in particular 'Dressing Up: Sartorial Extravagance in Early Modern London' and 'City Talk: Femininity and Commodification in Jonson's *Epicoene*' (pp. 109–27 and 129–43).

34. Lena Cowen Orlin, 'The Performance of Things in *The Taming of the Shrew*', *The Yearbook of English Studies*, 23 (1993), 167–88; esp. 167 and 183–5.

35. Fineman, 'The Turn of the Shrew', p. 125.

36. *OED*, 4:218.

37. In '"Sing Againe Syren": The Female Musician and Sexual Enchantment in Elizabethan Life and Literature' (*Renaissance Quarterly*, 42 [1989], 420–48), Linda Phyllis Austern notes that formal musical training was considered 'a mark of gentility' in the period insofar as it was both 'costly and time-consuming' (p. 430). It thus became 'a functional artifice' used by young women 'to attract socially desirable husbands' (p. 431). (Perhaps this is why Baptista seeks to have his daughter learn the lute.) In a contemporary treatise entitled *The Praise of Musicke* (1586), the art of music is specifically compared to other luxury commodities: 'so Musicke is as the most delicate meates, and as the finer apparell: not indeede necessary simply, but profitablie necessary for the comlinesse of life. And therefore *Socrates* and *Plato*, and all the *Pythagoreans* instructed their yong men and

maydes in the knowledge of Musicke, not to the provocation of wantonnesse, but to the restraining and bridling their affections under the rule and moderation of reason' (quoted in Austern, 'Sing Againe Syren', p. 428). The threat of 'wantonnesse', of excess, posed by the maids' consumption of musical cates is immediately tamed by the author of this treatise, who quickly shifts from a model of superfluous consumption to one of restraint or discipline. The defensive rhetoric of the treatise, as Austern argues, came in response to contemporary attacks on the playing of musical instruments by women as a form of untamed, 'Syrenesque' seduction.

38. Domestic manuals of the period manifest anxiety over the limits of a woman's right to dispose of household property. William Gouge's *Of Domesticall Dvties* (London, 1622), for example, devotes some fifteen chapters to defining the precise limits of the housewife's managerial role with respect to household goods. While it is the responsibility of the 'godly, wise, faithfull, and industrous woman', he maintains, to 'ordereth all the things of the house', he goes on to specify that this power must never exceed the scope of her husband's authority. In the dedicatory epistle of Gouge's treatise, however, we find that his attempt to limit the housewife's governance of household property was not overly popular with his parishioners: 'I remember that when these *Domesticall Duties* were first uttered out of the pulpit, much exception was taken against the application of a wiues subiection to the restraining of her from disposing the common goods of the family without, or against her husbands consent.' Gouge defends himself as follows:

> But surely they that made those exceptions did not well thinke of the *Cautions* and *Limitations* which were then deliuered, and are now againe expresly noted: which are, that the foresaid restraint be not extended to the *proper goods of a wife*, no nor overstrictly to such *goods as are set apart for the vse of the family*, nor to *extraordinary cases*, nor alwaies to an *expresse consent*, nor to the *consent of such husbands as are impotent, or farre and long absent*. If any other warrantable caution shall be shewed me, I will be as willing to admit it, as any of these. Now that my meaning may not still be peruerted, I pray you, in reading the restraint of wiues power in disposing the goods of the family, euer beare in minde those Cautions.

Gouge proffers so many mitigating exceptions to his own rule that perhaps it was more often honoured in the breach than in the observance.

39. *OED*, 6:185.

40. Baudrillard, *For a Critique*, p. 37.

41. Carol F. Heffernan, '*The Taming of the Shrew*: The Bourgeoisie in Love', *Essays in Literature*, 12 (1985), 3–14; esp. 5. On the gentry's increasing reliance on commerce in the period, see Lawrence Stone and

Jeanne C. Fawtier Stone, *An Open Elite? England 1540–1880* (Oxford, 1984).

42. On the 'economic and cultural symbiosis of land and money' in the period, see Stone and Stone, *An Open Elite?*, p. 26. The Stones conclude that the perceived symbiotic relation between the landed and merchant classes was more a 'question of values and attitudes' than of 'the facts of social mobility' (p. 211).

43. William Harrison's description of the 'great provision of tapestry, Turkey work, pewter, brass, fine linen, and thereto costly cupboards of plate' found in thc houses of 'gentlemen, merchantmen, and some other wealthy citizens' (*The Description of England*, p. 200).

44. Baudrillard, *For a Critique*, p. 40.

45. Stone and Stone, *An Open Elite?*, p. 185. On taste as a category of social distinction, see Bourdieu, *Distinction*, passim.

46. Stone and Stone, *An Open Elite?*, p. 187.

47. *OED*, 16:983. Note that this definition dates from the beginning of the sixteenth century.

48. According to Marx, it is 'the physical body of the commodity which is the use-value or useful thing' (*Capital*, p. 126).

49. 'Commodities first enter into the process of exchange ungilded and unsweetened, retaining their original home-grown shape. Exchange, however, produces a differentiation of the commodity into two elements, commodity and money, an external opposition which expresses the opposition between use-value and value which is inherent in it' (Marx, *Capital*, pp. 198–9).

50. The term *chattel* derives from the Latin *capitale* and in the sixteenth century meant either 'capital, principal', or, more commonly, 'a movable possession; any possession or piece of property other than real estate or a freehold' (*OED*, 3:59).

51. By the late sixteenth century the landed gentry had to a large extent adopted an emergent-market view of land and labour, though their view of their own society was still governed by residual concepts of feudal entitlement: see Stone and Stone, *An Open Elite?*, pp. 181–210.

52. [George Savile, Marquis of Halifax], *The Lady's New-years Gift: or, Advice to a Daughter*, 3rd edn (London, 1688), pp. 86–90.

53. Bourdieu, *Outline*, p. 181.

54. Ibid.

55. Ibid., p. 180.

56. Gouge, *Of Domesticall*, p. 297.

57. The early modern break with medieval cookery was marked by a shift from quantitative display to the qualitative refinement of 'conceited' dishes. For the first time, as Stephen Mennell notes in *All Manners of Food: Eating and Taste in England and France from the Middle Ages to the Present* (New York, 1985), 'knowledgeability and a sense of delicacy in matters of food' had come to function as markers of elite status – there was now 'food to be emulated and food to be disdained'. Differences in social standing were expressed not so much through the quantity or kind of food consumed by different social classes but 'more subtly through styles of cooking and serving' (p. 75). When it came to meat, the elite were no longer distinguished as those who ate game and fowl as opposed to 'gross meats' but as those who ate good cuts of meat as opposed to low-grade cuts. The 'cut' of one's meat, as Jean-Louis Flandrin puts it, literally took on a social function, that of 'dividing the vulgar from the distinguished'; see Jean-Louis Flandrin, 'Distinction through Taste' in *Passions of the Renaissance*, ed. Roger Chartier, Vol. 3 of *A History of Private Life*, ed. Philippe Ariès and Georges Duby, trans. Arthur Goldhammer, 5 vols (Cambridge, MA, and London, 1987–91), pp. 265–307; esp. p. 273. Cf. Fernand Braudel, 'Superfluity and Sufficiency: Food and Drink', in *The Structures of Everyday Life*, trans. Sian Reynolds (New York, 1981). On the refinement of table manners, cf. Norbert Elias, *The History of Manners*, Vol. I of *The Civilizing Process*, trans. Edmund Jephcott, 2 vols (New York, 1978).

58. According to Patricia Fumerton, the 'essential food value of banqueting stuffs ... was *nothing* ... the culinary referent of the void was zero' (*Cultural Aesthetics: Renaissance Literature and the Practice of Social Ornament* [Chicago and London, 1991], p. 133).

59. John Murrell, *A Daily Exercise for Ladies and Gentlewomen* ... (1617), quoted here from Fumerton, *Cultural Aesthetics*, p. 130.

60. Fumerton, *Cultural Aesthetics*, pp. 130–2.

61. In Marx's terms, Petruchio distinguishes a thing's 'stiff and starchy existence as a body' from 'its sublime objectivity at a value' (*Capital*, p. 144). 'Not an atom of matter', Marx writes, 'enters into the objectivity of commodities as values: in this it is the direct opposite of the coarsely sensuous objectivity of commodities as physical objects' (*Capital*, p. 138).

62. 'Commodities come into the world in the form of use-values or material goods ... This is their plain, homely, natural form. However, they are only commodities because they have a dual nature, because they are at the same time objects of utility and bearers of value' (Marx, *Capital*, p. 138).

63. Baudrillard, *For a Critique*, p. 93.

64. Bourdieu, *Distinction*, p. 55.

65. Bourdieu, *Outline*, p. 183.

66. Orlin, 'The Performance of Things', p. 185.

67. S. D. Amussen, 'Gender, Family and the Social Order, 1560–1725', in *Order and Disorder in Early Modern England*, ed. Anthony Fletcher and John Stevenson (Cambridge, 1985), pp. 196–217; esp. p. 196.

68. Amussen, 'Gender', pp. 201. Amussen cites the housewife's supervision of children and servants and her role in the household economy as instances of her joint governorship (p. 203).

69. Orlin, 'The Performance of Things', p. 185.

70. Baudrillard, *For a Critique*, p. 93.

71. Ibid., p. 101

72. Ibid., p. 96.

73. Robert B. Heilman was the first to speak of 'revisionist' readings of *Shrew* in his 'The *Taming* Untamed, or, The Return of the Shrew', *Modern Language Quarterly*, 27 (1966), 147–61. John C. Bean then divided *Shrew* criticism into both revisionist and anti-revisionist camps in his 'Comic Structure and the Humanizing of Kate in *The Taming of the Shrew*'.

74. The duplicitous shrew was a common topos in medieval literature. In William Dunbar's 'Tretis of the tua mariit Wemen and the Wedo', for example, the shrewd widow gets her way 'with her husband by feigning submission': '... I wes a schrew evir', she confides to her gossips. 'Bot I wes sehene [bright] in my schrowd [clothing] and schew me innocent; / And thought I dour wes and dane, dispitous and bald, / I wes dissymblit suuttelly in a sanctis liknes: / I semyt sober and sueit, and sempill without fraud, / Bot I couth sexty dissaif [deceive] that suttillar wer haldin.' The widow offers the following lesson to future shrews: 'Be constant in your governance and counterfeit gud maneris, / [...] dowis ay in double forme, / [...]. Be amy able with humble face, as angellis apperand, / [...] Be of your luke like innocentis, thoght ye haif evill myndis' (William Dunbar, *Poems*, ed. James Kinsley [Oxford, 1958], ll. 108–13 and 116–24).

    Anti-revisionist readings of the play remain equally within the medieval shrew tradition when taking Kate's final speech as evidence of her 'true' submission, giving credit to Petruchio's assertion that he will turn Katherina into 'a second Grissel'. In Chaucer's version of the story, Griselde's humble origins and predilection for hard labour position her as the very antithesis of the high-born, slothful, duplicitous shrew and lead her to suffer gladly her aristocratic husband's cruel tests. In contrast to the shrew's proverbial duplicity, Chaucer stresses

Griselde's unfeigned satisfaction with her degree; see Geoffrey Chaucer, *The Canterbury Tales*, ed. N. F. Blake (London, 1980).

75. Orlin in 'The Performance of Things' similarly proposes an alternative to traditional characterologic readings of the play, one that focuses on the 'performance of things' (p. 186).

76. Cf. Marx's assertion that '[exchangers'] own movement ... within society has for them the form of a movement made by things, and these things, far from being under their control, in fact control them' (*Capital*, pp. 167–8).

10

A Shrew for the Times

DIANA E. HENDERSON

Of all Shakespeare's comedies, *The Taming of the Shrew* most overtly reinforces the social hierarchies of its day. Lacking the gendered inversion of power and the poetic complexity of Shakespeare's romantic comedies, this early play might seem less likely to capture the imagination of modern audiences and producers; we might expect it, like its farcical companion *The Comedy of Errors*, to be filmed infrequently and almost obligatorily as part of canonical projects such as the BBC TV Shakespeare series. Quite the converse is true. More than eighteen screen versions of the play have been produced in Europe and North America, putting *Shrew* in a select league with the 'big four' tragedies, and outpacing those comedies scholars usually dub more 'mature'.[1] What accounts for this frequent reproduction of an anachronistic plot premised on the sale of women?[2]

Part of the answer lies in a venerable tradition of adaptation. Discussing David Garrick's *Catharine and Petruchio*, Michael Dobson points out that seemingly minor changes in the text 'mute ... the outright feudal masculinism of *The Taming of the Shrew* in favour of guardedly egalitarian, and specifically private, contemporary versions of sympathy and domestic virtue'.[3] Garrick's version provides the source for a performance tradition that tames not only the 'shrew' but also the text. Here 'Dr Petruchio' consciously assumes his boorishness as part of a therapy programme for a disturbed Katherina. This Petruchio is a far cry from Shakespeare's blusterer, knocking his servant Grumio soundly as he comes to wive it wealthily ('if wealthily then happily') in Padua. Such attempts to obliterate gender struggle ultimately collapse the leading couple into a single entity, 'Kate-and-Petruchio', replicating the play's narrative movement and its ideology. Viewing the story in a euphemised and relatively untroubled way from Petruchio's perspective remains the norm in almost all modern video versions – though not, intriguingly, in the two feature films starring Hollywood's most famous couples of their respective generations, Mary Pickford and Douglas Fairbanks Sr, and Elizabeth Taylor and Richard Burton. The film's differences derive not only from the unusual box office power of their leading ladies but also from their directors' cinematic choices.

These choices strive to create a female subject position for Katherine, adding gestures, glances, and private speech to the script's most notorious silences. The erasure of the Christopher Sly induction from filmed versions of *Shrew* removes the play's most common theatrical 'excuse' for its gender politics (i.e., it's all a prank, or a drunkard's wish fulfilment). In the very necessity of using the camera's eye to produce a second perspective on the story, modern film-makers both reveal the potential of their medium to provide an alternative 'frame' to the script's use of Sly and call attention to the text's troubled relationship to Katherina as shrew-heroine. Their choices also highlight the continuing difficulties involved in imagining a woman as the dramatic subject as well as object of narrative desire, and especially the interrelated muteness and mystery associated with woman-as-knower. Yet while the use of the camera to gesture at female subjectivity deserves special attention, ultimately each foray is displaced by a more conventional 'solution' in representing femininity.

Both modern theatre and film have removed the ironic potential of a cross-dressed boy playing Katherine. Thus they make all the more central their basic reliance on modern culture's enshrining of the heterosexual love plot and the presumed link between love and marriage. The familiarity and tug of this domestic fantasy helps explain *Shrew*'s obsessive return to the screen – particularly during the decades of 'backlash' when advances in women's political participation outside the home have prompted a response from those who perceive a threat. The timing of the *Shrew*s reinforces this cultural connection. In addition to five silent shorts between 1908 and 1913, 'spin-offs' such as *Taming Mrs. Shrew* attest to the popularity of the story during the heyday of suffragism.[4] Soon after suffrage came another silent (1923), and finally United Artists' *The Taming of the Shrew* of 1929, the only movie in which Pickford and Fairbanks co-starred. It claims pride of place as the very first of all Shakespeare 'talkies'.

Having been supplanted by more sophisticated remarriage narratives and screwball comedies during the Depression Era, *Shrew* returned as an ur-text for two musicals in the 1940s.[5] Soon after, the next set of 'faithful' *Shrew*s (as well as the filmed version of *Kiss Me, Kate*) coincided with the enforced return to domesticity of the women who had provided World War II's 'swing shift'; Rosie the Riveter was supplanted by Kate the Happy Housewife, as sponsored on television by Westinghouse and Hallmark. All these 1950s productions adopt Petruchio's perspective; on television he is a 'frame speaker' who gets the first or last word, while in *Kiss Me, Kate* his character doubles as the narrator for the titular musical-within-a musical. The new homeviewing technology gave *Shrew* new resonance, as it not only promoted female consumerism but quite literally kept women in their homes. And despite its stylistic innovations and dazzling tempo, Zeffirelli's feature film for the swinging sixties retained this emphasis on domesticity – though the motivation and effect of its domestic desires may be interpreted in a radically different way. Indeed, because of an unusual alliance between the director's and Katherina's perspective *vis-à-vis* the narrative, the unexpected subtext of this farcical film reveals female silencing and isolation, the issues that *Shrew* ballads of Shakespeare's era were quite blatant in promoting but which stage and film versions of the modern era have anxiously tried to suppress.

The third wave of *Shrew*s appeared not in the cinema but back on the TV screen, during the decade following the emergence of 'women's liberation'. Between 1976 and 1986, five *Shrew*s (including one parodic rewriting) appeared on North American television – setting a frequency record for productions during the era of sound recording. The most telling cinematic innovation in several of these is a post-'sexual revolution' directness in emphasising the erotic appeal of Petruchio's body as a motivation for Kate's conversion. The centrality of sex appeal is particularly powerful in two versions based on theatrical performances, both broadcast on PBS: the 1976 video of the American Conservatory Theater (ACT) production, and Joseph Papp's 1981 video repackaging of scenes from the New York Shakespeare Festival's Central Park production. By contrast, Jonathan Miller's putatively historicist and undeniably sober *Shrew*, made for the BBC Time-Life Series, was the perfect production to usher in the neo-conservative 1980s.[6] Miller set his production in opposition to what he perceived as 'American' 'feminist' versions less true to Shakespeare's text; he identified this foreign enemy with Papp.[7] Ironically, the stars of Papp's own video, *Kiss Me, Petruchio*, appear to share Miller's sexual politics: in interspersed backstage moments creating another version of a 'frame' story, Meryl Streep and Raúl Juliá deny that the play's gender representation constitutes a problem.[8] Indeed, by replicating Juliá's stage energy and sexual appeal through its angled close-ups and fast-paced intercuts, *Kiss Me, Petruchio* seduces. For very different reasons, so does the send-up of *Shrew* on the US network television series *Moonlighting* (1986), which seems wildly progressive in simply advocating marriage as a 'fifty-fifty' agreement. A sign of the times, indeed.

The clustering of filmed *Shrew*s correlates with those decades when feminism has induced conservative responses and when the media are actively encouraging women to find their pleasures in the home; moreover, *Shrew* occurs at moments of new viewing technologies and is promptly reproduced in the new media before most if not all other Shakespeare plays. The agents of culture seem anxious to make sure *The Taming of the Shrew* is preserved, even as our science progresses: from moving pictures, to the first Shakespeare talkie, to early television drama, to Zeffirelli's first popularised 'younger generation' Shakespeare film, to the world of network TV spoofs and home videos.[9]

In choosing to erase the Sly frame and use actresses for the female roles the film-makers increase the inset story's claims to social reality, already abetted by the transfer to a normatively realist medium. As Barbara Hodgdon has effectively argued, film's tendency to reify the voyeuristic and consumerist logic of the play's presentation of sexuality also reinforces the tendency to view Kate as a spectacle, bound by an economy in which her pleasure derives from placating 'her' man; the female spectator who identifies with Kate, not wishing to deprive herself of what is represented as the means to heterosexual pleasure, thus participates in her double-bind. Patriarchal inscription becomes inevitable and self-consuming for woman, with intended subversion revealed as always already inscribed as a subversion in the dominant discourse.

While finding this analysis compelling and descriptive of the narrative logic of most filmed *Shrew*s, I resist viewing patriarchal reinscription as a formal necessity, as this discounts some striking film moments as well as the agency (and responsibility) of the filmmakers. My aim is not to deny that all the *Shrew*s we currently have are works of ideological containment, but rather to suggest that despite their ultimate closing down of possibilities, their use of the camera and voice do temporarily work otherwise, and could be employed and extended in ways that might lead away from a co-opted and conservative gender politics. By looking closely at such moments of filmic adaptation and perspective play, my aim is not to argue about the prior existence of female subjectivity in Shakespeare's text nor to ignore the relative meagreness of those moments that catch my eye as causes for celebration within a bleak cultural canvas; rather, it is to affirm the significance and resonance of local artistic choices within our ideological frame, and hence the need to acknowledge their particular cultural agency and consequences.

To this end, I focus briefly on four films and four television shows that epitomise their generations' dominant patterns in representing *Shrew*; all are works that were constructed for screen viewing through editing and/or scripting, rather than being video recordings of theatrical performances. In *Kiss Me, Petruchio*, the actual scenes from *Shrew* are filmed theatre, but the intercutting of backstage interviews and commentary by audience members constructs a new narrative logic specifically for the camera. By combining a chronological discussion with emphasis on the use of the camera to create a second 'authorial' perspective, I hope to illuminate both the attempts to expand the representation of Kate as subject, and the particular cultural 'solutions' and frustrations tied to the eras of their production. Viewing these *Shrew*s historically, we can better understand their duplicitous, shrewd cultural work.

EARLY *SHREWS*

The silent short films and early talkies establish the basic filmic patterns and modifications to *Shrew* that have been reproduced throughout the twentieth century. D. W. Griffith's direction of

Biograph's brief 1908 *Shrew*, the first extant moving picture version, gains it a place in film history; Robert Ball regards it as one of Griffith's 'fumbling experiments to express himself artistically in a new form'.[10] Paving the way for several patterns in *Shrew* representation, Griffith's Petruchio laughs at Katherine's physical assaults and brings his whip to the wedding; in keeping with the 'improvement' of Petruchio on film, there is no final wager on Kate's behaviour but rather an offering of flowers. As interesting as the film is Biograph's promotional material, which begins with a moralising message clearly applied only to Katherine: 'If we could see ourselves as others see us what models we would become'.[11] This language foreshadows Jonathan Miller's 1980s statement that Petruchio gives Kate 'an image of herself'[12] and Meryl Streep's matching explanation of Kate's visual education. In each case, woman uses her eyes not to view (and hence potentially criticise and judge) others, but rather to see an objectification of her inadequate self. Through this 'proper' viewing of herself through the culture's eyes, Katherina is indeed transformed into a model of femininity.

The first *Shrew* produced in the era of women's suffrage, Edwin J. Collins's twenty-minute British & Colonial production of 1923, accounts for Katherine's transformation in terms superficially more amenable to independently minded women. One of the many narrative title cards explains: 'By noon the next day, though famished and weary for want of food and rest, the Shrew deep in her heart admired the man whose temper is stronger than her own.'[13] Here is the 'two of a kind' logic that some critics later apply to Zeffirelli's film, arguing that this wild couple stands in opposition to the tame, mercantile society of Padua; here too begins the representation of Katherine as the desiring subject erotically drawn to an alpha male, a pattern dominating the late twentieth-century *Shrew*s. Petruchio's strength is signified by the invulnerability of his body to her fists and fury, gendering the female as the one who is subject to physical suffering. When she hits him to punctuate her warning to 'beware my [wasp] sting', she hurts only herself: enacting a classic comic trope, he laughs while she nurses her own hand. Again deleting the final wager, the film ends with Kate firmly transplanted to her new home and cured of her 'vile' temper, laughing and kissing Petruchio as she sits in his lap.[14]

United Artists' feature film of 1929 shares this final image of the happy couple, but the backstage context informing Sam Taylor's movie is more complicated. Whereas the other silent *Shrew*s prefigure the norms that predominate in the sound era, this version reveals the struggles and momentary counterimages that encourage us to look closely. Made at the moment of transition from silents to talkies when many theatres were not yet equipped for sound, the movie was released in both formats; this knowledge helps explain the extreme gesturing and slow pace of the early scenes, and adds to one's appreciation of Douglas Fairbanks Sr's spirited entry and almost throwaway delivery. It does not, however, explain his bungling of famous lines ('I come to wive in Padua – wealthily'). For that, we must turn to Mary Pickford's autobiography:

> the strange new Douglas acting opposite me was being another Petruchio in real life ... I would be waiting on the set for him till nearly noon. ... When Douglas finally showed up, he wouldn't know his lines. They had to be chalked on enormous blackboards, and I had to move my head so he could read them. ... With dozens of eyes focused on us every minute of the day I couldn't afford to let my real feelings be seen.[15]

Pickford was hardly an impartial observer: during *Shrew* her marriage to Fairbanks was disintegrating. But even if read sceptically, her tale of the traumas of playing Kate (and play[Kat]ing Fairbanks, to invoke Hodgdon's pun) resonates in later actresses' accounts, most notably those of Fiona Shaw.[16] While director Sam Taylor's writing credit created an uproar at the time, more enduringly troublesome is the acting advice he had relayed to Pickford, against her own better judgement: 'We don't want any of this heavy stage drama; we want the old Pickford tricks.' The result, Pickford notes, was that 'Instead of being a forceful tiger-cat, I was a spitting little kitten'.[17] The 'set was tense with unspoken thoughts' as her suggestions were overridden: 'The making of that film was my finish. My confidence was completely shattered, and I was never again at ease before the camera or microphone.' Internalising *Shrew*'s dynamics, Pickford gave up her unpopular attempts to become something other than America's Sweetheart, soon abandoning her career as an actress for behind-the-scenes employment.

Despite her Shirley Temple timbre and pout, Pickford nevertheless was given equal time on screen, with added speeches and close-ups creating a sense of her ongoing agency, albeit in solitude or silence. The film's more equivalent representation of Kate and Petruchio includes giving them duelling whips, duelling soliloquies, and duelling eavesdropping scenes. Echoing Garrick's script, Katherine gets the last lines of the 'wooing scene' as a soliloquy (a form she lacks in Shakespeare), using Petruchio's animal-taming metaphors to refer equally to herself and her rider/falcon:

> Look to your seat, Petruchio, or I'll throw you.
> Katherine shall tame this haggard or if she fails,
> I'll tie up her tongue and pare down her nails.

Though the scene begins with a phallic parody in which Katherine visually assesses their respective whip-length and retreats upon discovering that Petruchio's is longer, both this and the previous scene broadcast an ironic send-up of the usual Fairbanks hero. Grumio and Hortensio exchange sidelong winks and glances behind Petruchio's back when he delivers his braggadocio catalogue of experience ('Have I not heard lions roar?'), and he breaks down in near-hysteria at the prospect of a 'woman's tongue'. In a remarkable dissolve, we continue to hear Fairbanks' laughing reiteration of 'a woman's tongue' as the scene shifts to the unhappy face of Baptista, being chastised by Katherina in her first speech of the film (earlier, we only *saw* her, and briefly). Thus the director's edit serves to mock Petruchio even as it confirms the narrative's logic that he plays a necessary role in taming Katherina's dangerous tongue.

Both through this visual choice and textual modifications, the following scene accentuates the fear of uncontrolled female speech, whose power is in some part confirmed as Katherina exits with a curse (borrowed from Gremio's part) which silences her father: 'you may go to the devil's dam.' She later uses her tongue as well as body parodically when waiting before the wedding, imitating Petruchio/Fairbanks' sweeping arm gestures, swagger, and incessant 'ha ha' as she describes his behaviour. Both speech and visuals collude in deconstructing Petruchio's dominance, reaching a climax when the man who began by leaping over walls ends up reeling in pain from her blow to his head (with a jointstool), murmuring 'Have I not heard lions' roar?' in woozy bafflement. While the film alters the story to undo Petruchio's harsh agency in effecting a change, Katherina's speech must nevertheless be tamed, a sign of her tender feminine heart when she discovers her husband's vulnerability.

Uniquely among screen *Shrew*s, Katherine's final assertion of voice does not require the disappearance or rejection of Bianca:

Pickford's famous final wink after her abbreviated last speech, the film model for later winks at the audience, is here clearly aimed at her *sister*, and is acknowledged as such: behind the patriarchal ventriloquising remains a conspiracy of 'unspoken thoughts', a female subculture whose bond is unbroken. Though her words have become tame, Katherine remains the one who sees more than her husband, creating a silent connection between her perspective and the film-maker's own. In concert with the shift from an invulnerable to a wounded Petruchio, these adaptations – while hardly presenting a challenge to the social world of Padua – preserve a 'separate sphere' for woman as agent. Kate thus sustains her own gaze and the illusion of self-creation from a subaltern position, becoming the sneaky servant rather than the Stepford wife of patriarchy. And in what seems on screen to be their 'merry war', Pickford and Fairbanks together provide a prototype for the great Hollywood comedies to come, in which equally important co-stars mix screwball antics with subtler repartee than this transitional film affords.

A *SHREW* IN THE HOME

The camera's eye works quite differently in US television's first *Shrew*, the Westinghouse Studio One production broadcast 5 June, 1950. Whereas the Pickfair film represents an ironic visual contest between the sexes, this *Shrew* suggests a gap between the viewer's expectations about a 'classic' and what the new technology will reveal. The hour-long video begins with a visual joke premised on our sense of historical distance from the past, a distance the immediacy of live, modern-dress performance will then work to deny. Beyond a stone arch labelled 'Padua', we survey a painted backdrop with a monumental column dominating an ancient townscape; then the camera tracks back to reveal the modern world of sidewalk cafés as Petruchio (Charlton Heston dressed in trenchcoat, hat, and sunglasses) enters on a bicycle and reiterates 'Padua'. Shorn of all that might distance this story from an American viewer (including the master/servant relations and class stratification that complicate the text's power relations), this version relentlessly reiterates conventional postwar ideas of gender difference. Even the radios Betty Furness hawks during a commercial break are gendered.[18] Having downed a beer in one gulp, pleased-with-himself Petruchio laughingly pronounces his modernised version of

Grumio's couplet: 'Katharine the curst!' / 'Of all titles for a woman, this one's the worst'; slapping her ass and chuckling to himself throughout the play, he appears entirely satisfied to embody those attitudes that two decades later would be called male chauvinism. The transformation of Lisa Kirk's Katherine, meanwhile, is played out through frequent costume changes. As if to replicate the recent displacement of the silver screen's strong women by 'softer' sweethearts, Kirk begins in a riding outfit clearly evocative of Katherine Hepburn's trousered look (she beats blonde Bianca, who wears an off-the-shoulder dress, with the riding crop), but with her courtship and marriage this Kate changes to the 'proper' dresses that accentuate her hourglass figure.

The new medium of television also accentuates a cartoonish vision of Katherine; Kirk's Broadway background ill prepared her to convey gesture subtly on screen, and she mugs in silent close-up while Petruchio talks in the middle distance. She is done a further disservice by director Paul Nickell's decision to give her a voice-over 'soliloquy' of lamentation in Act IV (the speech usually addressed to Grumio) while she silently gestures her hunger straight at the camera: in both cases, she appears less angry than mad. Nickell's treatment of Kirk could not be more remote from the use of voice-over for soliloquies in Olivier's films of himself as Henry V and Hamlet, in which the actor's pensive face becomes an occasion for aesthetic adulation. By contrast, this vocal/visual experiment in the new technology serves, like the production as a whole, to legitimate the domestication of women. Unlike Petruchio, who gets to speak directly to the camera in his soliloquies outlining his plan, Katherine is shown silently mouthing comments at the end of the 'wooing scene' and then close-mouthed at this moment of putative self-expression; but she does get to speak directly to the camera in the final speech, as she reminds all those happy homemakers about their duties to their husbands. Meanwhile, a grinning Petruchio casually eats grapes. The hour concludes with Kate's sustained wink to the camera while engaged in her third stolid kiss with Petruchio. She is thus allowed to address the TV audience as a unified speaking subject only when she has learned to manipulate the system and stand by her man.

Stylistically at the opposite end of the spectrum, the other US television *Shrew* of the 1950s nevertheless shares with the Westinghouse version an air of confidence and nonchalance in regard to its subject matter. Moreover, for all its visual wit and parody, the 1956 Hallmark Hall of Fame production starring Lilli Palmer and Maurice Evans concludes similarly to the 1950 'realistic' version.[19] The divide-and-conquer logic implicit in most productions, wherein Bianca must be revealed as the 'real' shrew when Katherine is tamed, is accentuated by transferring the widow's lines to the younger sister.[20] In this regard, both the 1950s television *Shrews* seem to have taken a step backward in time from Pickford's finale. And as in the 1950 production, Palmer's Katherine shifts her gaze from Bianca to the camera during her final speech when pronouncing that 'women are so simple'; deploying the new intimacy of the television screen to make herself a guest in our home, she smiles as she calls us 'unable worms'. The play had opened with an oblique use of lines from the Sly Induction, when Grumio invited the audience to watch these 'antic players', addressing the TV camera as he said 'Come, madam wife'. Now all the madam wives of middle America discover the purpose of their spectatorship as Katherine goes down on her knees, earning a final kiss from her husband and lord. Despite Maurice Evans's friendly reappearance after the curtain calls (in order to advertise subsequent programmes), the feminine mystique of the play's conclusion has not been ironised by this 'romp'.

A *SHREW* ALONE

Ten years later, Elizabeth Taylor similarly performed *Shrew*'s final speech without irony – and indeed without any lead-in request from her Petruchio, for she launches into her chastisement immediately upon re-entering the banquet hall (having dragged along the other women on her own initiative as well). The result was to naturalise Katherine's assertions as her own spontaneous feelings, flamed by her indignation at unruly wives and empathy for her husband's unexpressed desires. In this, art imitated life. For Taylor herself chose to perform the scene 'straight' to the surprise of both director Franco Zeffirelli and co-star Richard Burton, and her husband was touched:

> The usual trick is for the actress to wink at the audience ... Amazingly, Liz did nothing of the kind; she played it straight ... and she meant it. Full of that Welsh passion, Richard was deeply moved. I saw him wipe away a tear. 'All right, my girl, I wish you'd put that into practice.' She looked him straight in the eye. 'Of course, I can't say it in words like that, but my heart is there.'[21]

Complete with Taylor's stated inability to own the powers of language, this incident epitomises the paradoxical nature of Zeffirelli's film, in which Katherina is presented far more empathetically and with greater agency than in most video versions, yet employs that agency to naturalise a traditional sex-gender system all the more doggedly.

With similar irony, there is a surprising undercurrent of melancholy and nostalgia for home within this fast-paced lark of a film designed to appeal to the sixties younger generation. Those raised on MTV may find the contemporary reviews of this *Shrew* bemusing, for their worries about the disorientation caused by busy sets and camerawork seem almost quaint given the subsequent speed-up of our visual culture. Moreover, this concern with pace tends to displace detailed analysis of why the film makes unusual choices, such as presenting a predominantly boorish Petruchio and an often tearful Katherina, whose isolation is accentuated by sentimental music and lingering close-up shots. Some have regarded the movie solely as a vehicle for the co-producing star couple, but in this paradoxical tempo one finds marks of the director's own sensibility, representing through the images of *Shrew* the same emotions that his autobiography articulates regarding his fractured and romanticised childhood. His tendency to empathise with the social outcast becomes the occasion for cross-gender identification with Kate, as the camera repeatedly adopts her perspective and adds private moments in which we see her thinking.

An illegitimate child, Zeffirelli felt both beloved and abandoned. He was raised sequentially by a peasant wetnurse, his professional but socially ostracised mother (who died when he was six), and his unmarried aunt. His father, who occasionally visited his mother, at which time the 'family' all shared a bed, remained in other ways distant from the little boy; his father's wife memorably hounded the child as a 'bastardino' and haunted his dreams (her harassment becomes his autobiography's framestory). What Peter Donaldson notes in regard to Zeffirelli's other films also applies to his *Shrew*, providing a subtext for his empathetic representation of Katherina's perspective: 'Mourning for his mother's death and absence, grief for his own exclusion from the parental relationship ... and the effort to find a place in a fragmented family leave their mark on Zeffirelli's work in film'.[22]

Zeffirelli's sensibilities are split and seemingly contradictory, befitting the topsy-turvyness of life in the sixties. His favourite movie of the year was the Beatles' *Help!* and he got its buffoon-villain Victor Spinetti to play Hortensio, as well as hiring disaffected Roman *capelloni* ('long-haired ones') for the university scenes. At the same time, Zeffirelli insisted that the Italian premiere of his film be the English-language version, to please any of the old English ladies still surviving in Florence who had shared in his own youthful discovery of filmed Shakespeare through Olivier's *Henry V* – a film he credits with having liberated him from paternal authority by giving him the confidence to choose an artistic career.[23] In a version of subjectivity akin to that which the film grants Katherine, he became free to follow the master(s) of his own choosing. As director of *Shrew*, he creates a fantastic version of 'home' as screen image, displacing his own illegitimacy, his absent/present father, and the Florentine scandal that precipitated his mother's death, and replacing them with a cultural inheritance from the Bard, Italian *cinéma-verité*, and the visual splendours of the Italian Renaissance. Zeffirelli concludes the account of his childhood by remarking 'I still have difficulty in trusting love when it is offered. This is something that has marked my entire life.'[24] Within his representation, the farcical frenzy slows only when his camera lingers on those who are emotionally isolated, unsure, or far from home. The movie embodies the appeal of 'traditional values' for those self-creators who were only partially transformed by the sixties sexual 'revolution'.

The plaintiveness of the moments when one sees Katherine's isolation and sense of betrayal and the balancing tenderness of attention to gestures of gentleness provide an unexpected counterpoint to this *Shrew*'s energetic opening. Such moments also sentimentalise the story more thoroughly than does Taylor's particular (though consistent) choice in the banquet scene. Throughout the film, the pauses are pregnant, and sympathy goes to the outcast: Katherina hurt and crying in defeat after the protracted wooing chase, as she realises she has been betrothed against her will; locked in a darkened room while the men chortle in the public hall; looking anxiously to her father for support as she faces unfamiliar applause before her wedding; unintentionally witnessing the backroom transaction selling her (the transfer of the massive dowry her father has paid Petruchio); Katherine and Petruchio awkwardly preparing for bed; Katherina alone again, sobbing in the unfamiliar, wrecked bed in Petruchio's home; and then, in a key shift as she takes control of domestic space, a newly sympathetic Petruchio looking at his wife's working alliances with his re-clothed servants; melancholy

Katherina sitting amidst the wreckage of her promised clothes; Petruchio uncomfortably focusing on his drink at the banquet and waiting to see if Katherina will come at his bidding; and Petruchio surprised to find her gone after he finally achieves his long-desired kiss. All these extratextual moments create another layer of storytelling, allowing Katherina as much subjective presence as Petruchio.

The dynamics of power change radically at the moment when Katherina discovers her means to control: housekeeping. While it is easy enough for the critic to point out the patronising gender assumptions informing this means of attaining 'power' (and Zeffirelli's political pronouncements affirm his conservatism on some gender issues), it is also important to recognise the seductiveness of his representation, rooted in another aspect of Zeffirelli's social vision: his sense of allegiance to and nostalgia for peasant life. Not only does Katherina remake herself as the force of culture and domestic beauty in opposition to Petruchio's ruffian masculinity, but she does so through an alliance with servants. She transforms the dusty barrenness of Petruchio's bachelor home into a lively Arcadian villa, in which lady and grooms share featherdusters and wear similar homemade clothes. (Tellingly, the scene of Grumio's tormenting Kate with the prospect of beef and/or mustard is omitted.)

Here too Katherine's newly chosen way of life – not exactly 'slumming' but finding solace in a working vacation from her privileged social position – matches a powerful memory from Zeffirelli's youth. He had spent summers in Borselli with his wetnurse's family, in a world later lost through the parallel changes of his growing up (and the death of his individual caretaker) and the culture's development (the displacement of the age-old peasant economy). Ironically, it was only in that 'simple peasant town' that Zeffirelli 'had a sense of permanence'.[25] The director's affection for this world in which the children picked out dead ticks from the wool and all the clothes were homemade overdetermines the more obvious messages produced by similar actions on film (Petruchio's boorishness in proudly displaying his dog's ticks at Hortensio's table; Katherina's 'capture' in the woolbin; her rustic home decorating); it also deepens the film's nostalgic desire to embrace a past in which class as well as gender are mystified. After comically recording the scepticism of labourers who hear Lucentio's outburst of academic desire upon entering Padua, the rest of the movie presents the people as a jolly chorus to the public scenes – an energetic film correlate to a theatre audience's response, but also one that recreates feudalism as the good old days. It counters critical attempts to read Kate and Petruchio as carnivalesque opponents to a rigidly monolithic society: this jolly, frolicking Padua is not represented in a way so amenable to Bakhtinian schematisation.

Conversely, the ironies and wit of Zeffirelli's *Shrew* defy oversimple interpretation of this as a conservative film. In addition to its unusual crediting of Katherina with interiority akin to the director's own, it is also a work of pop art in postmodern style. For the film, as Holderness observes, is a minefield of parody. The fact that it is the giant prostitute who breaks into tears at the domestic fervour of Katherine's grand finale makes her action equally available for sentimental or ironic interpretation.[26] Moreover, the stress on Baptista's 'selling' of his daughters provides a countertheme to the romanticised home. This is especially true in the film's midsection, where Zeffirelli delivers a 1–2–3 punch showing Katherine isolated and silenced at her own wedding festivities. First Katherine, humiliated by Petruchio's loud, late arrival, tries to yell 'I will not' at the altar in response to her wedding vows – but Petruchio literally stops her mouth in an uneroticised kiss before the last word, at which point the entire congregation loudly celebrates. Then in a second shot Katherine is shown half buried by the congratulatory crowd, desperately yelling 'no' and 'father' despite the crowd's indifference to her will. We then appear to shift mood with Katherine as she graciously thanks guests at the reception while a musical consort plays; this, however, is merely the prelude to her witnessing, beyond a doorframe, the handshake and transfer of dowry funds from her father to her husband, an action confirming her isolation. She stands silently gazing from outside the space of a more orderly transaction than took place at church. This sequence of isolating moments, which highlights the culture's traffic in women, works in concert with an undercurrent of violence and the shifting use of the camera's perspective to create a more complicated film than has been fully credited.[27]

WHO'S ZOOMIN' WHO?

Zeffirelli's perspective play, in and out of Kate's vantage point, makes obvious the shaping potential – and ironic openendedness –

allowed by artful use of that other movie 'subject', the camera. Such play is especially appropriate for representing the subjectivity of a character who, though called a shrew, seldom gets a word in edgewise. Fiona Shaw observes, 'Along comes a man to tame the noisy one. And for almost five acts we never hear her speak'; but Paola Dionosetti rightly adds that although Petruchio gets the lines, 'Kate has eyes everywhere'.[28] The more socially progressive versions work to equalise the battle of wills by showing Katherine in thought, or by constructing visual matches. In Zeffirelli's film, the balance shifts in keeping with his visual priorities as well as emotional sympathies.

While critics swoon over her eyes and bustline, the camerawork not only accentuates Taylor's feminine beauty but mimics her positionality: showing her first as a single watchful eye above the street action; viewing her viewing; pausing to watch her pausing to think; concluding scenes when she concludes her sequence of emotions and decision-making. Indeed, it is Bianca's usurpation of Katherine's viewing position at the window that initiates Kate's attack on her sister, prompting the mock-horror sequence that actually unites the camera's perspective with Kate's own gaze. This affinity between the camera and Kate holds true after the wooing sequence, when the camera returns to join Katherina in her darkened room looking out rather than moving on with the men in the hall; gone is the scene of bartering over Bianca, leaving Katherine's solitary smile to close the narrative's first section. Similarly, in the wedding scenes her looks counterbalance Petruchio's blustering comedy and she again has a solo moment to end the sequence, when she pauses on donkeyback at Padua's gate recognising that neither direction holds much promise. She is seen last in the travel scene (in which Kate actively schemes to intercept the other riders, rather than merely suffering as in Grumio's textual account), and she gets both the nuptial bed and the last image on her wedding night – all the more remarkable since Petruchio's soliloquy is virtually cut.

By presenting Petruchio as a material creature at the start (a choice often criticised despite its textual defensibility and cinematic usefulness), Zeffirelli allows these camera shots to establish Kate as the movie's silent thinker. This subjectivity remains even after her gain in power causes a shift of empathy embracing Petruchio (now quieter, smarter, and sadder than before she started cleaning house). Because we have already seen Katherina plotting, acting unexpectedly, and only afterwards understood her motives, her final 'straight' delivery of her major speech benefits from that sense of anticipation: when Petruchio turns to find her gone, he experiences the surprise that we, filmically, have been trained to expect. Yet we do end up looking at the world from Petruchio's rather than Katherine's vantage. The ironies in this conclusion are legion: the actress's unexpected choice of sincerity is overridden by the director who thereby sustains his own vision by crediting the character with more artfulness than the actress professes. As such, this version shares with so many other productions a power struggle not only between the protagonists but also between director and actress. What remains indisputable is the complexity of cameraplay in the Zeffirelli film, and its crucial effect upon the representation of Katherine.

BACK TO THE FUTURE

The five television variations on the theme of *Shrew* appearing in North America between 1976 and 1986 demonstrate the range of stylistic interpretation the play continues to afford; they also reveal how meagrely the previous decade's political upheavals informed those productions deemed worthy to broadcast. Despite radical theatrical reinterpretations such as those of Charles Marowitz and Di Trevis, the hallmark of these TV productions (with the obvious exception of the last, a network spoof) is textual fidelity. The most notable shift has been an explicitly sexual one. In trying to make a recalcitrant text appeal to both sexes, the productions and camerawork for both the ACT and Papp videos celebrate the male body as erotic object; that body is well represented by the charismatic, slyly self-parodic figures of Marc Singer and Raúl Juliá.

For the 'me generation', sexual passion (leading automatically to true love) provides the quick-fix to explain away the societal dynamics of power in Katherine's 'taming' – or so Meryl Streep's backstage commentary seems to imply in the video aptly entitled *Kiss Me, Petruchio*.[29] Raúl Juliá's Petruchio plays the sexual Svengali, his perspective credited as fully reasonable and his body the prize worth any price; as Juliá himself asserts (in comments that shift between the third and first person), Petruchio 'is very self-confident ... [and] feels he can make the best husband in the world, and he *can*, too ... I'm here to make money ... and any father with the money for a dowry, he's getting a good bargain'. The video seems to confront the potentially offensive aspects of the play right away, with Petruchio performing his post-wedding assertion of ownership ('she is my goods, my chattel ...') – the only speech recorded twice, in and out of context. What we are soon told, however, is that we should not have been identifying with the audience members who boo – or if we do, our protest has already been as domesticated as Katherine herself (Streep: 'They boo because they don't *see* it'; Juliá: 'I love it when they boo and hiss Petruchio, because that means Petruchio is making them feel something.'). Throughout, offstage cuts deflect potential criticisms of the production, as do camera pans of the audience (we are shown women laughing at the end of the 'wooing' scene as Petruchio sits on Katherine announcing she will become as 'conformable as other household Kates'). Because the actors are commenting during a performance, they understandably adopt the perspective they have created for their characters. In Juliá's case this adds an unintended layer of comedy; however, Streep's replication of Katherine's 'conversion' – seeing the world through the eyes of patriarchy – is more disturbing, particularly because she does not show comparable imagination in understanding Katherine's former 'shrewish' identity. On-stage, she performs a cartoon catalogue of 'masculine', anti-social behaviour (stomping on flowers, 'pumping up' for a fight); although she always appears smart and funny, none of these actions is presented with the nuanced psychological realism she accords to the reformed Katherine. The video accentuates this by allowing her voice-overs to explain the latter part of the play, whereas Juliá's comments dominate during the first half. In a voice-over during the tailor scene, as Kate sits with the torn gown in hand, Streep asserts 'Really what matters is that they have an incredible passion and love; it's not something that Katherine admits to right away but it does provide the source of her change.' Then, as Katherine silently gives the dress to Petruchio, Streep makes the leap to his perspective (thereby legitimating what she never directly confronts, the inequity of behavioural reformation and her infantilisation in this putatively mutual scene of passion and love): 'What Petruchio does is say I'm going to take responsibility for you, and I'm going to try to change you *for your better*, make you as great as you can be.' Both actors presume throughout that Petruchio does not need to be (could not be?) improved.

The focus solely on the leads and the constant need for the actors to justify the narrative testify to the play's intractability; Streep's exasperated attempts ultimately underscore the interpretive work necessary to make sense of Kate's fate, and leave one agreeing instead with Ann Thompson's sense that 'we can no longer treat *The Shrew* as a straightforward comedy but must redefine it as a problem play in Ernest Schanzer's sense: ... "so that uncertain and divided responses to it in the minds of the audience are possible or even probable"'.[30] Perhaps the video's most appealing choice is to allow audience members to voice the tensions that the actors try so hard to erase. In the viewers' responses a gender gap appears. None of the men interviewed expresses discomfort, whereas the women divide: most express reservations, though one (speaking in concert with her male partner) fully enjoys this 'fabulous love story'.

A jolly conclusion recapitulates the performance's emphasis on Petruchio as sexual prize, as if to defuse the social hierarchy: Kate begins to drag him off to bed during the final lines, and then he concedes to exit in her direction during curtain call. While a woman in the audience gets the last word (noting that 'It's a fantasy that is dangerous for men' and that she feels 'very ambiguous'), the last image is Streep patting Juliá's ass as they exit – as if this role-reversal of Heston's fifties' slaps constituted a restoration of equality.

WHEN A WOOER GOES A WOOING ...

Comparison between this production's and Zeffirelli's rendering of the climactic scene of *Shrew*'s first two acts, the initial encounter between Katherine and Petruchio (II.i.178–269), reinforces the crucial role of the camera in establishing empathy and shaping the script's significance.[31] To achieve the dowry that has motivated his suit, Petruchio must obtain 'the special thing ... That is, her love' which her father regards as 'all in all' (II.i.124–5). Nevertheless, as in the parallel 'wooing scene' in *Henry V* it is not clear that Katherine's consent is actually required: Petruchio's reply 'Why, that is nothing' (II.i.126) not only indicates his confidence that he will make her yield but also how little evidence it takes for the men of Padua to decide she has been won. Both in the play and in criticism, Katherine's own last words of the act, her refusal to marry ('I'll see thee hanged on Sunday first!' [II.i.288]), are overridden and supplanted by Petruchio's brazen assertion – directly contrary to what he knows of her 'private' behaviour, and consistent with his decision to invert the truth verbally to get his way – that "tis incredible to believe/ How much she loves me' (II.i.295–6). Indeed, to make *Shrew* into a romantic comedy, one needs to make Petruchio a truth-teller in spite of himself or else motivate an even more 'incredible' reversal later (having Katherine fall for him when he deprives her of all forms of ownership). Neither subtext is psychologically implausible in a world of contorted desires and socially endorsed abjection, but to say so removes the lightheartedness associated with farce and may make a viewer uneasy. Once the complexity of real-life psyches intrudes, slapstick can look distressingly like domestic violence, and the problem of Kate's consent is not evaded but compounded.

In the Papp production, the eroticised male body which provides an explanation for Kate's desire is thus invoked most insistently in the initial encounter. The scene allows Juliá to dominate playfully and seductively without seeming overtly violent. Thus Petruchio tickles, carries, and encloses Katherine, but only she actually slaps, hits, and spits; nevertheless, she is the one who is left breathless and lying on the floor, while he retains his poise and humour. When Kate strikes Petruchio to 'try' whether he is a gentleman (the scene's only scripted violence), he does not flinch. When she spits in his face in response to his request to 'kiss me, Kate', he pauses and then delightedly licks his lips to ingest her spittle. Although Streep makes the most of her wittier lines, she is clearly confronted with a superior force here, whose apparent invulnerability to abuse or opposition is only a step less absolute than Fairbanks's laughter as he is whipped. The tide of inevitability that Petruchio had predicted is thus for the most part fulfilled in these performances through the men's delighted embodiment, and Kate's resistance seems both doomed and counterintuitive. These are the sexual dynamics captured by the camera most frequently in twentieth-century *Shrew*s.

By contrast, the extended farcical chase in Zeflirelli's movie defuses the scene's focus, transforming Petruchio's relentless verbal enclosure of Katherine into an unpredictable game in which neither words nor rooms can effectively enclose energy: both their bodies hurtle precariously through space, walls, and ceilings. Petruchio does show his persistence, using his head to raise the trap door upon which Kate heavily sits (thus giving a visual punch to the bawdry of his 'tongue in [her] tail' retort). But the camera's giddy tracking from room to courtyard to barn to roof and back down through roof to woolbin conveys the film's ongoing message that Kate may eventually be trapped but not easily tamed. The end of the scene brings a shadow of violence, but in doing so acknowledges a change of mood as well: when Petruchio pins down Katherine in the woolbin, the stick in her hand (with which she has been pounding his head) is forced across her throat, while the camera angling down upon her head and heaving breast comes close to Petruchio's perspective of dominance. This eroticised shot puts Katherine in the position of countless female victims in movie thrillers, cowering with a knife at the throat. Zeffirelli earlier used a conventional horror movie sequence in open parody, with Kate in the unseen killer/monster position of the camera closing in upon Bianca as the screaming victim. Thus the shift in Katherine's placement underscores her succumbing to the superior force of Petruchio and the coincidence of that position with eroticised femininity. She will later reclaim equanimity through her greater intelligence and her adoption of a matron's role, but here – and in her subsequent collapse on the floor in tears – she is first revealed as vulnerable in body and spirit. Even as Petruchio looks on tenderly and helps her to her feet, this 'wooing' concludes by uneasily signalling his power and her abjection, not her consent. Here again Zeffirelli's practice implies the possibility of a more extensive use of the camera to suggest another perspective on Shakespeare's story.

CODA: ALL'S WELL ...?

The silliest of the 1980s *Shrew*s constantly parodies Zeffirelli's film, and goes further in modifying Shakespeare's text to create a space for modern love. Replacing the Sly frame with a homework-resisting schoolboy who wants to watch television, the *Moonlighting Shrew* begins with some self-reflexive comedy about the most widespread modern addiction and its target audience. And by placing the series' stars in Shakespeare's plot (sort of), we get a market-pleasing three-for-the-price-of-one dose of character deconstruction: when Cybill Shepherd plays Maddie Hayes plays Kate, and Bruce Willis plays David Addison plays Petruchio, who can say what's 'really' going on? One joke involves Willis/Addison/Petruchio presenting his parchment list of dowry demands, which includes a winnebago, rights to direct, and other TV contract items; having earlier quoted other Shakespeare lines ('wrong play') he now realises 'wrong scroll'. As much a send-up of contemporary media as of Shakespeare, the show nevertheless displays a commonsense consciousness of the textual tensions scholars spend so much energy explaining away, and uses its over-determined characters to comment on how times do change (as in Willis's comic aside after his pre-wooing soliloquy, which devolves into the Steinian mantra 'the man is the man is the man ...': 'if you're a man, you gotta love the sixteenth century'). Willis's rock-n-roll wedding number, 'Good Lovin'', invokes the familiar medical trope but converts Dr Petruchio into the patient ('I said doctor, Mr M.D., "can you tell me what's ailin' me? ... he said all I really need is good lovin"'). Of course, singing 'I got the fever, you got the cure' to a Katherina bound and gagged at the altar takes 'commentary' over the top. The loonery-tunery of his post-wedding courtship (at which point Shakespeare's plot is entirely rewritten to replace coercion with mutual respect) reanimates a classic cartoon sequence: upon Petruchio's third gift offering at a hostile Katherine's door, her hand shoves a stick of dynamite into his suit-of-armour's visor; he 'looks' at us, walks off camera, and then the picture jiggles with the unseen explosion. Inverting the sun and moon speech to allow Katherine her own eyesight, the show carries further Shakespeare's comic logic, allowing hierarchies (artistic as well as gendered) to evaporate without pain. Unlike the Papp video so titled, when Kate here says 'Kiss me, Petruchio' and sweeps him into her arms, role reversal gives the story a new lease on life, without victims. And for those who wish to find a Petruchio motivated by true love rather than money, this version makes his culminating gesture the renunciation of the dowry (which here is involved with the wager). An unabashed American wishfulfilment of painless change resulting in equality for all, this sunny moonlit *Shrew* announces it is now the best of times, when the messages a schoolboy learns from his 'Atomic Shakespeare' resemble those in 'Free to Be ... You and Me'.

As Graham Holderness concludes, if historical analysis 'fails to engage with contemporary sexual politics, then the play will continue to speak ... for the same repressive and authoritarian ideology'.[32] In Zeffirelli's emphasis on the visual, he suggests that artful camerawork and conceptual adaptation could yet produce a textually grounded but truly modern *Shrew*: a fully filmic version that would address rather than replicate the gender hierarchy that continues to haunt most screen versions. Until that time, viewers may take solace in the farcical throwaways of the *Moonlighting* grapple:

Petruchio   Where there's a will –
Katherina   There's a won't.

Perhaps it will take a new millennium to produce a more experimental filmic rendering of this resistant tale. For the present, by studying the subtler differences and historical reflections of the many twentieth-century *The Taming of the Shrew*s, we may learn more – if not about a golden world, at least about this brazen one.

From *Shakespeare the Movie. Popularizing the Plays on Film, TV, and Video*, ed. Lynda E. Boose and Richard Burt (London, 1997), pp. 148–68.

NOTES

[Diana E. Henderson's essay was originally published as one of a collection of essays in *Shakespeare, the Movie* edited by Lynda E. Boose and Richard Burt (London, 1997), in which several plays are traced through a much more optimistic and inventive series of film productions. This essay, however, clearly demonstrates the difficulties of filming a play which appears to support outmoded values and thus comments not only upon *The Taming of the Shrew*, but also on the power of changing values to dominate screen versions of Shakespeare's plays. Ed.]

1. This number excludes spin-offs.

2. While aware of the shiftiness of meaning in comedy and of the ways people ironise or evade some of the text's less pleasant implications, the work of Boose, Newman, and Marcus has demonstrated, and companion plays such as Fletcher's *The Woman Prize* confirm, that the text responds to the particular gender issues of its time. [The essays by Lynda Boose and Karen Newman referred to here are reprinted in this volume; see above pp. 166–91 and pp. 148–65 – Ed.]

3. M. Dobson, *The Making of the National Poet: Shakespeare, Adaptation and Authorship, 1660–1769* (Oxford, 1992), p. 190.

4. A link with contemporary gender issues occurs in the spin-off *The Taming of the Shrewd* (Knickerbocker, 1912), in which a suffragist who has neglected her housework is 'tamed' by her husband's arousal of jealousy when he escorts another woman to one of her political meetings (R. Ball, *Shakespeare on Silent Film* [New York, 1968], p. 149).

5. See C. Hirschhorn, *Hollywood Musical* (New York, 1981), p. 236 on *Casanova in Burlesque* (1944). The famous musical was *Kiss Me, Kate*, debuting on Broadway in 1948 and made into a film in 1953.

6. Radical only in its departures from theatrical tradition, this BBC-TV museum piece unabashedly celebrates the order achieved through female submission – and makes John Cleese seem not very funny as part of that project. The show was broadcast on the BBC in June 1980, soon after Thatcher's election; in the US on 26 January 1981, at the beginning of Reagan's presidency.

7. J. Miller, *Subsequent Performances* (New York, 1986).

8. Although the stage director was Wilford Leech, I refer to this as the Papp *Shrew* because the video foregrounds Papp's proprietary control.

9. In a related 'first', in 1964 *Kiss Me, Kate* was the first US musical to be adapted for British television (K. Rothwell and A. Melzer, *Shakespeare on Screen: An International Filmography and Videography* [New York, 1990], p. 275).

10. Ball, *Shakespeare on Silent Film*, p. 62.

11. Ibid., p. 63.

12. Miller, *Subsequent Performances*, p. 122.

13. Cited from the Folger Shakespeare Library Archive's 35 mm print. Another title card tells us that this Petruchio follows in the tradition of Garrick's 'masked' educator: 'In order to tame the Shrew, Petruchio determines to be more unreasonable than her in all things'.

14. Visually, this *Shrew* epitomises the style Collick characterises as quintessentially and conservatively British, replicating the Victorian stage spectacle in its elaborate costumes, proscenium-like sets, and statically full-front camera work. J. Collick (*Shakespeare, Cinema and Society* [Manchester, 1989], pp. 33–57) interprets it as symptomatic of a desire to define an English, as distinct from a US, style and tradition; see also Rothwell and Melzer, *Shakespeare on Screen*, pp. 270–1.

15. M. Pickford, *Sunshine and Shadow* (New York, 1955), pp. 311–12.

16. Shaw remarks upon her parallelism with Kate as an actress alone among men in rehearsal, a gendered isolation which men don't [often] experience: 'the sense of the terribly clouded confusion that overwhelms you when you are the only woman around. That was Kate's position, and it was mine: she in that mad marriage, me in rehearsal. Men, together, sometimes speak a funny language' (C. Rutter, *Clamorous Voices: Shakespeare's Women Today* [New York, 1989], p. xvii).

17. Pickford, *Sunshine and Shadow*, p. 311. The 1966 version removes 'with additional dialogue by Sam Taylor', replacing it with 'Adaptation and Direction by Sam Taylor'. Although the cutting of lines and variation from 'pure' Shakespeare aroused criticism in 1929, the development of film theory and practice would confirm the

necessity of true screen adaptation – including line cuts as well as the discovery of visual equivalencies and distinctively filmic motifs.

18. These radios are rhetorically and physically differentiated: the young man wants the 'swell-looking job in the dark green cabinet' with the 'powerful' reach; whereas the ivory compact is a 'big favourite with the girls because it's light as a feather'. Having been given the properly sexed radio, the couple dances away together.

19. Extending a pattern introduced by the 1929 film's opening with a Punch and Judy puppet show, this production uses *commedia dell'arte* techniques; the constant movement of acrobats, dancers, and clown-nosed servants combines with active camerawork to create an energetically three-dimensional look within the bare studio 'setting'.

20. Miller, *Subsequent Performances*, p. 122.

21. F. Zeffirelli, *Zeffirelli* (New York, 1986), p. 216.

22. P. Donaldson, *Shakespearean Films/Shakespearean Directors* (Boston, 1990), p. 147.

23. See Zeffirelli, *Zeffirelli*, p. 224 and G. Holderness, *Shakespeare in Performance: The Taming of the Shrew* (Manchester and New York, 1989), pp. 55–6 on *Help!*, and Donaldson, *Shakespearean Films*, pp. 148–9 on the role of Olivier's film.

24. Zeffirelli, *Zeffirelli*, p. 9.

25. Ibid., pp. 10–11.

26. On the use of metafilmic parodies, see Holderness, *Shakespeare in Performance*, pp. 64–7.

27. None of this undermines the farce or enjoyment that the film affords.

28. Rutter, *Clamorous Voices*, p. 1.

29. The stage directors' motivations for emphasising the male body lie outside the scope of this essay. My aim is to outline the filmic effects of such choices, and how (even if informed by alternative sexualities and unconventional desires) when combined with a traditional narrative they reflect the dominant ideology of their times – in this case, making a patriarchal text more palatable to a predominantly heterosexual public affected by the 'sexual revolution'.

30. A. Thompson (ed.), *The Taming of the Shrew* (Cambridge, 1979), p. 41.

31. Line citations for *The Taming of the Shrew* refer to the Cambridge edition edited by Thompson in her 1979 edition.

32. Holderness, *Shakespeare in Performance*, p. 117.

Further Reading

The Further Reading is divided into two sections in order to help those readers who are studying the plays separately. However, it is worth pointing out that several works in both lists cover a broad range and could provide useful and interesting reading for *Much Ado About Nothing* and *The Taming of the Shrew*. This is particularly true of those texts that focus upon theatre history and film criticism.

MUCH ADO ABOUT NOTHING

S. Beauman, *The Royal Shakespeare Company: a History of Ten Decades* (Oxford: Oxford University Press, 1982).

J. R. Brown (ed.), *Much Ado About Nothing and As You Like It: A Casebook* (London: Macmillan, 1979).

C. Cook, '"The Sign and Semblance of Her Honor": Reading Gender Difference in *Much Ado About Nothing*', *Proceedings of the Modern Language Association*, 101 (1986), 186–202.

J. Cook, *Women in Shakespeare* (London: Harrap, 1980).

J. F. Cox, 'The Stage Representation of the "Kill Claudio" sequence in *Much Ado About Nothing*', *Shakespeare Survey*, 32 (1979), 27–36.

C. Dennis, 'Wit and Wisdom in *Much Ado About Nothing*', *Studies in English Literature*, 13 (1973), 223–37.

J. Hays, 'Those "soft and delicate desires": *Much Ado* and the distrust of women', in *The Woman's Part: Feminist Criticism of Shakespeare*, ed. Carolyn Ruth Swift Lenz, Gayle Greene, and Carol Thomas Neely

(Urbana, Chicago and London: University of Illinois Press, 1980), pp. 79–99.

R. Henze, 'Deception in *Much Ado About Nothing*', *Studies in English Literature*, 11 (1971), 187–201.

J. D. Huston, *Shakespeare's Comedies of Play* (New York: Columbia University Press, 1981).

E. Krieger, 'Social Relations and the Social Order in *Much Ado About Nothing*', *Shakespeare Survey*, 32 (1979), 49–61.

P. Mason, *Much Ado About Nothing: Text and Performance* (London: Macmillan, 1992).

J. R. Mulryne, 'Shakespeare: *Much Ado About Nothing*', *Studies in English Literature*, 16 (1965); reprinted in *Shakespeare: Much Ado About Nothing and As You Like It: A Casebook*, ed. J. R. Brown (London: Macmillan, 1979), pp. 117–29.

C. Neely, *Broken Nuptials in Shakespeare's Plays* (New Haven, CT, and London: Yale University Press, 1985).

C. Prouty, *The Sources of 'Much Ado About Nothing'* (New Haven, CT: Yale University Press, 1950).

C. Rutter, *Clamorous Voices: Shakespeare's Women Today* (London: The Women's Press, 1988).

J. H. Sexton, 'The theme of slander in *Much Ado About Nothing* and Garter's *Susanna*', *Philological Quarterly*, 54 (1975), 419–33.

THE TAMING OF THE SHREW

M. Andreson-Thom, 'Shrew-taming and other rituals of aggression: Baiting and bonding on the stage and in the wild', *Women's Studies*, 9 (1982), 121–43.

R. H. Ball, *Shakespeare on Silent Film* (New York: Theatre Art Books, 1968).

J. C. Bean, 'Comic Structure and the Humanizing of Kate in *The Taming of the Shrew*', in *The Woman's Part: Feminist Criticism of Shakespeare*, ed. Carolyn Ruth Swift Lenz, Gayle Greene, and Carol Thomas Neely (Urbana, Chicago and London: University of Illinois Press, 1980), pp. 65–78.

J. C. Bulman and H. R. Coursen (eds), *Shakespeare on Television* (Hanover, NH: University Press of New England, 1988).

P. S. Donaldson, *Shakespearean Films/Shakespearean Directors* (Boston: Unwin Hyman, 1990).

P. Erickson, *Patriarchal Structures in Shakespeare's Drama* (Berkeley, CA: University of California Press, 1985).

J. Hartwig, 'Horses and Women in the *Taming of the Shrew*', *Huntington Library Quarterly*, 45 (1982), 285–94.

T. Hating-Smith, *From Farce to Metadrama: A Stage History of 'The Taming of the Shrew', 1594–1983* (Westport, CN: Greenwood Press, 1985).

C. F. Heffernan, '*The Taming of the Shrew*: The Bourgeoisie in Love', *Essays in Literature*, 12 (1985), 3–14.

R. Heilbrun, 'The Taming Untamed, or, the Return of the Shrew', *Modern Language Quarterly*, 27 (1966), 147–61.

R. B. Heilman, 'The *Taming* Untamed, or, The Return of the Shrew', *Modern Language Quarterly*, 27 (1966), 147–61.

G. Holderness, *Shakespeare in Performance: The Taming of the Shrew* (Manchester: Manchester University Press, 1989).

R. Hosley, 'Sources and Analogues of *The Taming of the Shrew*', *Huntington Library Quarterly*, 27 (1963–4), 289–308.

C. Kahn, '*The Taming of the Shrew*: Shakespeare's Mirror of Marriage', *Modern Language Studies*, 5 (1975), 88–102.

K. McLuskie, 'Feminist Deconstruction: Shakespeare's *Taming of The Shrew*', *Red Letters*, 12 (1982), 15–22.

M. Novy, 'Patriarchy and Play in *The Taming of the Shrew*', *English Literary Renaissance*, 9 (1979), 273–4.

L. C. Orlin, 'The Performance of Things in *The Taming of the Shrew*', *The Yearbook of English Studies*, 23 (1993), 167–88.

P. Parker, *Literary Fat Ladies: Rhetoric, Gender, Property* (London and New York: Methuen, 1987).

J. A. Roberts, 'Horses and Hermaphrodites: Metamorphoses in *The Taming of the Shrew*', *Shakespeare Quarterly*, 34 (1983), 159–71.

C. Rutter, *Clamorous Voices: Shakespeare's Women Today*, ed. Faith Evans (London: Routledge, 1989).

A. Thompson (ed.), *The New Cambridge Shakespeare. The Taming of the Shrew* (Cambridge: Cambridge University Press, 1984).

V. Wayne, 'Refashioning the Shrew', *Shakespeare Studies*, 17 (1985), 159–88.

Notes on Contributors

Harry Berger Jr is Professor Emeritus of Literature and Art History at the University of California, Santa Cruz. He is the author of *Imaginary Audition: Shakespeare on Stage and Page* (Berkeley, CA, 1989) and *Making Trifles of Terrors. Redistributing Complicities in Shakespeare* (Stanford, CA, 1997).

Lynda E. Boose is Professor of English and Women's Studies at Dartmouth College. She is the co-editor, with Betty Flowers, of *Fathers and Daughters* (Baltimore, MD, 1988), and, with Richard Burt, of *Shakespeare, the Movie: Popularizing the Plays on Film, TV, and Video* (London, 1997), as well as of many articles on Shakespeare. She is working on a study of shrews and scolds in early modern England.

S. P. Cerasano is Professor of English at Colgate University. She is currently writing a biography of the Renaissance actor and entrepreneur Edward Alleyn. With Marion Wynne-Davies she is co-editor of *Gloriana's Face: Women, Public and Private, in the English Renaissance* (Hemel Hempstead, 1992), and of *Renaissance Drama by Women: Texts and Documents* (London, 1996).

Barbara Everett has held Fellowships and Lectureships at both Oxford and Cambridge, and is now Senior Research Fellow at Somerville College, Oxford. She has delivered both the Lord Northcliffe Lectures at University College, London, and the Clark Lectures at Trinity College, Cambridge. She has published on a wide variety of subjects. Shakespeare editions include *Antony and Cleopatra* (Signet) and *All's Well That Ends Well* (New Penguin). Her most recent books are *Poets in Their Time: Essays on English Poetry from Donne to Larkin* (London, 1986: Oxford, 1991) and *Young Hamlet: Essays on Shakespeare's Tragedies* (Oxford, 1989, 1990).

Joel Fineman was Associate Professor of English at the University of California, Berkeley. He was the author of *Shakespeare's Perjured Eye: the Invention of Poetic Subjectivity in the Sonnets* (Berkeley, CA, 1985) and of essays on Shakespeare and on literary theory.

Penny Gay is an Associate Professor in English at the University of Sydney, where she also teaches in Performance Studies. She has published extensively on Shakespeare's women in performance, and has a study of *As You Like It* forthcoming in the *Writers and Their Work* series. She is currently writing a book on Jane Austen and the eighteenth-century theatre.

Diana E. Henderson is Associate Professor of Literature at MIT, where she also teaches in the Women's Studies and Comparative Media Studies Programs. She has been an Honorary Visiting Fellow at the Open University (UK). Her first book was *Passion Made Public: Elizabethan Lyric, Gender, and Performance* (Urbana, IL, 1995). In addition to articles on works by Spenser, Peele, Heywood, and Joyce, recent essays include 'The Theatre and Domestic Culture' and 'Female Power and Devaluation of Renaissance Love Lyrics'. Her current book project, *Uneasy Collaborations: Transforming Shakespeare Across Time and Media*, includes a longer version of her essay in this collection.

Jean E. Howard is Professor of English and Director of the Institute for Research on Women and Gender at Columbia University. Her recent publications include *The Stage and Social Struggle in Early Modern England* (London, 1994) and, with Phyllis Rackin, *Engendering a Nation: A Feminist Reading of Shakespeare's English Histories* (London, 1997). She is also one of the four editors of *The Norton Shakespeare* (London, 1997) and is presently working on a book entitled *Theater of a City: Generic Innovation and Social Change in Early Modern English Drama*.

Natasha Korda, Assistant Professor of English at Wesleyan University, is currently working on a book entitled *Household Stuff: Shakespeare's Domestic Economies* and is co-editing with Jonathan Gil Harris a critical anthology entitled *Staged Properties: Props and Property in Early Modern English Drama*.

Karen Newman is University Professor and Professor of Comparative Literature and English at Brown University. She is the author of *Shakespeare's Rhetoric of Comic Character* (London, 1985), *Fashioning Femininity and English Renaissance Drama* (Chicago, 1991) and *Fetal Positions* (Stanford, CA, 1996), as well as articles on early modern culture and on literary theory. She is at work on a new book on cultural production in early modern London and Paris.

Index

New Casebooks

MUCH ADO ABOUT NOTHING

and

THE TAMING OF THE SHREW

New Casebooks

(continued overleaf)

DRAMA

BECKETT: *Waiting for Godot* and *Endgame* Edited by Steven Connor
APHRA BEHN Edited by Janet Todd
SHAKESPEARE: *Antony and Cleopatra* Edited by John Drakakis
SHAKESPEARE: *Hamlet* Edited by Martin Coyle
SHAKESPEARE: *King Lear* Edited by Kiernan Ryan
SHAKESPEARE: *Macbeth* Edited by Alan Sinfield
SHAKESPEARE: *The Merchant of Venice* Edited by Martin Coyle
SHAKESPEARE: *A Midsummer Night's Dream* Edited by Richard Dutton
SHAKESPEARE: *Much Ado About Nothing* and *The Taming of the Shrew* Edited by
   Marion Wynne-Davies
SHAKESPEARE: *The Tempest* Edited by R. S. White
SHAKESPEARE: *Twelfth Night* Edited by R. S. White
SHAKESPEARE ON FILM Edited by Robert Shaughnessy
SHAKESPEARE IN PERFORMANCE Edited by Robert Shaughnessy
SHAKESPEARE'S HISTORY PLAYS Edited by Graham Holderness
SHAKESPEARE'S TRAGEDIES Edited by Susan Zimmerman
JOHN WEBSTER: *The Duchess of Malfi* Edited by Dympna Callaghan

GENERAL THEMES

FEMINIST THEATRE AND THEORY Edited by Helene Keyssar
POST-COLONIAL LITERATURES Edited by Michael Parker and Roger Starkey

---

New Casebooks Series
Series Standing Order
ISBN 0–333–71702–3 hardcover
ISBN 0–333–69345–0 paperback
(outside North America only)

You can receive future titles in this series as they are published by placing a standing order.
Please contact your bookseller or, in case of difficulty, write to us at the address below with your
name and address, the title of the series and the ISBN quoted above.

Customer Services Department, Macmillan Distribution Ltd
Houndmills, Basingstoke, Hampshire RG21 6XS, England